Social History of Africa

IN PURSUIT OF HISTORY

Social History of Africa Series
Series Editors: Allen Isaacman and Jean Hay

African Workers and Colonial Racism
JEANNE PENVENNE

Agriculture and Apartheid
JONATHAN CRUSH AND ALLAN JEEVES (EDITORS)

Are We Not Also Men?
TERENCE RANGER

Burying SM
DAVID COHEN AND ATIENO ODHIAMBO

Colonial Conscripts
MYRON ECHENBERG

Cotton is the Mother of Poverty
ALLEN ISAACMAN

Cotton, Colonialism, and Social History in Africa
ALLEN ISAACMAN AND RICHARD ROBERTS (EDITORS)

Cutting Down Trees
HENRIETTA MOORE AND MEGAN VAUGHAN

Drink, Power, and Cultural Change
EMMANUEL AKYEAMPONG

Feasts and Riot
JONATHAN GLASSMAN

Gender, Ethnicity, and Social Change on the Upper Slave Coast
SANDRA GREENE

In Pursuit of History
CAROLYN KEYES ADENAIKE AND JAN VANSINA (EDITORS)

Insiders and Outsiders
BILL FREUND

Law in Colonial Africa
KRISTIN MANN AND RICHARD ROBERTS (EDITORS)

Money Matters
JANE GUYER (EDITOR)

The Moon is Dead—Give Us Our Money!
KELETSO ATKINS

Peasants, Traders, and Wives
ELIZABETH SCHMIDT

The Realm of the Word
PAUL LANDAU

"We Spend Our Years as a Tale That is Told"
ISABEL HOFMEYR

Women of Phokeng
BELINDA BOZZOLI

Work, Culture, and Identity
PATRICK HARRIES

IN PURSUIT OF HISTORY

FIELDWORK IN AFRICA

Edited by
Carolyn Keyes Adenaike
and Jan Vansina

HEINEMANN
Portsmouth, NH

JAMES CURREY
Oxford

Heinemann
A division of Reed Publishing (USA) Inc.
361 Hanover Street
Portsmouth, NH 03801-3912
Offices and agents throughout the world

James Currey Ltd.
73 Botley Road
Oxford 0X2 OBS
United Kingdom

© 1996 by Heinemann
All rights reserved. No part of this book may be reproduced in any form or by any electronic or mechanical means, including information storage and retrieval systems, without permission in writing from the publisher, except by a reviewer, who may quote brief passages in a review.

ISBN 0-435-08990-0 (Heinemann cloth)
ISBN 0-435-08992-7 (Heinemann paper)

ISBN 0-85255-676-4 (James Currey cloth)
ISBN 0-85255-626-8 (James Currey paper)

British Library Cataloguing in Publication Data

In pursuit of history : fieldwork in Africa. — (social history of Africa)
 1. Africa — Social conditions — Field work 2. Africa — History — Field work
 I. Adenaike, Carolyn Keyes II. Vansina, J. (Jan), 1929–
960'.00723

Library of Congress Cataloguing in Publication Data

In pursuit of history : fieldwork in Africa / edited by Carolyn Keyes Adenaike and Jan Vansina.
  p. cm. — (Heinemann social history of Africa series)
 Includes bibliographical references and index
  ISBN 0–435–08990–0 (cloth : acid-free paper). ISBN 0–435–08992–7 (paper : acid-free paper)
  1. Africa—History—Research. 2. Africa—Description and travel—1977– 3. History—Field work. I. Adenaike, Carolyn Keyes. II. Vansina, Jan. III. Series: Social history of Africa.
DT19.I5 1996
960'.072—dc20   96-30779
                                              CIP

Cover design by Jenny Jensen Greenleaf
Cover artwork by Carolyn Keyes Adenaike
Maps by Claudine Vansina and Carolyn Keyes Adenaike

Printed in the United States of America on acid-free paper.
99 98 97 96 DA 1 2 3 4 5 6

CONTENTS

List of Maps vii

Notes on Contributors ix

Prologue
The Editors xi

Reading the Pursuit: An Introduction
Carolyn Keyes Adenaike xvii

1 Life During Research
  Carolyn Keyes Adenaike, Nigeria, 1989–1992 1

2 Fieldwork among Neighbors: An African's View of
  Another African Country
  Tefetso Henry Mothibe, Zimbabwe, 1990–1992 11

3. Both Sides of the Border: The Impact of the Political Milieu
   on Field Research in Burundi and Tanzania
   Michele D. Wagner, Burundi, 1985–1987; Tanzania, 1991–1993 18

4 Women's Work in Kano
  Beverly B. Mack, Nigeria, 1979–1980; 1982–1983 29

5 Learning the Dance, Initiating Relationships
  Sheryl McCurdy, Tanzania, 1992–1993 41

6 Suspected of Sorcery
  Z. S. Strother, Zaïre, 1987–1989 57

7 Falsehood, Truth, and Thinking Between:
  Histories of Affiliation and Ethnogenesis
  Paul Stuart Landau, Botswana, 1989–1990 75

8   A Moment in the Middle: Fieldwork in the Nuba Hills
    Janet J. Ewald, Sudan, 1977–1978 94

9   A Double Exile: Extended African Residences and the
    Paradoxes of Homecoming
    Richard A. Shain, Nigeria, 1979–1987 104

10 Venture into Tio Country
    Jan Vansina, Congo, 1963–1964 113

Epilogue: Fieldwork in History
    Jan Vansina 127

References 141

Index 148

LIST OF MAPS AND FIGURES

General Location of Research Described in this Book xvi

Burundi and Buha 19

Kigoma 42

Three Communities in East Central Botswana and the Transvaal 78

Genealogies of Actors in Madala and Ngwato Ruling Houses 80

NOTES ON CONTRIBUTORS

Carolyn Keyes Adenaike, now at Vassar College, taught African history at Hunter College (New York), at the University of Wisconsin–Madison, and at Johns Hopkins University as a visiting lecturer. She obtained her Ph.D. in history at the University of Wisconsin–Madison in 1993. She resided in Nigeria (1989–92, 1995) and has written several articles on Yoruba history and society.

Janet Ewald is associate professor of history at Duke University. She received a Ph.D. in history at the University of Wisconsin–Madison in 1982. She resided in Sudan (1976, 1977–79) and in Yemen (1994–95). She has written *Soldiers, Traders, and Slaves: State Formation and Economic Transformation in the Greater Nile Valley, 1700–1885* (Madison, 1990), a book about Taqali within the Greater Nile Valley, as well as several articles examining the use of oral sources.

Paul Landau is assistant professor of history at Yale University and has taught at the University of New Hampshire. In 1992 he obtained his Ph.D. in history from the University of Wisconsin–Madison. He resided in Botswana (1988–90) and in South Africa (1995, 1996), and is the author of *The Realm of the Word: Language, Gender, and Christianity in a Southern African Kingdom* (Portsmouth, NH, 1995) and a number of articles concerning the history of Christianity in Southern Africa.

Beverly Mack is associate professor in African and African-American studies at the University of Kansas. She has taught at Bayero (Kano), Georgetown, George Mason (Fairfax), and Yale Universities. She obtained a Ph.D. in African Languages and Literature at the University of Wisconsin–Madison in 1981. She resided in Nigeria (1977, 1979–80, 1982–83). In addition to many articles about Hausa women, she edited a volume with Catherine Coles, *Hausa Women in the Twentieth Century* (Madison, 1991) and co-authored with Jean Boyd two forthcoming books about the life and writings of Nana Asma'u.

Sheryl McCurdy is completing her Ph.D. in Sociomedical Sciences at Columbia University. She resided in Tanzania (1981, 1984–86, 1992–93) and Madagascar (1990). She has written on women's associations in Ujiji and on health and development in Tanzania.

Tefetso Henry Mothibe teaches at the University of Lesotho. His Ph.D. in history from the University of Wisconsin–Madison dates from 1993. A native of Lesotho, he currently lives and works in Lesotho. In 1990–92 he did fieldwork in Zimbabwe. He has written on labor history in Southern Africa.

Richard Shain is assistant professor of history at the Philadelphia College of Textiles and Science. He has taught at the Universities of Jos and Cross River and at Rutgers University–Newark. He obtained his Ph.D. in history from Johns Hopkins University in 1992. He has resided in Nigeria (1978, 1979–1987), and has written articles on religious history and regionalism in Nigeria.

Z. S. Strother is assistant professor of art history at Columbia University and has taught at the University of Michigan as a fellow of the Michigan Society of Fellows. She received her Ph.D. at Yale University in 1992. She resided in Zaïre from 1987 to 1989. Her book about Pende art history, *Inventing Masks*, is forthcoming.

Jan Vansina is professor emeritus of history and anthropology at the University of Wisconsin–Madison. His Ph.D. in history at the University of Leuven (Belgium) dates from 1957. He resided in Zaïre (1954–56, 1966–67, 1971), Rwanda and Burundi (1953–54, 1957–60), Congo (1963–64), Libya (1978), and Gabon (1980). He has published extensively, including studies on historical method.

Michele Wagner, now at the University of Georgia, has taught history at Williams College and at the University of Wisconsin–Madison. She worked for the United Nations Human Rights Field Operation in Rwanda (1994–95) and for Human Rights Watch–Africa (1995). She obtained her Ph.D. at the University of Wisconsin–Madison in 1991. She resided in Burundi (1985–87), Tanzania (1991–93), and Rwanda (1994–95). She has published on Rundi history, Ha history, and conflict resolution in Rwanda.

PROLOGUE

Carolyn Keyes Adenaike and Jan Vansina

Fieldwork is a magic word for aspiring scholars from outside the region who plan to do research in African history, especially those interested in social history. They have all heard stories related by veterans, but with a few exceptions, most of the published discussions of fieldwork are written by and for anthropologists, not historians.[1] Graduate students, especially those in social history, know that fieldwork can be the crucial test for the success of their research projects, yet sometimes they are unaware of what challenges might be involved beyond obtaining funding and making travel plans. In particular, they underestimate how much personal commitment may be required and how stressful that can be. Moreover, during the last two decades significant changes have taken place in the experience of fieldwork itself.

Like any other practice, fieldwork changes over time and has a history. This book does not deal with that history, but a brief discussion will help form a context for the essays that follow. From the late 1950s onward, some historians of Africa began to engage in field research themselves, rather than relying on data collected by others, usually anthropologists. From the mid-1960s onward, the practice of field research became common and was institutionalized in most North American universities granting Ph.D. degrees in African history.

The earlier historians within Africa and from outside sought to establish an overall framework and overarching narrative for African history. In the 1960s and early 1970s many of them chose ambitious subjects, often covering sizable areas, and they focused predominantly on political and economic history. Typical topics included the political history of a precolonial kingdom or the economic history of trade networks. In contrast to colonial and imperial historiography, the new historians also wanted to privilege inside sources and thus focused on gathering oral traditions. At that time, therefore, young scholars went to Africa to experience firsthand the societies whose history they studied, to consult archives, and to "recover" relevant oral traditions before they died out. Hence "collecting oral traditions" and "pursuing fieldwork" became almost synonymous. Because they wished to gather

---

[1] The most notable exceptions are David Henige, ed., "Fieldwork in Zambia," *History in Africa*, 5 (1978), 273–326; David Henige, ed., "Silences in Fieldwork," *History in Africa*, 17 (1990), 319–58; and Janet Ewald, "Foxes in the Field: An Essay on Historical Methodology," *African Studies Review*, 30, 2 (1987), 9–15. See also the discussion in David Newbury, *Kings and Clans: Ijwi Island and the Lake Kivu Rift, 1780–1840* (Madison, 1991), 239–47.

oral traditions concerning a large area, many scholars had to be peripatetic, rather than settling for a long time in a single community. A few historians, however, focused on narrower topics to be explored in greater depth within a single community or small region.

Most scholars prepared specifically for the field by studying the relevant language beforehand and practicing their interview skills. Although language skills were necessary, a middle level of fluency was considered sufficient in most cases. Researchers should know enough of the local language to find their way around and to check the reliability of one's assistant or translator. Data were to be obtained by the formal interview of "informants," recorded on tapes wherever possible; ideally these tapes and/or transcripts would be copied and deposited for the ultimate use of other researchers. In the slipstream of independence, researchers were faced with few logistical difficulties and few problems of access related to war, famine, or epidemics, and suffered less interference from local and national authorities.

From the 1980s on, the fieldwork experience began to change. Later researchers built on the achievements of their predecessors and chose to pursue narrower subjects in greater depth. Whereas Fred Cooper, Charles van Onselen, or Charles Perrings dealt broadly with the history of labor, younger scholars such as John Higginson, Jeanne Penvenne, or Keletso Atkins concentrated on the study of particular cultural expressions of labor consciousness among workers.[2]

Many of the contributors to this volume also followed in the footsteps of earlier researchers. Numerous studies already existed about Hausa, Pende, Rundi, Tswana, Yoruba, and Rhodesian history, for instance, before they undertook their own research. After about 1980, scholars whose primary goal was to collect oral traditions became a minority while more recent fieldworkers have focused on social history—especially on that kind of social history that links the subject to particular expressions of mindsets or *mentalités*. Such topics require an advanced knowledge of the local language and more intensive fieldwork: stays of a year or longer in the same place. These requirements sometimes produce significant difficulties for researchers. Grants are often insufficient for the projected length of fieldwork. There may be problems learning the needed languages. Of the languages spoken in the research areas mentioned in these essays, Arabic, Hausa, and Swahili are commonly taught in North America to an advanced level, while Shona, Tswana, and Yoruba may be studied to an intermediate level at a few institutions or during intensive summer programs. But serious instruction in such other languages as Pende, Rundi, Tio, or Etulo is not available. These languages have to be learned in the field, and time for this has to be added to the time required for fieldwork. Staying longer, and staying within a single community, exerts a greater impact on the person and personality of the researcher, and claims a significant emotional

---

[2] Frederick Cooper, *Plantation Slavery on the East Coast of Africa* (New Haven, 1977); Charles van Onselen, *Chibaro: African Labour in Southern Rhodesia, 1900–1933* (London, 1976); Charles Perrings, *Black Mineworkers in Central Africa* (New York, 1979); John Higginson, *A Working Class in the Making: Belgian Colonial Labor Policy, Private Enterprise, and the African Mineworker, 1907–1951* (Madison, 1989); Keletso Atkins, *The Moon is Dead! Give Us Our Money: The Cultural Origins of an African Work Ethic, Natal, 1843–1900* (Portsmouth, NH, 1993); Jeanne M. Penvenne, *African Workers and Colonial Racism: Mozambican Strategies and Struggles in Lourenço Marques, 1877–1962* (Portsmouth, NH, 1995).

toll. Finally, internal turmoil is now more common than in the past, and affects the very possibility of carrying out research. Such conditions make it difficult or impossible to broach "sensitive" topics and inflect the course of research, while the prevailing tensions infect the researchers themselves. All these characteristics of conducting intensive fieldwork today are reflected in some way in the following essays.

An awareness of the lack of discussion of fieldwork in the methodological literature and of the changing conditions in Africa led Jan Vansina to organize a one-day symposium on fieldwork at the University of Wisconsin–Madison on March 20, 1993. Its goal was to explore how fieldwork contributes to the collection and especially the interpretation of historical evidence from Africa. Clearly, a deeper understanding of both local historical consciousness and historical evidence results from personal immersion in the society and internalization of the culture studied. But how exactly is this understanding to be developed during fieldwork, and how is fieldwork to be structured so as to attain its optimal effects? Intensive fieldwork exerts a considerable effect on the personality of the researcher. But does that not also mean that the precise effects of such fieldwork will vary considerably from person to person, and that perhaps no single recipe for fieldwork would even be desirable?

Prompted by the interest awakened by the symposium, Carolyn Keyes Adenaike then proposed to follow it up by publishing an edited volume about the subject. Five of those who had presented papers at the symposium agreed to rework them—Carolyn Adenaike, Janet Ewald, Henry Mothibe, Jan Vansina, and Michele Wagner. The editors then recruited the other contributors to this volume. Two among these came from Madison—Paul Landau in history, and Beverly Mack in African languages and literature—while the three others had studied at other institutions: Sheryl McCurdy in sociomedical science at Columbia, Z. S. Strother in art history at Yale, and Richard Shain in history at Johns Hopkins. The editors strove to assemble a set of contributors most of whom would report on intensive fieldwork carried out during the 1980s and 1990s, so that their collective experience would be of value to those who are about to go into the field themselves.[3] The goal was to gather enough diversity of experience to throw light on the fundamental processes by which fieldwork leads to the production of historical information and to better informed interpretations of that knowledge. It was therefore not necessary to assemble a statistically representative sample of all scholars who have recently carried out fieldwork. Still, we regret that only one among the contributors is African, and that despite our efforts, we did not succeed in enlisting African-American scholars as well; their perspectives on fieldwork are therefore absent from this collection.

The younger writers in this volume all found intensive fieldwork to be an absolute requirement for studying African social history. Michele Wagner and Richard Shain examined historical consciousness and changes in community identity; Sheryl McCurdy focused on healing practices, Beverly Mack on gender, and Paul Landau on the social context of conversion; while Z. S. Strother explored the social meaning and use of art objects, Carolyn Adenaike the complex interrelations of

---

[3] In eight cases, grants from Fulbright programs made such intensive fieldwork possible.

social categories and fashion, and Henry Mothibe aspects of labor history at the national level. They all worked within the framework of social history, because they investigated the social and cultural dynamics of communities. As may be typical for social historians, most focused on subordinate and often "mute" groups, including local communities (McCurdy, Shain, Wagner), trade unions (Mothibe), or people considered to be of lesser account (Landau). A few investigated a social web from bottom to top (Adenaike, Ewald, Strother, and Vansina). Only Mack's research focused squarely on an elite, but the emphasis was on women and thus on a "silent" and subordinate group within that elite.

The experience of intensive fieldwork is not only crucial to the endeavors of *a priori* social historians, but its practice fosters a strong consciousness of social history in any historian, whatever the topic studied. Even though the initial topics of research involved in the earlier fieldwork mentioned here (by Ewald and Vansina) were originally conceived as straightforward political history, the practice of intensive fieldwork showed social history to be so important that it transformed both projects into studies of social history. Hence it is a fallacy to think that historians who do not study social history or who focus on a much larger arena than a local community have little use for fieldwork and can be content to collect relevant local archives and traditions. To the contrary, such historians also stand to gain a greater depth of understanding as they are immersed in the culture they study and gradually uncover how local actors affected and shaped dynamics found in the wider arena.

The ten essays in this collection share an additional similarity, derived from the high degree of personal involvement in the communities studied, consisting of the researchers' disregard of earlier prescriptions requiring the maintenance of distance between researcher and researched in the name of objectivity. Instead, most of these writers used their own subjective involvement as an effective pathway to achieve an enriched and more nuanced understanding of the past than would otherwise have been possible.

These essays have been written first and foremost for those about to follow us in the field: young historians, and especially those engaged in social history. So far no book-length discussion exists about the pursuit of history in the field. The available works about fieldwork are written by and for anthropologists and do not meet the needs of historical researchers. The editors also realized how counterproductive it would be to construct a narrow manual of methods ("How To Gather Historical Evidence in the Field") because contingencies of time and space matter so much, the nature and intensity of the interactions between researchers and hosts is so crucial to the whole endeavor, and the impact of fieldwork on those who carry it out is so strong and varies so much according to personality. Thus we concluded that aspiring fieldworkers would be best served by a series of essays touching on various aspects of personal experience in the field. We therefore asked our collaborators if possible to discuss one striking and revealing episode in their fieldwork as a paradigm of their relationships with their local hosts, rather than to give a potted account of their research plans and the concrete unfolding of their research activities. The resulting essays intend to give future researchers at least some idea of how much their personalities will be challenged and engaged by others in the field and show them how much such encounters can contribute to a deeper understanding of the culture studied.

Readers may well ask how the experience described in these chapters relates to the input of fieldwork in formal academic results. They can find out by comparing the essays in this volume with the contents of the books, articles, and dissertations that have resulted from the research described here. In every instance, the major contribution of fieldwork was not the addition of oral evidence to written evidence, although that did happen. Rather, the major value of fieldwork lies in the ability to understand and interpret a mass of sources from a new and more valid perspective, informed by local culture and its collective historical consciousness as much as by the expertise in evaluating evidence from disparate sources that academic training imparts to all historians.

Although these essays are primarily written for foreign graduate students about to go to the field, they will also be of interest to African historians involved in fieldwork at home or in neighboring countries. Certainly language difficulties and "culture shock" will pose fewer problems for them, but local tensions, poverty, deteriorating health services, and lack of financial support are of much greater and lasting significance for them than for outsiders. Yet our African colleagues may well find relevance in the intellectual and methodological issues raised here, and be better informed about the goals and activities of foreign researchers. Perhaps ultimately this volume may serve to foster better understanding and communication between African scholars and the foreign researchers in their midst.

XVI IN PURSUIT OF HISTORY

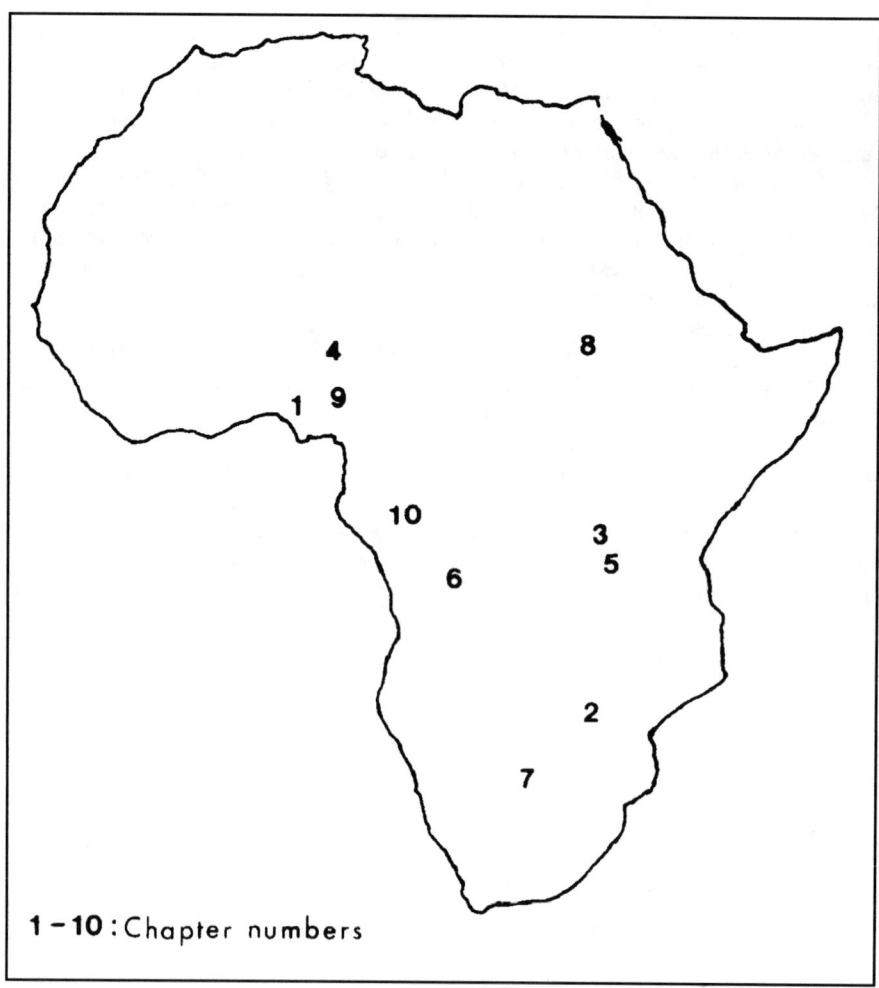

Map 1: General Location of Researcg Described in this Book

READING THE PURSUIT: AN INTRODUCTION

Carolyn Keyes Adenaike

"No event, no history," says the slogan emblazoned on the side of a passing bus in Lagos, Nigeria. At first sight, most historians today would disagree with this statement in principle, yet it is simply an observation about an event in the life of a bus driver. Like the acquisition of a bus, historical fieldwork in Africa is nothing if not an event in itself. It is a moment in time, a place, a project, a group of people, a memory. It is a major event in the lives of those who undertake it. It is an event undertaken in the pursuit of history, an event which shapes the contours and contents of the history derived from it and of the scholars emerged from it. It is the subject of this book.

Fieldwork, as popularly conceived, is an event more usually associated with anthropology than with history. In the popular imagination, the archetypal anthropologist is an intrepid soul with a marked resemblance to Indiana Jones, armed with a notebook, tape-recorder, and sturdy shoes, who heads off to some exotically remote area to perform the anthropological ritual of fieldwork. Equally archetypal and equally imaginary is the image of the historian as a bookish type, reminiscent of Mr. Chips with a laptop, who performs another day of scholarly labor by ferreting historical facts from dusty and disused local archives.

Improbable though it may appear, only the bus is real. The archetypal characters are purely fictional, although good fiction persuades with its resemblance to popular conceptions of reality. Ostensibly an archaeologist, Indiana Jones probably owes more of his popularity to the accumulated bulk of field memoirs written by ethnographers than to the monographs published by archaeologists. Mr. Chips, actually an English teacher, is here relegated to the archives because historians have not, for the most part, written about their experiences in the field.

The essays presented here are all written by historians, and the events they describe are as diverse and as real as the buses in Lagos. Stepping into the breach between the abundance of field research manuals on the one hand and the memoirs of anthropologists on the other, these collected essays present the experiences of ten historians in the field. In so doing they respond to an acute need in African history today. The need is acute because field experiences shape what historians learn about history, how they understand it, and how they present it. Individually and collectively, we in this volume are examining our work in the field, and thus we are examining how we practice history. We are examining how we learn and what we learn, in ways that do not otherwise appear in scholarly literature.

The types of learning that we are discussing in this volume are the types that cannot be referenced the way we reference other sources in footnotes. These are the kinds of learning that are experiential, personal, subjective by definition, and often deeply challenging to our concepts of ourselves. These are the experiences that shape not only the history we write, but also the individuals and historians that we become.

These experiences, by definition, go far beyond the paradigm of participant observation. They participate in much more than that paradigm ever intended to include, and they often merge the observer with the observed. As such, these are experiences for which no manual on field methods can provide preparation. At issue are personal adaptations to situations and environments. In describing our own adaptations, we ten are describing the contingencies, challenges, and difficulties too often glossed over in memoirs.

Being mostly younger scholars, we are describing parts of our pasts still colored by a sense of immediacy to our present lives. The young among us especially are writing from a position very close to the material. By the same token, we are describing encounters with an Africa in the grip of economic crisis, ethnic strife, and political turbulence. As much as our experiences are not those for which the field manuals were written, our Africa is not the one which those manuals envisioned.

Anthropological field manuals enjoin us to be objective, to maintain an intellectual detachment, to draw up careful interview schedules, to practice wisely the art of participant observation, to choose thoughtfully our "informants" and translators.[1] Existing grant and funding structures implicitly expect us to be able to accomplish our objectives in nine months, or less.[2]

Recently, some historians have begun to critique these expectations in print. The inadequacy of interview schedules for eliciting historical information has been underscored on the grounds that they leave no room for the historian to learn what questions need to be asked.[3] The fact that historical information may be intentionally withheld in the absence of a firm relationship of personal trust has been highlighted.[4] The inherent contradiction in the study of life histories has been pinpointed as an inability to obtain information about experiences which one does not share.[5]

---

[1] For example, R. F. Ellen, ed., *Ethnographic Research: A Guide to General Conduct* (London, 1984), and Pertti J. Pelto, *Anthropological Research: The Structure of Inquiry* (New York, 1970).

[2] Currently, most of the major grants applicable to African area research in history stipulate a period of nine months for dissertation research. In most cases, dissertation research is the first fieldwork experience for Africanist historians. In the past, visits of even less than nine months were considered fieldwork. For example, John J. Honigmann describes as fieldwork three months in 1944 in "Field Work in Two Northern Canadian Communities," 40; and Norman E. Whitten Jr. includes as fieldwork six weeks in the summer of 1966 in "Network Analysis and Processes of Adaptation among Ecuadorian and Nova Scotian Negroes," 381; both in Morris Freilich, ed., *Marginal Natives: Anthropologists at Work* (New York, 1970).

[3] Richard Roberts, "Reversible Social Processes, Historical Memory, and the Production of History," *History in Africa*, 17 (1990), 348.

[4] James Lance, "What the Stranger Brings: The Social Dynamics of Fieldwork," *History in Africa*, 17 (1990), 335-37.

Reading the Pursuit: An Introduction XIX

Anthropologists have long debated the theory and praxis of field research, but less commonly queried the stresses involved in the practice. Implicit research expectations have been critiqued on the grounds that the quality of material obtained ultimately depends on the experience of the individual researcher. It has been noted that the fieldworker's understanding of the subject under study is dependent on his or her own life experiences, whether in the field or out of it, as it is this life-experience which, in the final analysis, forms the researcher's frame of reference.[6] More trenchantly, it has been suggested that the current anthropological concern with concepts of self may be at least partially attributed to the "excruciating experiences" undergone by anthropologists during fieldwork, provoking an inevitable and necessary introspection and "confusion" as an integral part of the process of research.[7]

From psychologists, for whom the debate centers on emotion in relation to cognition, the criticism has been scathing. One writer has argued that such unpleasant emotions as embarrassment, shame, guilt, and even contempt are an integral part of the fieldwork enterprise, inevitably human consequences of the confrontations between culture and self inherent to fieldwork itself. The author of this critique further noted that the dissimulation or withholding of such personal information means that, in practice, deceit is also an integral part of scholarly field research. Carrying this to its logical extreme, he concluded that this throws the notion of scholarly "evidence" into disarray.[8]

While a handful of scholars have been shining flashlights on these and other qualitative problems, a sociologist has turned on the floodlights. Motivated by her own encounter with tragedy to quantify such incidences for field researchers as a whole, Nancy Howell has produced the first comprehensive study of the risks researchers face in the field. Her data range from the minor and mundane to the major and dangerous, but a cursory glance at her statistics will show that Africa is not the safest of fields in which to do research. Although based on a self-reported survey of anthropologists, her findings give pause for thought, and merit more than passing consideration here.[9]

The Africanists in her study, compared to specialists of other world areas, were the least likely to have access to creature comforts in food and lodging. Most did not have access to such basics of health and hygiene as safe drinking water or

---

[5] Leslie H. Townsend, "Out of Silence: Writing Interactive Women's Life Histories in Africa," *History in Africa*, 17 (1990), 355.

[6] Anthony P. Cohen, "Post-Fieldwork Fieldwork," *Journal of Anthropological Research*, 48 (1992), 339, 349, 351.

[7] Elvi Whittaker, "The Birth of the Anthropological Self and its Career," *Ethos*, 20, 2 (1992), 205, 207.

[8] Benjamin Kilborne, "Fields of Shame: Anthropologists Abroad," *Ethos*, 20, 2 (1992), 238, 242, 244–45. The deceit he describes is reciprocal, occurring on the parts of both the researcher and the researched. For the metamorphosis of such introverted feelings as shame and embarrassment to a range of externally-directed hostile emotions, the reader is referred to the relevant psychological literature, some of which is referenced in Kilborne.

[9] Nancy Howell, *Surviving Fieldwork: A Report of the Advisory Panel on Health and Safety in Fieldwork, American Anthropological Association* (AAA Special Publication No. 26, 1990). All percentages given here are for the personal experiences of respondents to her survey, 70 percent of whom were anthropologists and 30 percent archaeologists (p. 27).

toilets or medical facilities.[10] This notwithstanding, the overall impression given by the data is that of an odd sort of optimism among the Africanists surveyed, as few visited other scholars in the field for advice, even fewer took out life insurance or made out wills before heading off, and fewer still planned for emergency evacuations.[11]

This apparent optimism seems not to have been warranted by actual experience in the field.[12] Predictably, the figures show the hazards of disease in Africa to be genuine. The Africanists in the survey took first place not only for malaria, but also for typhoid and hepatitis A. Most contracted diarrhea and many contracted *E. coli* infections, while cholera afflicted over one third.[13] Disturbingly, most Africanists encountered criminal interpersonal hazards in the field, particularly violent assaults. Many reported personal experience of living through political turmoil and local factional conflict. Many also reported such accidental forms of violence as car crashes, and only a minority left the field without any type of injury.[14]

As might be expected from the foregoing, the Africanists also reported undergoing a number of affective disturbances ranging from hallucinations to depression, including rather high incidences of anxiety, manic states, and culture shock. The Africanists surveyed were in addition subject to the highest rate of repatriation stress and ran the highest incidence of personal relationship problems caused by fieldwork.[15] These statistics should be enough to make an Africanist think twice before dismissing the arguments of the psychologists. Clearly there is no basis on which to claim a special occupationally-selected resistance to the effects of stress.

In light of all the foregoing, it comes as no surprise to read ethnographic memoirs that recount extreme feelings of loneliness and unhappiness,[16] or even extreme feelings of dislike for the people being studied.[17] Rather, the surprise is how many memoirs gloss over such unpleasantnesses as if they were minor, or pass over them

---

[10] An alarming 55 percent resorted to self-treatment and only 24 percent reported consulting physicians. Howell, *Surviving Fieldwork*, 55–58, 60, 63. Why this should be so is beyond the scope of this essay. The interested reader can find comparative statistics on standards of living in UN publications and incidences of diseases in WHO publications.

[11] A mere 26 percent of Africanists sought advice from other scholars in the field, while only 12 percent planned for emergency evacuations. Specialists of other world areas did all these things more routinely. Howell, *Surviving Fieldwork*, 63.

[12] Among other hazards, Africanists also ran the highest incidences of fieldworkers anywhere for dehydration, severe weight loss, snake bites, scorpion and bee stings, attacks by army ants, and mosquito bites. Howell, *Surviving Fieldwork*, 65, 68, 77, 81, 83–86.

[13] More surprisingly, Africanists caught plenty of colds, got more sore throats, bronchitis, and toothaches than fieldworkers elsewhere, came in second to colleagues in the Pacific for headaches and migraines, took first place in allergies, and came in second to researchers in the Indian subcontinent for rashes. Howell, *Surviving Fieldwork*, 116, 130, 132, 134, 147–48.

[14] The figures are as follows: 52% reported experiencing criminal interpersonal hazards of which the single largest category (17%) were violent assaults, 30% reported political turmoil and 13% factional conflict, 17% were involved in car accidents, and the uninjured amounted to 22%. These statistics were higher than those reported by researchers for any other world area. Howell, *Surviving Fieldwork*, 89, 92, 99, 101, 113.

[15] The reported rate of repatriation stress was 22 percent, twice the average, while 35 percent reported relationship problems. Howell, *Surviving Fieldwork*, 152–155, 160, 168.

[16] Laura Bohannan [writing as Elenore Smith Bowen], *Return to Laughter* (New York, 1954; reprint, 1964).

[17] Bronislaw Malinowski, *A Diary in the Strict Sense of the Term*, trans. N. Guterman (New York, 1967).

altogether in silence.[18] Most memoirs, as most field manuals, seem to pass over both the quantitative and the qualitative difficulties as if they were of little importance.

Recently, some scholars have begun to challenge the effects of little or no or low-quality fieldwork on scholarship, arguing the need for research based on long-term residence in the field.[19] In one such critique, after eight years of residence in her research area, an anthropologist has taken to task the literature of that area, laying bare a collective web of inadequacies in field research and advocating that scholarship be based on the intimate and long-term knowledge of extended residence.[20] Whether or not the potential benefits outweigh the potential risks of extended residence in the field is perhaps a matter of personal decision, but it is important to note that research findings are beginning to be queried on the basis of the length and quality of fieldwork.

These preceding pages can easily be interpreted as describing a continuum, from the most conservative of field manuals at one end to the advocates of "immigrant" anthropology at the other extreme.[21] The contributors to this volume are situated at various points along this continuum. The shortest doctoral research included here is one year, and that follows previous in-country residence. The longest, at eight years, approximates an "immigrant" sort of history. The majority fall in the range of two to three years. As these chapters will make clear, our respective research experiences were all in one way or another related to our lengths of stay, and the latter were all well beyond those expected by funding agencies.

The Chapters

These research experiences have made their imprint on the scholarship of the authors of this volume. The depiction of this imprint and of its effects on the authors' understandings and presentations of history is best left to the chapters themselves and to the conclusion, but a few preliminary observations will not be out of place. All of the contributors to this volume have encountered the kinds of difficulties that Howell enumerates. All of us have been deeply marked in one way or another by our time in the field, and we all share a belief in the need to discuss our experiences. As these chapters will show, we have all stayed long enough in one place to sort through many of the difficulties and to conclude with a strong attachment to the places and people which defined and with whom we shared our experiences.

These chapters collectively document this process and its contributions to historical scholarship. Each in our own way, we are all describing challenges encountered. More importantly, we are describing how we responded to these challenges,

---

[18] Morris Freilich, "Field Work: An Introduction," in Freilich, *Marginal Natives*, 27–28, states that "Anthropologists, either consciously or unconsciously, attempt to forget the more stressful and unhappy times of field work," and provides his own explanation of why accounts of fieldwork are "selectively weighted toward the pleasant."

[19] As one example: Hermann Forkl, "Publish or Perish, Or How to Write a Social History of the Wandala (Northern Cameroon)," *History in Africa*, 17 (1990), 77–94.

[20] Lynn Hirschkind, "Redefining the 'Field' in Fieldwork," *Ethnology*, 30, 3 (1991), 237–49.

[21] Ibid., 238–39.

what we learned from them, and how they affected our research. It is our hope that these essays will be of interest and use not only to colleagues, but that they may also and especially benefit students contemplating field research.

The first chapter (Adenaike, "Life During Research") opens this collection with a presentation of adjustments made during the first six months of a thirty-month stay. Although it is an individual account anchored in a particular place and time (Southwestern Nigeria in 1989–1990), its interest lies primarily in the portrayal of an initial phase through which the fieldworker must pass. This is a stage which begins immediately upon arrival and lasts as long as necessary for the individual to begin to adapt to a new physical, personal, and cultural environment.

Approaching overall adaptations to the research area from a different perspective, Chapter 2 (Mothibe, "Fieldwork among Neighbors") moves to Zimbabwe and to the experience of an African researcher in a place unfamiliar yet close to home. Welcomed as a "brother" by those whose history he has come to study, the fieldworker must still negotiate the shifts of political, economic, social, and linguistic contexts inherent to the fieldwork experience itself. In this essay, distance and proximity are not geographical or cultural absolutes but relationships viewed through the telescoping lens of lived experience. Traversing social distances, the author provides a unique portrayal of research in a situation where both differences and similarities produce unexpected challenges.

Depicting the encounter with the research environment from another angle, the third chapter (Wagner, "Both Sides of the Border") describes fieldwork under the political conditions of a repressive regime. The author's experiences in Burundi between 1985 and 1987 draw a compellingly individual portrait of a general problem, one too familiar and too little discussed among Africanists today. Crossing the border four years later into Tanzania, she remains within the same cultural area yet enters a radically different working environment. Contrasting the impact of these two political climates on research strategies and relationships, this chapter links the large national picture to the smaller, local, and personal settings.

Moving to Northern Nigeria in the late 1970s, Chapter 4 (Mack, "Women's Work in Kano") addresses gender and social identity in the field. This is the account of a woman doing research among and about women in a Muslim society, at a time when this sort of endeavor is still a novelty. The author enters a community of women, inside an Emir's palace. Tracing her progress and position within and outside the palace over three years, the narrative depicts as well the development of personal relationships in research, the insertion of the researcher in the community, and the unexpected reward of life histories for research in oral literature.

Set in Tanzania in the 1990s, Chapter 5 (McCurdy, "Learning the Dance") explores relationships and trust in another kind of closed community of women. The context is a woman's initiation, and the initiated is the researcher herself. In a vivid and sensitive portrayal of individuals and situations, the writer describes a journey in which what is learned must not be revealed. Her narrative brings large ethical issues into a specific and local scene, describing also the balance of control between researcher and researched over the content of the study.

The sixth chapter (Strother, "Suspected of Sorcery") presents an unexpected encounter with the power of rumor in Zaïre. After two years in the field, the researcher is accused of witchcraft. In a thoughtful and thought-provoking essay, she traces the development of the events and factors leading up to the eventual accusation, exposing multiple layers of interpretation and their latent potential for manipulation by individuals with competing interests. Her chronicle raises complex issues of the interplay between the researcher's dual social identity as both insider and outsider, and of the double-edged effects of extended residence.

The seventh chapter (Landau, "Falsehood, Truth, and Thinking Between") examines a single relationship formed in the course of fieldwork in Botswana. This is an account of the researcher's conversations with one elderly man, and of the tension between information and interpretation on which their relationship pivots. Gently probing the nature and dynamic of their discussions, the writer describes a thin line between information and misinformation, between interpretation and manipulation, and between truth and falsehood. In so doing, the author delineates the impact of the circumstances of present situations and individual objectives on accounts of the past, questioning the relationships between divergent views of the past and the meanings of history.

Balancing personal experience with academic implications, Chapter 8 (Ewald, "A Moment in the Middle") looks back on research in Sudan in the 1970s and discusses how the work done in the field shapes the history written. This is a view of a time and place in which local and academic histories share no common ground, and in which the gap is bridged by writing the history after leaving the field. With the clarity of mature reflection, this chapter directs its gaze to the meaning and nature of fieldwork and its relationship to historiography.

In Chapter 9 (Shain, "A Double Exile"), reflecting on his eight years in Nigeria, the writer sets forth the implications of long-term residence. Narrating a journey not yet completed, this essay exposes in potent and immediate terms the deepening chasm which separates historiography on the two sides of the Atlantic. This is an account in which there is no functioning bridge, and where a heavy toll is exacted from those attempting to cross. Questioning the location of "home" and the meaning of exile, this chapter depicts the difficulty of finding and defining the audience for whom it is possible to write a history so long researched.

The tenth and final chapter (Vansina, "Venture into Tio Country") describes how the author comes to appreciate the historical consciousness of the people whose history he proposes to study in Congo Brazzaville in the early 1960s. Expecting to gather data about an old kingdom steeped in political traditions, the researcher finds instead that what matters and is remembered about the past is not a kingdom history writ large, but social and family histories, writ small. This is an account of changing the research to fit and describe local conceptions of history; it is also an account of the reaction to this from the academy. Thirty years after the fact, this chapter raises questions about the relationships between fieldwork and history that are still keenly contemporary in their pertinence.

A Forest of Themes

Separately and together, these chapters embrace a forest of themes large and small of historical fieldwork in Africa. While some of these themes may appear to be universal to fieldwork, many are located in historical changes in fieldwork practices over time.[22] Some are specific to fieldwork in history and still others are delimited by the subject matter of the research itself. As an elephant walking through the forest, the discussion here is but a preamble to "open the road" for the contents to follow. A preliminary foray, these introductory observations serve a purpose of opening to discussion many of the themes embedded in this volume.

To cut the broadest of swaths through the forest is to expose the soil in which the trees first took root. It may begin with the observation that the practice of fieldwork germinated as part of the production of knowledge by Europeans for Europeans about the areas and peoples of the world under European colonial domination. Fieldwork's deepest roots sprouted from a situation of European hegemony. From the outset, the practice of fieldwork was both predicated on that hegemony and integral to an academic discipline which was itself an outgrowth of the same hegemony, the field of anthropology.[23]

There was an initial and inherent contradiction between the purpose of fieldwork as it was originally conceived and that of African history. African history pushed its own roots in the formulation of knowledge by Africans for Africans about the African past. Only later did the intended readership of this history shift to include European academics.[24] From the outset, African history developed as a reaction to and challenge of European hegemony. Yet despite this goal, when it grew into an academic discipline during the first flush of independence for African nations in the 1960s, its practitioners borrowed the practice of fieldwork from anthropology. The first generation of academic Africanist historians adapted the practice of fieldwork to their aims of gathering oral sources. The present generation built upon the work of their predecessors. Using the previously established framework of history as a basis, the generation of the 1980s–1990s demonstrated an overall trend towards a new kind of social history. A shift towards a search for meanings, mentalities, and perceptions of mind became apparent.

The requirements of such an approach are reflected in fieldwork practices. The shortest research periods of the younger participants in this volume (one year, eighteen months) both follow previous stays in the country of research. All share in common a longer and deeper involvement in the research area than used to be the

---

[22] No history of fieldwork has yet been written. George W. Stocking Jr., "History of Anthropology: Whence/Whither," in *Observers Observed: Essays on Ethnographic Fieldwork* (Madison, 1983), 7, defines the topic of the volume as "the development of ethnographic fieldwork in sociocultural anthropology," but falls far short of achieving a history of fieldwork. J. Urry, "A History of Field Methods," in Ellen, *Ethnographic Research*, also fails to provide a history of fieldwork. Robert Lawless, Vinson H. Sutlive, Jr., and Mario D. Zamora, "Introduction," in Lawless, Sutlive, and Zamora, eds., *Fieldwork: The Human Experience* (New York, 1983), xiii–xiv, gives a brief synopsis/periodization of types of writing about fieldwork, but points out that "the history of fieldwork is a sadly neglected area." John Clammer, "Approaches to Ethnographic Research," in Ellen, *Ethnographic Research*, 65, notes that fieldwork practices are a product of history, both the intellectual history of anthropology as a discipline and the sociopolitical history of colonialism; he addresses many of the issues a history of fieldwork might fruitfully include.

[23] Some discussion of the colonial impact may be found in Ellen, *Ethnographic Research*, and in Stocking, *Observers Observed*.

[24] Samuel Johnson, *The History of the Yorubas* (Lagos, 1921) is a good example of this early period of African history. Some discussion of the early histories and their role in the African nationalism of the day can be found in Robert July, *The Origins of Modern African Thought* (London, 1968). Later, the work of such scholars as Cheikh Anta Diop, *Nations nègres et culture* (Paris, 1954) and I. A. Akinjogbin, *Dahomey and its Neighbours 1708–1818* (Cambridge, 1967) targeted a European academic audience.

case. From the longer stay and the closer relationships that develop within it grows a new approach to interpretation. Out of praxis not theory flow changes in epistemology and beliefs about the roles of objectivity, responsibility, and interpersonal relationships in research. From this it follows naturally that scholars should strive for collective interpretations of history (Shain) or for empowerment of elders and teachers to research the community history on their own (Wagner). What this approach to research yields in terms of our experiences and ideas about fieldwork is the primary focus of this book.

As the following chapters will make clear, the experiences presented here are not so much representative of a generation as of a particular type of fieldwork. The most important common denominator in the group is doubtless our lack of detachment. This feature first and foremost characterizes the type of fieldwork represented here, and most sharply distinguishes us as a group from both our predecessors and many of our contemporaries. Among the hallmarks of this new research is that the interpretation of history flows from the internalization of experiential learning during fieldwork. Other features of this type of fieldwork may be drawn out by a preliminary foray through the forest of themes implicit in these chapters.[25]

On the surface, fieldwork may be defined as a process undertaken in the pursuit of knowledge, a process in which the researcher must make certain psychological, cultural, and physical adjustments to a new human environment in which the fieldworker is assigned a gender and a social identity by the collectivity, and within which the knowledge obtained depends on cooperation between the researcher and the researched. On closer inspection, however, even such grand themes as ethics, adaptations, cooperation, gender, and social identity have been subject to historical changes in the practice of fieldwork.

In the classical period of anthropology, the researcher was an outsider.[26] Later, the social identity of the researcher became some locally specific role into which she or he could almost, but not quite, be made to fit. At best, some anthropologists have described being identified as someone's daughter,[27] or as the secretary of a professor.[28] At worst, others have described being defined as personally deviant from local norms,[29] or as a government official, or a spy.[30]

---

[25] Historians have not shown much tendency to write about their fieldwork experiences. David Henige's questions in "Fieldwork in Zambia," *History in Africa*, 5 (1978), 273–74, went unanswered.

[26] George W. Stocking Jr., "The Ethnographer's Magic: Fieldwork in British Anthropology from Tylor to Malinowski," in Stocking, *Observers Observed*, 97, notes that although Malinowski advocated participating in the life of the study area, "total immersion was not easy for him"; instead of living in a village, he lived in a tent "sixty meters" outside of it, where "he could to some extent shut out the native world."

[27] For example, see Jean Briggs, "Kapluna Daughter," in Golde, *Women in the Field*.

[28] Ernestine Friedl, "Field Work in a Greek Village," in Golde, *Women in the Field*, 214.

[29] Aram Yengoyan, "Open Networks and Native Formalism: The Mandaya and Pitjandjara Cases," in Freilich, *Marginal Natives*, 412, reports being identified as "a homosexual" in the Philippines.

[30] Howell, *Surviving Fieldwork*, 97–98, says 13 percent of her respondents reported being suspected of spying, and further observes that "sometimes the suspicion is correct: after the crisis, Louis Leakey openly admitted that he had been working for the Kenyan government, as Mary Leakey put it, 'broadcasting propaganda to the loyalists and gathering intelligence about Mau Mau groups and their leaders'" (citing Mary Leakey, *Disclosing the Past* [Garden City, NY, 1984], 111). Pertti J. Pelto, "Research in Individualistic Societies," in Freilich, *Marginal Natives*, 276–77, working in rural northern Minnesota in the 1960s, records non-cooperation from an interviewee who regarded his questionnaire as "part of what she believed to be

In the past, it was common for anthropologists in the field to attempt to create an identity for themselves by offering verbal definitions of who they were and what they were doing. The truth or falsehood of these statements was not considered to be important. One self-definition particularly popular among previous generations of anthropologists was that of "historian."[31] In light of such intentional dissimulation in the past, it is no surprise to find skepticism regarding the self-presentations of researchers in the present. In the essays in this volume, the researchers' identities are clearly not created by the fieldworkers alone but are rather arrived at by a process of negotiation over time.

In the chapters to follow, social identity is a constant theme, and one rich with nuance. Each person's identity is unique, multivalent, and subject to change over time. Each is the product of specific historical factors in the area of study (including memories of previous researchers), perceptions of the individual researcher by members of the community, and the behavior of the fieldworker. The interplay between these three factors is the common thread in these highly individual experiences. Together, these chapters show that social identity is established by consensus, with gossip on the one hand and negotiations by the researcher on the other; subject to change over time, social identity usually progresses from more stereotypical to more personal.

Several of these papers highlight the effects of different aspects of the historical context in defining the identity of the foreign researcher. Factors here include memories of the colonial past (as noted by Landau; Strother; Vansina), contemporary racial politics (Landau; Mothibe), and perceptions of expatriates, Europeans or Americans (Strother; Vansina).[32] Depending on past experiences, foreign researchers may be regarded as people who do not work, get angry (Adenaike), and should

---

an already widely developed Communist plot to take over the United States," and accused Pelto of "being an undercover worker for the 'conspiracy.'" Cora Du Bois, "Studies in an Indian Town," 224, describes suspicions of spying in India as being so common, and accentuated by the "ineptitude of our Central Intelligence Agency, as well as the Chinese and Pakistan hostilities," that she came to view these suspicions as "normal."

[31] As early as 1971, at least one anthropologist declared all misrepresentations of self and project to be categorically unethical: Joseph G. Jorgenson, "On Ethics and Anthropology," *Current Anthropology*, 12, 2 (1971). A perusal of published memoirs, however, shows such admirable standards to have been more often practiced in the breach than in the observance, as the following examples illustrate. Morris Freilich, "Mohawk Heroes and Trinidadian Peasants," in his *Marginal Natives*, 188, explained his research as "a great interest in Mohawk history" and (193) concealed his true research because he felt people would not cooperate if he behaved openly as an anthropologist. Paul Rabinow, *Reflections on Fieldwork in Morocco* (Berkeley, 1977), 90, presented himself as a historian because this was "understandable and acceptable to the villagers." Nicola Goward, "Personal Interaction and Adjustment," in Ellen, *Ethnographic Research*, 115, says that "an anthropologist may satisfactorily explain an interest in the contemporary lives of informants as part of a fascination for their history and the way of life of their ancestors." In a rare presentation of the other side of the coin, Mary Ellen Conaway, "The Pretense of the Neutral Researcher," in Tony Larry Whitehead and Mary Ellen Conaway, eds., *Self, Sex, and Gender in Cross-Cultural Fieldwork* (Urbana, IL, 1986), 57–58, an anthropologist, recounts the effects it had on herself and her research when she arrived in Venezuela in the 1970s and found she was following on the heels of "a woman in the Peace Corps" who had "told everyone she was an anthropologist on a research assignment."

[32] Specific page references for the themes discussed in this introduction will be found in the index. References given here are by chapter only.

be viewed with suspicion (McCurdy; Vansina).[33] In the present context, it is common for local people to have relatives who are university graduates (Ewald) or professors (McCurdy), rendering the category of student a natural and innocuous fit in some cases (McCurdy; Strother) and in other cases providing a comfortable niche at the university (Mothibe; Shain).

Several chapters report the active role taken by others in shaping the fieldworker's identity. In two cases, this is accomplished by friends who decide how to present the researcher to others, when the researcher agrees (Adenaike) and when she objects to the content of the introduction (McCurdy). In one case, the insistent and unwanted attentions of a state security agent play an important role in shaping the researcher's identity (Wagner). Rumor, too, appears in these chapters as a factor in the social construction of identity (McCurdy; Strother), with the rumor mill being at times employed to transform the identity of the researcher to the benefit of others (McCurdy).

The interplay between insider and outsider facets of the fieldworker's identity is an essential theme. Two chapters describe having different social identities in different local areas (McCurdy; Strother), the result of different degrees of familiarity but also and especially the result of voluntary association with certain individuals. McCurdy's initiation thus does not automatically make her an insider in the community, but it does immediately make her an outsider to the rivals of those who initiate her; becoming an insider in the community occurs separately from the initiation. Similarly, Strother's association with a particular chief makes her an insider with one group, outsider with another, and thus potentially useful for political rivalries; the dynamic at work here is in some ways reminiscent of Laura Bohannan's experience.[34]

Often, identities shade fluidly between two or more roles. Mack's association with the women of the palace renders her "a known member of the palace community" in some situations and an "envoy of the emir of Kano" in others. Shain, although on the one hand an outsider as a foreign student, is simultaneously quite the insider as a university lecturer. In his words, "the multidimensionality of my life made it impossible for me to limit myself to any one particular role." Mothibe, welcomed by both old and new university-mates as the first African researcher

---

[33] On the subject of perceptions of previous researchers, Robert J. Maxwell, "A Comparison of Field Research in Canada and Polynesia," in Freilich, *Marginal Natives*, 466–67, records receiving a visit during his fieldwork in Samoa from a delegation of chiefs who instructed him not to follow the example of Margaret Mead and "shame the Samoan people." Laurie Krieger, "Negotiating Gender Role Expectations in Cairo," in Whitehead and Conaway, *Self, Sex, and Gender*, 121, describes encountering in Cairo in 1978–1980 a prevailing image of Western women as "loose," a view derived from television shows like "Charlie's Angels" and "tourists clad in shorts and bathing suits." In an unusually detailed account of remembered perceptions of foreigners, Michael V. Angrosino, "Son and Lover: The Anthropologist as Nonthreatening Male," in Whitehead and Conaway, *Self, Sex, and Gender*, 71, describes research in Trinidad in the early 1970s on an island where American troops had been stationed during World War II, and how their presence combined with later waves of American "cruise-ship tourists" had taken on legendary proportions and produced an image of Americans as all in search of a good time. Du Bois, "Studies," 225 describes encountering "a feeling that we foreign academicians come to India to exploit local scholars and go home to advance our careers at their expense"; she comments that "exploitation of this sort is not unknown in the United States, where professional ethics are rarely insisted upon."

[34] Bohannan, *Return to Laughter*, 84, 232–37.

from south of the Limpopo, is accorded far greater respect for that achievement than probably befits the average foreign student. He records his ability to mix with both senior academics and other graduate students, observing that influential interviewees with doctorates treat him as an equal while those with less formal education offer him deferential regard. Although ostensibly remaining "a stranger," the theme of polyvalent, situationally-specific identity resurfaces in Landau's chapter.

Intangibles factor in as well. Often remarked in these pages are one or several points at which a change in identity makes itself felt. In some cases this is a subtle shift in the behavior of others (e.g., McCurdy notes a series of changes in the comments she overhears about herself), or in terms of address (e.g., Mack becoming "Hajiya;" or Adenaike becoming different types of "wife"). At times the change takes a more overt form as protective behavior on the part of the neighbors (Adenaike; Mack; Vansina). In each case the shift has an ineffable quality to it, and cannot be reduced to any specific single event or set of events.

The importance of the behavior of the researcher in the construction of identity is made most evident in two chapters. Mack points out the subtle differences in dress and behavior which set her apart and by which others set her apart. It is important to note however that there is a vast difference between these little tinkerings and the oft-encountered attitude that a foreigner can do whatever s/he wants. The tinkerings Mack describes are the little differences that fall within the parameters of the socially acceptable (norms) and the personally acceptable (individual variations within the context of those norms); they are the products of her individual negotiation of the dual status of insider and outsider. Thus, although not a Muslim, she demonstrates knowledge of the Holy Book and a willingness to fast, and so acquires the Muslim honorific of "Hajiya." Similarly, Adenaike attempts to express the proper balance of status and respect in dress and behavior for her research, and finds herself in turn respectfully addressed as "wife."

Enmeshed with social identity is gender identity. It has long been a commonplace of fieldwork folklore that the woman researcher becomes "an honorary man."[35] Concrete evidence of such an identity is, however, hard to find in the memoirs of women fieldworkers, and is often conspicuously inapplicable even to the accounts of early women anthropologists. To note one such conspicuous example, Ruth Landes' fieldwork experience was marked by such extreme sexual harassment that she ultimately paid the price with her career—hardly evidence of a masculine gender identity.[36]

In favor of the "honorary man," two principal arguments have been advanced. The more common view holds that by the very fact of doing academic research the

---

[35] For example, see Carol A. B. Warren, *Gender Issues in Field Research* (Newbury Park, CA, 1988), 21.

[36] Ruth Landes, "A Woman Anthropologist in Brazil," in Golde, *Women in the Field*. Carolyn Fluehr-Lobban and Richard A. Lobban, "Families, Gender, and Methodology in the Sudan," in Whitehead and Conaway, *Self, Sex, and Gender,* speaking of fieldwork in Sudan in 1970-1972 and 1975, Fluehr-Lobban states: "As a woman with a husband and later a young daughter, I was not afforded the status of 'honorary male' which many Western female professionals living alone in the Sudan receive." A striking exception is that of Elizabeth Faithorn, "Gender Bias and Sex Bias: Removing Our Cultural Blinders in the Field," in Whitehead and Conaway, *Self, Sex, and Gender,* 276, 281, who records having been viewed "as a man" when she first arrived in Papua New Guinea in 1971, to the point where women "insisted that I lift my blouse for them all to see the positive proof of my female sex."

female scholar crosses gender lines, by virtue of having an education and a profession that women in the study area do not have.[37] The less common view holds that a loss of gender identity is an internal psychological phenomenon experienced by the researcher herself, part of a range of psychological adaptations to a radically different cultural environment in which she feels herself to be an outsider.[38]

In light of these views, it is interesting to note that only one woman in this collection expresses any doubts about her gender. Mack describes herself as having a "dubious female status" and says "neither wife nor mother, and very much in the public realm, I could only be classed as ambiguous." These statements, however, are presented in an overall context of patently feminine situations. Her use of the word "status" rather than identity must be highlighted, as her youth, singleness, and childlessness all clearly place her in junior feminine roles of child care and errands. Her gender identity does not appear to be in doubt, and her relatively low status conferred by that identity is equally apparent.[39] Perhaps most importantly, as she points out, a woman doing what she was doing in the 1970s was a novelty. In Africa today, the study of women's issues is no longer a novelty, and neither are women academics; on the contemporary situation it is pertinent to note the facility with which McCurdy is identified as a "medical student."

Of the six women included in this volume, only Strother records overt transgression of gender roles, and this is not a function of her person but of her research. Art history, in the area where she works, is defined as a masculine subject, as are both the art objects themselves and their spiritual significance. Pursuing the topic requires crossing gender lines, and she notes women's complaints that she is "neglecting them." In one of the more striking instances of this traversal of gender, men protect her from the punishment that would ordinarily be inflicted on women who do not keep out of sight of the boys' initiation, an initiation she is given permission to witness. Such instances, including her eventual accusation of possessing a masculine power, might be construed as evidence of "honorary man" status.

---

[37] One example is provided by the statement, included in John L. Wengle, *Ethnographers in the Field: The Psychology of Research* (Tuscaloosa, 1988), 91, from one of his informants, that "women don't behave like you have to. They don't live alone, they don't even dress the way you do. They're not intellectuals. They don't carry little notebooks around. They have children—so what's the matter with you?" Regina Smith Oboler, "For Better or Worse: Anthropologists and Husbands in the Field," in Whitehead and Conaway, *Self, Sex, and Gender*, 36, states: "A male researcher is unambiguously coded as male," but a woman researcher by virtue of her education, "has higher status than the average woman in a traditional community" and is thus "able to move to some extent toward the higher status sex/gender role. It is said that a female researcher working alone can establish a somewhat androgynous gender identity and gain equal access to both sexes." This claim was not borne out by her own experience, accompanied by her husband, in Kenya in 1976–1977.

[38] This interpretation is given in Wengle, *Ethnographers*, 91–92, supported by the statement from one of his informants that "One important aspect of fieldwork was that I had to become sexually neuter. In their eyes, I wasn't what a woman is. I couldn't quite be what a man is either, and so I was neuter. I was a neuter in role and over time in that identity as well. Really, I felt asexual in my inclination. I just lost my sexuality. I was nothing."

[39] Jean Jackson, "On Trying To Be an Amazon," in Whitehead and Conaway, *Self, Sex, and Gender*, 271, records feeling "both elated and irritated" that, after some time in Colombia and Brazil (c. 1970s), "My femaleness had superseded my status as an affluent and high-status outsider. Although more of an insider, I was being assigned to my proper place on the inside—second place."

However, as she herself points out, even for this a feminine archetype does exist, an archetype with which she is explicitly identified.[40]

A number of points militate in favor of a firmly feminine gender identity for the women in this volume. Four of the six report instances of sexual harassment in the field (Adenaike; Mack; Strother; Wagner), and this is certainly not something one would expect to occur in the absence of a strong gender identity.[41] Also indicative of a definitely feminine identity are instances of male discouragement, attempts to gain male approval, and cases of unwanted, unwarranted or otherwise dubious male involvement (Mack; McCurdy; Wagner). Equally indicative, and again a clear departure from previous literature, none of these women record any expressions of doubt about their marital status.

The classic paradigm of marital status in the field is that the woman researcher, single or married, is never believed to be married, regardless of what she claims.[42] This again, in light of the essays in this volume, appears to be largely a function of the behavior of the researcher.[43] Carrying one's own water (Adenaike; Strother), doing one's own cooking and/or housekeeping (Adenaike; Strother), expressing an interest in other women's children (Mack; McCurdy); all of these are doubtless involved. Perhaps most importantly, none invent elaborate lies about non-existent husbands (only Mack has a wedding-like band thrust upon her) and all attempt not only to conform to feminine behavior, but to emulate a model of a virtuous woman. This is precisely McCurdy's rationale for seeking initiation, Adenaike is "determined to do" what many Nigerian women routinely do, and Mack invests herself in becoming the good woman, while Strother carries out as many womanly chores as her research permits.[44]

---

[40] Warren, *Gender Issues*, 17, 21, notes that women have often sought access to men's worlds in the field. This may be another factor in the "honorary man" tradition. Shirley Ardener, "Gender Orientations in Fieldwork," in Ellen, *Ethnographic Research*, 124–25, also notes that women have often gained access to men's domains in fieldwork, but attributes the myth of the "honorary male" to gender roles in the researcher's own culture and in the academy.

[41] Ardener, "Gender Orientations," 120, observes that sexual harassment is suspiciously uncommon in fieldwork literature, due to a "reluctance" on the part of women to discuss it, thus rendering its importance or frequency "difficult to establish." Howell, *Surviving Fieldwork*, did not even include it in her survey. While some may view my choice of phrase here inappropriate or too strong, in my opinion the issue is too important to be left in silence.

[42] Even though her husband lived with her for the duration of her fieldwork, Friedl, "Field Work," 211, describes being considered not as his wife, but as his secretary, because "Looking young, especially by the women's standards (they kept commenting on how smooth my hands were), and having no children seemed to outweigh the fact that I was married." Wengle, *Ethnographers*, 92, includes a description from one of his informants of creating a fictional fiancé during her fieldwork because, as she put it, "women had always been asking me about marriage and children and so on"; the more women asked her for details, the more fictional details she created, which "near killed me. That was hard. It was far from harmless, which is how I first thought about it. . . . I just kept replaying a scenario that wasn't true, and I was conscious of the lies in all this. That was an enormous psychological burden."

[43] Warren, *Gender Issues*, 16–17, notes that "women's worlds are not necessarily open to all women. Gender alone is not enough to win full acceptance into female concerns," and makes the parallel observation for men. On the importance of behavior, Warren, 20, further notes: "Laura Nader's behavior, outside the frame of traditional female, so puzzled the Zapotec Indians that they decided that she was able to turn herself into a man or woman at will" (citing Laura Nader, "From Anguish to Exultation," in Golde, *Women in the Field*, 104–105 (Chicago: Aldine, 1970).

[44] An earlier echo of such behavior is provided by Oboler, "For Better or Worse," 37, in her statement: "In my attempt to conform I had only to practice the public reserve of a good Nandi wife."

A Forest of Themes XXXI

Corollary to gender are age and race, both of which are also socially constructed aspects of identity. While both may appear to be understated in these chapters, neither is absent.[45] Although all of the contributors recount in these pages episodes from their chronological youth, not all are socially coded as equally youthful (contrast the relative maturity accorded to Vansina with the rather extreme youthfulness attributed to Strother). In some cases, social age is subject to fairly dramatic shifts, independently of chronological age (e.g., Adenaike; Mothibe). Similarly, complexion and race are independent variables in these essays, conceptions about them varying from place to place, and race being generally less primary a factor in the social construction of identity in the research areas included in this collection than it is in North America. As physiological characteristics alone may not be enough to create a gender or an age identity, so they may not alone be sufficient to create a racial identity.

Where race emerges as an explicit theme in these chapters, it does so in divided communities. Hence, McCurdy is a "foreign *mzungu*" at every turn, in a community deeply divided and suspicious of outsiders (in contrast to the term *"oyinbo"* in Adenaike). Hence, Landau is not just "a white man forty miles from the Transvaal border" but a "tax collector" or "government official" in momentary temporal lapses of memory. Complexion most strongly becomes race in areas where it is politicized and thickly overlaid with power relations, whether in the form of "Arab slave traders" of the past (McCurdy) or in the form of temporal and geographic proximity to white supremacist regimes (Landau, Mothibe). In most of these accounts, complexion does not surface with the political and conceptual overtones of race, but rather trickles quietly beneath the surface of chapters, entwined with various aspects of insider/outsider identities and facets of foreign-ness, from which it is nearly indistinguishable.

In only one chapter is race clearly pervasive to the social identity of the researcher. Mothibe is received as a "brother" when he arrives in a country which just ten years previously had achieved independence from a white supremacist government. His remark that race relations had since significantly improved can as well be read as an indication that the issue remains very much alive. Much as the warmth of his reception is influenced by the situation he meets on arrival, it is also shaped by his coming from that vast area "south of the Limpopo" then still under (in the words of Landau) "the last white supremacist regime in Africa." The combination of his complexion and origin produces a high regard for his achievement from the people with whom he works. So high is this regard that it transcends ethnicity (in marked contrast to the politicization of ethnicity in other chapters, e.g., McCurdy, Shain, Wagner). It does not, however, automatically grant him insider status and even as "an educated African child" he remains subject to challenge as a foreigner.

A given identity is based largely on behavior. Lifestyle is an enormous aspect of behavior, and one which influences strongly the ways in which fieldworkers are

---

[45] Efforts to recruit an African-American scholar willing to address the theme of race in fieldwork having been unfortunately unsuccessful, this potentially rich area of analysis does not receive in this volume the attention the editors had hoped for. The interested reader may wish to compare Gloria Marshall, "In a World of Women: Field Work in a Yoruba Community," in Golde, *Women in the Field*, with chapter one of this volume, as both write about research in the same cultural area albeit three decades apart. Age was not one of the planned themes for this book.

perceived by members of the communities in which they work. The classical practice in colonial times for many anthropologists was that of the scholar living in a European-style house, with as many of the amenities as could be obtained, and with a retinue of servants to perform the mundane chores of living. The argument has been made that this freed the scholar's time for work, as if one "would have had time for nothing else"[46] without servants to do the housekeeping, but it is equally clear that this freed the researcher's time for leisured teas and dinners with the colonial expatriate community.[47]

Such a lifestyle was a product of a specific historical period, dependent on colonial infrastructures or their survival in a neo-colonial context. In contemporary Africa, any such context is conspicuously lacking, its absence rendering such a lifestyle extremely difficult, if not impossible, to maintain. None of the contributors to this volume attempt to maintain it. These accounts show a variety of living situations. The variety runs from lodging with the family of an alumnus of the researcher's home university (Ewald) to living in symbiosis with the local crazy woman (Strother) to house-sitting or living in a rented flat with or without one's husband (Adenaike; McCurdy), to renting an ordinary house in an ordinary neighborhood (Landau; Mack), to living in a graduate student residence hall (Mothibe), to living in a converted shop (Vansina). None of these experiences occur in a colonial context, and distance from any expatriate community is a tacit theme as is distance from the local academic community (Adenaike; Mack). On the reverse of the same coin, two contributors immerse themselves as fully as possible in the local academic community (Mothibe; Shain).

To some extent these choices about living arrangements and lifestyle may reflect individual preferences, but to a large extent they are the product of the circumstances of each particular place and time. This combination of circumstance and choice has strong effects on the physical health and well-being of the researcher. Long treks on foot between sparse settlements (Strother), bicycling down rutted roads in the rain (Wagner), getting about by public transport (Adenaike; McCurdy; Mothibe; Shain) or by car (Landau; Mack) or not getting about at all (Vansina),

---

[46] Friedl, "Field Work," 208, complaining of mud, dust, kerosene cookers, and carrying water from a well, says "Obviously we needed some domestic help. Anthropologists in the field always have some such need, but for a woman anthropologist running a household, such help is utterly indispensable. Had I had to do the housework under these primitive conditions, I would have had time for nothing else." Angrosino, "Son and Lover," 67, echoing this view, asserts that: "As a single person and an impecunious graduate student, I had learned to fend for myself as cook and housekeeper, but in the interests of saving time and energy, I was not willing to do all that in the field," and so decided to live with a family, where the wife/mother would do "all that" for him.

[47] Stocking, "The Ethnographer's Magic," 100, 108, notes that Malinowski lived in the Trobriands with a "retinue of two or three New Guinean 'boys,'" in a colonial style, and that he made frequent trips for "refuge" to the company and houses of Europeans. Nicola Goward, "Publications on Fieldwork Experience," in Ellen, *Ethnographic Research*, 94, says of Malinowski that "Fieldwork itself seems to have been a part-time occupation, secondary to the pursuit of pleasure, leisure, and exercise, fitted in between novels and *Punch*, taking tea or an enema, or confined to the period before breakfast," and defines this as characteristic of a colonial context. See also Goward, "Personal Interaction," 108. Bohannan, *Return to Laughter*, 9–13, 238–39, 241–43, describes living in a "hut" but still maintaining this lifestyle as much as possible. Anthony P. Cohen, "Informants," 227, in Ellen, *Ethnographic Research*, considers such a lifestyle and its accompanying social distance from members of research communities as symptomatic of fieldwork in the "colonial era."

A Forest of Themes

carrying water (Adenaike; Strother), fasting during Ramadan (Mack), reading by candlelight or lanternlight (Landau; McCurdy), clearing the bush (Adenaike), and converting a shop for habitation (Vansina) probably sound more like the activities of Peace Corps volunteers than graduate students in history, but these are a product of the conditions. In an environment, even an urban environment, in which malaria is both endemic and one step ahead of medical advances, it also just goes with the territory (Adenaike), as do typhoid (Mack) and yellow fever (McCurdy).

The observations of one contributor about the political context apply as well to the conditions of daily life, that "the time period when the research is conducted makes an enormous difference in the kind of experience one has" (Wagner). These conditions have an equally great impact on the lessons the historian learns, as all of the contributors speak of learning by doing. Whether the doing is locating ruins (Ewald; Strother), dyeing textiles (Adenaike), spending one's days in seclusion (Mack), avoiding security agents (Wagner), being initiated (McCurdy), driving a treacherous road (Landau), teaching classes (Shain), attending community events (Vansina), participating in recreational activities (Mothibe), or doing housework (Adenaike), all of the contributors underscore the importance of practical, lived experience in the learning process. The result is a blurring of the boundaries of research and an overwhelming quantity of material, as one writer notes (Mack).

As contributor Janet Ewald observed, "fieldwork is not a time or a place or a personal experience, but a type of work in its human context." Living daily life is part of that work. It is important to note that the type of work described in this volume differs in significant respects from the "participant observation" of anthropological method. The early participant observers, as noted above, did very little participating.[48] Later, "participant observation" came to be defined as "simulating" the enactment of a role.[49] Where daily life intersects with work, as it does in different ways in all of these chapters, the type of work done parts company with the model of participant observation. As one result, the work fits differently, more deeply, into its human context.

The human context of fieldwork is one of social and interpersonal relationships. This milieu is what fieldwork is all about. It is in beginning to understand this human environment that we begin to understand our research topics (Adenaike;

---

[48] Rabinow, *Reflections*, 79, characterizes participant observation as "oxymoronic," with the qualification that "However much one moves in the direction of participation, it is always the case that one is still both an outsider and an observer." Clammer, "Approaches," 68–69, considers "participant observation" a myth because "many anthropologists who claim to use the method actually live apart from the people studied, often in a house or apartment with much better facilities than those of the informants, and surround themselves with equipment (justified as being 'necessary' to the fieldwork) and comforts (often characteristic of their own culture)," because language facility is usually not achieved by fieldworkers but "is a primary requirement of genuine participation," and because "many anthropologists in the field actually represent themselves as something else."

[49] According to Friedl, "Field Work," 196, "simulated rank . . . is what participant observation always involves." Barbara Harrell-Bond, "Studying Elites: Some Special Problems," in Michael A. Rynkiewich and James P. Spradley, eds., *Ethics and Anthropology: Dilemmas in Fieldwork* (New York, 1976), 120, in reference to her fieldwork (1967–1968, among persons with equivalent levels of education to her own, in Freetown, Sierra Leone), notes the moral difficulties posed by this, saying: "I suspect that they are inherent in all the participant observational research conducted by anthropologists. It is simply always a great deal easier to avoid facing up to them when our field research is conducted among a remote and nonliterate group."

Shain; Strother; Vansina). It is also in attempting to understand and fit into this setting that we must make our most challenging adjustments. From the first flush of excitement/shock on arrival (Adenaike; Wagner) through trying to accomplish the necessary practicalities to get settled in (housing, official documents, language training, and so on: compare Adenaike; Vansina; Wagner), the process is really about adapting to a new human context, and adjusting one's expectations and objectives to the new context (Mack; Wagner). This is a process in which the researcher often has a sense of becoming like a child, learning the basics all over again (Adenaike; Mack; Strother). It is a process in which new friends give cues on how to behave in public, and offer explanations in private (Adenaike; McCurdy). It is a process of learning whom to fear and whom to respect (Wagner), of learning to "be just one in a crowd," and to accept respect when it is offered (Mothibe).

The process of adapting to a new human situation is greatly eased by some measure of linguistic facility, the absence of which was once regarded as a prerequisite for fieldwork.[50] Although not all achieve the same degree of competence, all of the contributors to this collection have some linguistic preparation. The importance of language facility is thickly underscored in these essays (Landau; Mack; McCurdy). An ability to speak the language may be regarded as proof of sincerity of the researcher's interest (Mack), and the ability may not matter as much as the evident effort expended in learning. The type of language spoken may locate the researcher in social space (Landau; Mothibe). A knowledge of riddles and proverbs may earn one points and provide a socially acceptable means of verbal self-defense (Adenaike; Mack). Language training at its best may also be a kind of cultural training (Adenaike).

The political context can exert great influence on the formation of relationships. This again is a product of historical change in the area of research, a major contemporary factor in many parts of Africa. National politics have always some relationship to the local area (Ewald), and security agents may be a fact of life even in remote rural areas (Strother), and even when they appear relatively innocuous (Vansina).[51] As one contributor observes, "the political milieu imposes itself at every step of historical research whether the historian wants to admit it or not" (Wagner). Security agents may behave at times like a personal nuisance to the fieldworker, but it is prudent to realize the risk such attentions can pose to those who associate with the researcher; hers may be an extreme example, but Wagner argues the need for caution and awareness in all cases.

It may be a truism that we see ourselves at least partially as others see us. A sense of being not merely seen but actively watched is evident in some chapters (Adenaike; Mack; McCurdy). What Mack calls "Life in a Fishbowl," McCurdy describes as a sense of isolation from the outside world. Being observed in our fish-

---

[50] An inability to speak the language was one of the hallmarks of fieldwork in the classical period of anthropology, part of a methodological construct in which the scholar was supposed to be distant and different from the people in the area of study. Helen Codere, "Field Work in Rwanda, 1959–1960," in Golde, *Women in the Field*, 143–44, still argued in 1970 for an absence of language facility as a necessary precondition for fieldwork.

[51] Says Du Bois, "Studies," 224: "I consider it desirable to leave my notes freely accessible to any intelligence officer who may wish to examine them during my absence from my room. Such is his duty, and I feel I should make no attempt to outwit him."

bowls, we are aware of a need for self-control, to behave properly, to contain curiosity, and to be patient (Mack; McCurdy). We may fear becoming socially unacceptable, outcast, or shut out (McCurdy). We may be confronted with dependence (Adenaike), or with a sense of helplessness, of being pulled along by people and events more or less in spite of ourselves (McCurdy). Our self-concept can hardly avoid being changed by the experience (Adenaike; Shain).[52]

Such difficult emotions as frustration and embarrassment (Adenaike) may be our constant companions at first, until we learn to cope. In situations where those around us have much to fear, we may find ourselves internalizing those fears (Wagner). When we adjust, we may do so with what Mack defines as "patient acceptance" and what Wagner describes as "learning to take the quiet road." The sense of adjustment is implicit to all these accounts, as is the end result of feeling "at home" (Strother; Shain).

It is significant that none of us describe the sort of deep social isolation in the field of which older writers often spoke:

> I would like to be able to report that . . . people came to love and trust me completely, helped me sympathetically when I needed it, and freely opened their hearts and minds; the truth is far from that rosy ideal. I carefully had to calculate a strategy for almost every piece of information I gleaned, and I bartered, cajoled, and wheedled or bluffed knowledge I didn't have in order to get more.[53]

As this passage so clearly shows, part of the difference lies in historical change in the values and procedures of fieldwork. In the past, fieldworkers have spoken often of values centered on work, on the accuracy of the data, and the career that hinged upon the careful recording of data.[54] The extent to which this has changed is perhaps most sharply rendered by the fact that all the contributors to this vol-

---

[52] Wengle, *Ethnographers*, 7–8, describes an individual's sense of identity as dependent on many factors, including links with a familiar physical and interpersonal environment, observing that "when an individual's social or physical environment changes rapidly, his sense of identity will be threatened." Considering that such changes of environment are inherent in fieldwork, Wengle, 8–9, asserts that "the initiate anthropologist experiences an attack against his sense of identity during fieldwork," because "the student's entire world, as mirror, has changed radically," producing "a psychological climate that is hardly conducive to maintaining a sense of selfsameness and continuity in time and a feeling of embeddedness in a wider environment." From these considerations, Wengle, 19, concludes that "the fieldwork experience may produce psychological changes ranging along a continuum from the minor and superficial to the major and profound." Surprisingly, however, in his study of anthropologists, Wengle, 42, finds that the majority of people "undergo no such significant personality change."

[53] Peggy Golde, "Odyssey of Encounter," in Golde, *Women in the Field*, 75.

[54] Laura Nader, "Professional Standards and What We Study," 169–70, describes fieldwork in the 1950s as part of a system of professional prestige in which the values are "tied into the system of ranking one anthropologist's work over that of another." Wengle, *Ethnographers*, 12–16, makes the point that many anthropologists react to the identity-challenges of fieldwork by creating a new identity for themselves as anthropologists, as members of a special professional group. Hazel Hitson Weidman, "On Ambivalence and the Field," 241, said of her fieldwork: "It meant becoming an anthropologist," and "In essence, anthropology helped me to establish an identity." An informant in Wengle, *Ethnographers*, 14, said of her fieldwork: "I'm an anthropologist now. I don't have to wait for the Ph.D., for an academic job, to be one. That's immaterial. I am one now. And the fieldwork, that's why." Stocking, "The Ethnographer's Magic," 109, notes that the true hero in Malinowski's monograph on the Trobriands was not the Trobriand islanders but Malinowski himself.

ume seem to take a certain set of values so much for granted that explicit statements about these concepts are rare in these essays. Implicitly, however, we collectively demonstrate that ours are not work-centered but person-centered values.[55] Expressed in our individual ways, these essays share in common this one crucial trait.

This contrast between the work-centered and the person-centered views of fieldwork is made most explicit by Wagner's refusal to do anything that might jeopardize the people with whom she associates, even at the price of her research. It is equally apparent in Strother's refusal to give an amulet when requested to do so, even though its refusal cannot be expected under the circumstances to further her research. Strother phrases her refusal in terms of fidelity to her own self-concept, and contrasts it to advice she later receives. That hers is a professional decision as much as a personal one is made clear by comparison to Bohannan who, under similar pressures, not only fabricated "amulets" but publicly announced their "powers" and proceeded to use the belief in those "powers" to her own benefit.[56] The contrast shows that a work-centered value system allowed the researcher to manipulate others, while in these chapters a person-centered value system gives control to others. Thus McCurdy acknowledges that her own values give to the people with whom she works an effective means of "silencing" her on certain topics and aspects of research, a fact she simply accepts as morally necessary.

This sense of personal responsibility is doubtless a factor in creating a climate of interpersonal trust. McCurdy describes the young woman who "put her reputation on the line" and "vouched for me as a trustworthy and honest person." To gain trust, the researcher needs to be trustworthy. The researcher must be available to hear people's concerns, and accountable to those concerns, as Shain notes. The importance of keeping one's promises is highlighted by the delivery of another historian's photographs (McCurdy). It is also underscored by one contributor's efforts to protect the people who help her (Wagner). Reciprocally, the researcher needs to trust others for their advice (Adenaike). And, of course, people must trust the researcher in order to share information (Mothibe; Shain; Wagner).

Entwined with trust is cooperation. As one contributor states, "where we get our best information is often where we make the best friends" (Strother). Even when working in archives, the assistance of "good friends" may be instrumental (Mothibe). While it may appear idealistic to assert that cooperation must be voluntary (Adenaike), these are realistic accounts. The importance of previous acquaintance is noted (Mack; Mothibe) as are gender and generational differences in cooperation (Vansina). People cooperate for different reasons, and the researcher may

---

[55] Wengle, *Ethnographers*, 21, distinguishes two principal types of responses to the identity-challenges encountered in the field, which he terms "defensive" and "reparative" behaviors. Defensive behaviors are attempts to maintain links "with the home world," through food, language, leisure activities, or whatever "offers the possibility of establishing a sense of symbolic continuity" with home, and can be used "by the fieldworker as a means of identity maintenance." These "defensive behaviors" all serve to maintain distance from the human and physical environment in which the fieldwork is conducted. Along the same lines, the usual "reparative" behavior, as noted above, is the creation of a new identity as a professional. Put in different terms, these are part of a complex of behaviors belonging to a conception of fieldwork in which the achievement of a professional goal is paramount. The alternative "reparative" behavior is what Wengle, 31, defines as "secondary identification with the native culture," as will be discussed below.

[56] Bohannan, *Return to Laughter*, 250–63.

earn cooperation by being useful (McCurdy). Usefulness may represent a means to accomplish something for one individual (McCurdy). It may represent an extra pair of hands for child care and errands (Mack), or it may represent an opportunity to have one's story be told (Mothibe). At times, cooperation may be given not only when the researcher serves no apparent useful purpose, but even when cooperation with her represents a clear and present risk, as is demonstrated by the disclaimers repeated to Wagner that the risks do not matter.

In the older ethnographic literature, the persons with whom the scholar established associations in the field were called "informants."[57] The term has become a linguistic convention, and one not absent from these pages (Ewald; Landau; McCurdy; Mothibe). However, to take one example where the term is used, the degree of nuance in the written evocation of individual women (McCurdy) says clearly that these are not relationships of the type one expects to find attached to the word "informants."

Described in these chapters are complex, individual, and highly varied relationships, and it is the very individuality of these ties which forms one of the most salient and important themes of these collected essays. Connections may be sought by the fieldworker or by people in the community, or they may be formed by accident (e.g., a flat tire, as in Wagner). Factors here may include persistent daily visits by the researcher (Mack), and they may include common friends among graduates of the researcher's home university (Mothibe). Relationships may be shaped by the fieldworker's position in the long-standing rivalries of others (McCurdy; Strother), or by the dictates of politics (Wagner). They may be initiated by personal introductions or by letters of introduction given by others (Ewald; Mothibe).

These are relationships in which one both gives and receives respect (Adenaike; Mack; Mothibe), in which others give the researcher the strategies she lacks (Adenaike; Mack), in which others decide what the researcher will do and how much she will learn (McCurdy), or whom he will meet (Mothibe). These are alliances in which the fieldworker may be pulled in different directions by competing social obligations (McCurdy) and in which the boundaries of public and private may need to be carefully distinguished (McCurdy). These relationships are the crucible in which the research is formed, and a change in them produces a change in the information received (Strother). Certain topics can be discussed only within a firmly established personal relationship (Wagner). It is in a context of such firmly established bonds that one writer encounters the histories of women's lives, richly textured with unexpected frankness, personal perspectives, and generational differences (Mack).

The common emphasis on the personal qualities of the relationships in this volume shows them to be based on far more than what older ethnographers sought and defined as "rapport." Described in these pages are individual feelings of personal rapport, in its common-usage meaning as an intimate and unspoken understanding between two people who know and care for each other. Absent from these pages is any reference to or description of the "rapport" of older anthropological literature in which the word defined the point at which an informant and a researcher reached a common understanding of the topic under study, with the result that the informant began to

---

[57] For example, see Pelto, *Anthropological Research*.

produce the information desired.[58] This change is indicative of a historical shift from work-centered field relationships to person-centered relationships in the field.[59]

Also indicative of this shift are the descriptions, a common denominator in these chapters, of particularly important individuals, persons with whom the researcher obviously shares especially close ties. From the descriptions, it is evident that these individuals are very different from the "key informants" of the past. "Key informants" were the people on whom older anthropologists relied for the bulk of their data and analyses.[60] By contrast, the persons painted in special detail in these accounts appear in the roles of facilitators and friends. They introduce the researcher to others, sharing their social networks and offering advice and friendship, but they do not, and are not expected to, fill key data-giving roles in the research.

In straying so far from the models of the types of relationships established by our predecessors in the field, these chapters share another common feature: the authors have no illusions about objectivity, and no desire to distance themselves in its name. In the words of one contributor, what some call "objectivity" is but "studied avoidance," a "convenient reprieve" from the "morally painful burden" of involvement (Wagner). In the view of another contributor, the promotion of "scholarly objectivity" is intended not to improve fieldwork, but to facilitate re-entry to "North American academic life" (Shain). As another puts it, writing about her experience in the field amounts to describing "my own life, in all its complexity, confusion, and subjectivity" (Adenaike). Another describes her research as a process of "personalities" and "trying to cope" (Mack). In the words of yet another, it is the essence of fieldwork that one "develops sympathy" for the people and issues involved, and thus gains "insights" about the realities of life for the people most directly concerned (Mothibe).[61]

---

[58] Morris Freilich, "Toward a Formalization of Fieldwork," in Freilich, *Marginal Natives*, 539–56, devotes a lengthy section to "rapport," defining it as the ability of the anthropologist to procure information from informants. Freilich, 540, distinguishes the anthropological meaning of "rapport" from its common-usage meaning, stating that, "Achieving great rapport does not necessarily mean having good relationships," but it does mean having "an agreement to communicate"; he discusses several ways in which such "an agreement" may be achieved, pointing out, 545, that one "obvious and very useful" means of establishing "rapport" is the payment of cash for information. These views, including the payments of cash or kind, are echoed in Goward, "Personal Interaction," 109, 117–18.

[59] Warren, *Gender Issues*, 59, notes: "The 1920s–1960s language of objectivity in ethnography has given way to a discourse of 'immersion and distance,' but still the distance remains—the explicit or implicit instruction to the fieldworkers not to get too close to informants."

[60] Cohen, "Informants," 224, notes a tendency over the years for ethnographic researchers to rely "heavily" on a few "key informants." Wengle, *Ethnographers*, 28–31, discusses how key informants tend to be marginal people in their own societies, people with whom the anthropologist can identify to some extent. Rabinow, *Reflections*, 73, describes his own key informants as "marginal." Pelto, "Research," 257, says that his own "first important informant" in Finland in the 1950s was "marginal" in the community; he further observes, 257n.1, that anthropologists commonly find that the individuals most willing to associate with them "may be deviants, social outcasts, persons who are particularly critical of their own community, or . . . who have had more than the usual amount of contact with outsiders."

[61] John Van Maanen, Peter K. Manning, and Marc L. Miller, "Editor's Introduction" to Warren, *Gender Issues*, 5, observe: "Fieldworkers would like to believe that whatever they see, hear, and write up as a result of their research experience in a particular setting is what any other similarly trained and situated fieldworkers would also see, hear, and write up. This is the ethnographic conceit and, to a certain extent, it has kept the enterprise going for the past fifty or so years. Such a conceit has had its day, however. Increasingly, fieldwork is regarded as a highly and almost hauntingly personal method for which no programmatic guides can be written."

In Wagner's account, so keenly aware is she of the possible consequences her actions might have for people, that not only is objectivity about these people a myth but it is also impossible to be "detached" from the politics of the time and place. We internalize the biases of the areas in which we work (to the point where the types of patience described by Mack and Adenaike are non-transferable between our respective areas). We internalize also the fears of the area in which we work (Wagner), and the specters (Landau). Our personal involvement with people may provoke in us depression when they are unhappy or when tragedy strikes (McCurdy). In describing one such instance, McCurdy reacts to her sense of being "pulled" into women's lives by "relationships," by responding with a felt need to "gain some distance" in order to "function as a researcher." Yet the whole narrative is in contradiction with the objective scientific researcher as an ideal.[62]

Abandoning "rapport," "participant observation," and "key informants," and throwing objectivity to the winds, amounts to violating the Prime Directive of the previous generation, an imperative which even Captain Kirk found impossible to maintain on his interplanetary fieldtrips.[63] Older fieldwork literature frowned on this sort of thing, enjoined researchers not to do it, and admonished those who did it anyway for "going native." The phrase was a component of a methodological construct in which one was supposed to remain internally true to the distanced (and superior) stance of a detached scientific observer while externally and temporarily using whatever locally-specific role-playing seemed necessary; the point at which one internalized or truly felt one's local role was the point at which one violated the prime imperative of fieldwork and "went native."[64] Fortunately, the contributors to this volume have collectively abandoned both the unhappy phrase and the impractical methodological framework of which it was a part, relegating both to the colonial past from which they sprang.

---

[62] Pelto, *Anthropological Research*, devotes several pages, 21–30, to defining anthropology as a science. Stocking, "The Ethnographer's Magic," 74–75, 80, notes that late-nineteenth-century anthropologists first trained as scientists and that the term "field work" itself "derived from the discourse of field naturalists." The ideal of the detached scientific observer is echoed in Wengle, *Ethnographers*, xvi, by the statement: "Anthropologists participate in the cultural life of their people yet also maintain enough distance from it to record its features more or less objectively."

[63] John Gulick, "Village and City Field Work in Lebanon," in Freilich, *Marginal Natives*, 138, advocates an ethic of non-interference. Michael A. Rynkiewich, "The Underdevelopment of Anthropological Ethics," in Rynkiewich and Spradley, *Ethics and Anthropology*, in particularly illuminating passages on pp. 49 and 58–59, describes how, during the course of his fieldwork in 1969–1970 in the Marshall Islands, the "nonintervention" he held as central to his sense of professional ethics was severely buffeted by the presence of the United States military. Ultimately, this experience forced him to redefine his own ethics, thus: "I see my responsibility to the people I study to be to deal with the problems that concern them as well as with those that interest me" (59).

[64] In brief, "going native" describes an internal, psychological, and intellectual process in which the researcher identifies with the local area of research rather than with the profession of anthropology. This is what Wengle, in *Ethnographers*, 31, calls "secondary identification with native culture," pointing out that this permits the researcher "to feel once again that he has a place where he belongs, that he is again a member of a larger, more enduring whole." Fuller definitions and discussions will be found in: Freilich, "Toward a Formalization," 530–33, and in I. C. Jarvie, "The Problem of Ethical Integrity in Participant Observation," *Current Anthropology* 10, 5 (1969), 505–508. Jarvie sharply admonishes the "honest anthropologist" not to forget that "as well as being a scientist he is a member of the society he came from and will return to."

It is our personal involvement which allows us to internalize the intellectual frameworks and "categories of experience" of the areas in which we work (Landau; Shain). By so doing the researcher strives above all to achieve a history that will not only be intellectually acceptable to the people with whom s/he works, but that will be faithful to what is felt and experienced as important about that history for the people most directly concerned. Yet this goal, and the level of personal investment from which it is inseparable, does not come without exacting a price. Nowhere is the price tag more vivid than in Shain's account of his personal "exile." As he observes, the result of a high level of personal investment is far from an achievement of "bicultural fluency" and more likely to be a sense of isolation from North American academe. Indications of this occur but rarely in these essays, obliquely couched in the interstices of some chapters, and even in Shain's writing they can be presented only in the third person impersonal. The core issue here is neither reducible to repatriation stress nor unique to long-term research, but indicative of a tension between the goals of a particular type of fieldwork and mainstream North American academic convention. It is symptomatic of a deepening rift between academic agendas and concerns for African history on the American side of the Atlantic and the meanings of African history in Africa. Perhaps the greatest challenge lies not in striving to learn history for its own sake and on its own terms during fieldwork, but in finding some means of presenting the history thus learned on the American side of the divide.

Historical Methods

The methods and the goals of research must be consistent. As historians, our methods differ from those of even contemporary anthropologists, because the intellectual contexts of our disciplines differ. Not bound by the theoretical propositions of anthropology, the historian is free to follow the direction of the data. If the goal of the historian's research is to create a history consistent with the concerns of the people with whom s/he works, it then follows that the methods as well as the direction of the study must be shaped on the ground. Not surprisingly, one of the most salient features of these essays is their collective emphasis on historical methodology. Historical fieldwork shares with every other kind of historical research the common need to evaluate information, to assess its value as evidence, and to cross-check it with other types of evidence. The processes of collecting, evaluating, and assembling historical evidence are described in particular detail in three chapters (Landau; Mothibe; Vansina).[65] The essential difference however, is that archives cannot talk back, but people can, and do.

---

[65] This is not intended as a discussion of historical evidence for non-historians, or as an analysis of the differences between anthropology and history. It is, however, important to note that history and anthropology require different types of fieldwork and that these produce different types of data. For example, Elizabeth Tonkin, "Participant Observation," in Ellen, *Ethnographic Research*, 222, includes a puzzling passage about the "historical importance" and validity of the data produced by anthropological fieldwork. In contrast, Clammer, "Approaches," 67–68, 84, points out that anthropological fieldwork and the data it generates have limited utility for history, as the fieldwork itself is based on concepts of space ("village

Contributors describe evaluating information on the basis of the level of trust the teller reposes in the researcher and substantiating all information with other information (Wagner). In these accounts, it is primarily personal knowledge of the teller that produces belief (or skepticism: Landau; Vansina) in the sincerity of the account told (Strother), and reciprocally it is personal knowledge of the listener that makes the teller trust enough to tell (Strother). Practical experience is also used to both obtain and evaluate more formal sources of historical information (Adenaike).

Living in the present, we can use that present to understand the past (Adenaike; Ewald). Understanding and experiencing daily life can be used to understand data about the past in archives (Adenaike). It can also be used as a means of understanding the ways in which history is reinvented in the service of the present (Ewald; Landau). It can as well be used as a means of detecting the influence of accounts written in the past on accounts told in the present (Mothibe; Vansina). By living the "daily routine" we learn the "idioms and languages" used to conceptualize and discuss the past (Shain). We learn also the realities of "people's lives as lived" (Landau), and we hear "the real voices of the African people" (Mothibe).

The data about specific methods in these chapters are as varied as the individuals and situations which shape them. All are shaped by specific situations, and some seem to grow so organically from their settings as to be almost invisible as methods. In the words of one contributor, "things never go as planned, and things always happen the way they should" (Mack). Research designs need to be changed to match actual situations (Adenaike; Mack) or to reflect "the wishes of my informants" (McCurdy). This changing of the research project to match the lived-in context is a constant theme in all the chapters, although in each it happens a little differently, as circumstances require. Thus, one contributor speaks of rewriting the research proposal "based on the realities that I could see all around me" (Adenaike), and another notes exchanging his "university-bought categories" for those that matter to the people concerned (Landau). One contributor describes the process of arriving at a history which shares the perspective of the local area (Ewald), while two others describe changing their views of history to match those of the areas in which they work (Shain; Vansina).[66]

The paths followed to reach these goals are as varied as the situations to which they are adapted. One contributor speaks of learning by watching and doing, allowing her friends to formulate research methods for her, and verifying friendly advice as one would historical data (Adenaike). Another speaks of the advantages

---

community") and time ("ethnographic present") that can be viewed as effectively "obviating the necessity of worrying about history." He concludes that "there are certain kinds of questions that one simply cannot ask of traditional fieldwork data, since the techniques inherent in that method have no way to answer or even discover them. When one is concerned, for example, with social change or with the working of politico-economic structures in the wider society on the smaller community, the limitations of fieldwork are glaringly revealed." As such concerns are the stuff of history, so also must be certain research methods.

[66] Some anthropologists have also recorded changes in research; for example, Gulick, "Village," 150, describes changing his topic while in the field because "reality was more complex than I had originally envisaged"; Jackson, "Amazon," 267, notes changing her research topic in the field "after realizing my original proposal was impossible to carry out."

of seclusion and of becoming as silent and taken-for-granted as the walls (Mack).[67] Another speaks of the benefits of being welcomed as a "brother" and yet being placed outside of the national political arena by his foreign nationality (Mothibe). One describes the advantages of his wife's artistic ability in attracting and appealing to people's interest (Vansina). Another speaks of learning indirectly knowledge which she is honor-bound not to use in order to better understand the evidence she can obtain from formal interviews and thus be permitted to use (McCurdy). Yet another describes the rewards of a university teaching position as a process in which his own conception of history is "fundamentally altered" (Shain).

Three writers describe conducting group village-assembly type interviews at first and then following up individually later (Strother; Vansina; Wagner). In Wagner's account, the public group interviews were intended to "emphasize that I had nothing to hide," a necessity dictated by circumstance. Hiring assistants to transcribe tapes yields a security agent/employee, who then cannot be fired, another product of the situation. A delicate approach to emotionally or politically sensitive aspects of the past is also adopted, allowing the speaker to set the tone and direction of the discussion and offering graceful ways to change the subject when it becomes difficult to speak. Close attention to the psychological dynamics of human interactions becomes routine. In a freer context, "town-meeting-style gatherings" become the norm of interviews in which "public discussion" is both "lively and vivid," and where the elders themselves convene the "history gatherings." In this more relaxed setting, the "research team" is able to set the tone of the interviews and the research project transforms itself into a community effort (Wagner).

In another situation, it is the researcher's sensitivity and awareness of the psychological dynamics of interviews that allows Landau to disentangle the threads of divergent accounts of the past. A careful textual and interpersonal analysis of interviews becomes the norm here, with close attention to phrasing and choice of words. Analyzing the motivations that interviewees may have for putting across particular versions of the past, Landau turns the same analytic method on himself, examining the ways in which he inadvertently prompts for certain types of answers through his demeanor and verbal cues in his questions. His attempts to reconcile irreconcilable versions of the past lead to an attention to detail, and to an avoidance of subsuming the details under some artificially reconstructed "version of 'the' whole." The path in this case leads not to a whole but to a "narrative" of details, and to the question of truth in historical narrative.

The need to collect and compare data from many and different sources is a commonplace of historical method. In these accounts, it is based also on an awareness that the practice of history should not be partisan and on an awareness that traditions change. One contributor mentions the importance of asking many people for "exegesis" (Strother). Another mentions the importance of staying long enough

---

[67] Warren, *Gender Issues*, 18–19, describes the advantages of women's invisibility in many field settings, and gives several examples from her own experience in which her presence seemed simply not to be noticed, as well as the following (at a treatment center), when it was noticed: "I vividly remember one day deciding to go upstairs, an action expressly forbidden to anyone not resident in the facility. Someone started to protest; the protest was silenced by a male voice saying, 'Ah, what harm can she do, she's only a broad.' Upstairs I went."

Historical Methods

in one place to hear more than the official version of history, and describes talking to many people, asking about family histories as well as kingdom history, and visiting outlying areas in order to go beyond the official Muslim history of the center (Ewald). What these different strategies all share in common is summed up well by Ewald's description of collecting pieces of information which exist as pieces rather than as a coherent history, and then putting the pieces together.

It is clear in these accounts that as much as perceptions of the researcher shape the way the project is seen, so also do perceptions of the project shape the way the researcher is seen. Thus, a topic on art leads to witchcraft because power is "associated with all talents and abilities" (Strother). A topic on women leads to life in a women's world and to statements by men that the topic is impractical because women do nothing of interest (Mack). A topic on textiles shapes friendships and produces a heightened sense of the importance of personal appearance (Adenaike). A topic on community leads to a rocky relationship with national politics and the impossibility of pursuing the subject (Wagner). The common thread here is one of legitimacy and of the reciprocal relationship between the legitimacy of the topic and that of the researcher. To this, two chapters add the caveat that legitimacy on the ground does not imply legitimacy in the eyes of the academy (Shain; Vansina).

In these days of research restrictions and research clearances which must often be obtained before a grant is even awarded,[68] it may be easy to assume that legitimacy is *a priori*, but these accounts show this to be too facile an assumption. A sensitive topic, even a funded one, may produce intractable problems with research clearance after the funds are awarded and the researcher is arrived in-country (Wagner). Likewise, research clearance (Mack) and research affiliation (Adenaike; Mack) may pose problems in-country even for such apparently innocuous topics as women's literature and textiles. On another level, what seems an innocuous topic may still lead to personal challenges from local authorities (Strother). In more than one case, research which is accepted locally leads to later challenges, not to say attacks, from academic colleagues (Adenaike; Shain; Vansina). Perhaps one cannot choose one's topic too carefully, but perhaps also the greatest lesson is simply to expect the unexpected with an attitude of "patient acceptance" (Mack).

In assembling this volume, we began with a symposium[69] and afterwards actively sought contributions that would emphasize, each in one chapter, some particular theme of historical fieldwork. Although some themes have had to be dropped along the way for lack of a writer willing to address them, the broad aim of capturing in print a sense of the variety of the experience has been achieved. Individually and collectively, these assembled chapters speak to a range of themes and experiences exceeding even that for which we had hoped.

Separately they may be read as selected aspects of individual experiences; together they may be read as a single account of a journey told in many voices, from the first flush of excited arrival through the initial adjustments and mini-odysseys of personal relationships to writing up and reflecting on the meanings of history

---

[68] As early as 1970, Du Bois, "Studies," 224, noted that fieldwork, "if allowed at all, involves elaborate procedures and clearances. More than ever good briefing and tact are professional obligations."

[69] "Historical Fieldwork in Africa," African Studies Symposium, University of Wisconsin–Madison, March 20, 1993.

and historical scholarship. It would take an entire book to fully address the experience of any one chapter, and this lengthy introduction touches only the surface of these richly textured reflections. Hence, these are not chapters to be read quickly or once and never again; rather the reader will find more in them on returning to them again and again. Separately and together, they incorporate many more aspects of historical fieldwork than this introduction can mention. While it may be true that the reader will find in these pages what s/he looks for, s/he will find no fiction.

1

Life During Research

Carolyn Keyes Adenaike

At the outset, I should probably say that I was in Nigeria, living in Ibadan, for two and a half years under the combined auspices of a Fulbright and a Mount Holyoke College alumnae grant. I was there to do the research for my dissertation on textile history, focusing on hand-dyed fabrics (*adire*).[1] More importantly, before going to Nigeria, I had the extraordinary good fortune of being taught by Michael Oladejo Afolayan. Dr. Afolayan taught me far more than the basics of the Yoruba language. He taught me how to be polite, and somehow managed to equip me with the skills necessary to negotiate all sorts of situations. I still made mistakes of course, but the fact that I managed to avoid the worst ones, and that I managed to have the kind of success I did, is very greatly due to the preparation that Dr. Afolayan gave me.[2]

The title ("Life during Research") means exactly what it sounds like it means: this essay is about the two and a half years of my life that happened while I was in Nigeria to do research for my dissertation. Fieldwork was not time out from life. Those two and a half years were an eventful and important part of my life. My intention here is to describe, however briefly, the life part of doing fieldwork, and the effects of that on the research results.

I went to Nigeria with two fixed ideas in my mind. First, I was determined to love the place. Second, I was going, to the best of my ability, to do a good job at my research. To me, doing a good job meant three things: (1) that I would stay for a minimum of two years, (2) that whatever came out of it would be openly and hon-

---

[1] The resulting dissertation, "*Adire*: Cloth, Gender, and Social Change in Southwestern Nigeria, 1841–1991" (University of Wisconsin–Madison, 1993), is deposited under the name of Carolyn Keyes. The term *adire* includes all fabrics to which the color and design are added by local artists after weaving. The focus on *adire* led my research in many different directions, one of which is described in "Putting the Color Back in the History," in Robert W. Harms and others, eds., *Paths toward the Past: African Historical Essays in Honor of Jan Vansina* (Atlanta, 1994), 415–25. The dissertation used the evidence provided by textiles to reconstruct a history of technology, art, economics, production, and social change.

[2] A complete list of acknowledgments for the research described here would exceed the length of the chapter itself. I am grateful to all those who helped along the way, and wish especially to thank the two people who figured most prominently in preparing me to make the adjustments described in this chapter, M. O. Afolayan and J. Vansina.

estly based on relationships formed between myself and individuals I met there, and (3) that people would cooperate because they wanted to cooperate, and for no other reason. Those ideas were crucial to my experience of Nigeria, and to the success of my research.[3]

Ibadan is supposed to be the largest city in sub-Saharan Africa.[4] Driving up from Lagos, my first view of it was stunning. The car reached the top of a hill, and suddenly the whole city was spread out before my eyes. Fading into the horizon, in all directions, were brown houses in a haze of red dust, punctuated by the occasional green dots of palm trees. The rusted tin roofs of the houses, very few with a second storey, seemed to house a population as great as that of New York City, but all spread out horizontally. For the duration of my stay in Ibadan, the views from the tops of the hills would not cease to amaze me.

On that first day, as the car descended the hill into the city, we soon found ourselves stuck in traffic. As we moved slowly along, it seemed to me that thousands of people were all crowded into and around the streets. People of every variety and description, dressed in clothes of so many types and every imaginable color, all seemed to be going somewhere, doing something, with all the hustle and bustle of a major market area. From the inside of the air-conditioned, bulletproof diplomatic vehicle, the streets seemed to be a panorama of swirling, colorful costumes. Trying to watch all the sights of the city streets go by was a sensory overload for me.

That was my first impression of Ibadan, but this essay is not about scenery. It is primarily about adjustments, of which the sensory overload was only a small part. This is about an on-going, long-term process of a whole set of adjustments, of which culture shock was only an initial phase. This is a process which I have still not really completed, so I cannot approach it with a distanced, objective eye. It is about life, my own life, in all its complexity, confusion, and subjectivity.

One of my biggest shocks on arrival in Nigeria was the idea that people could spend years viewing everything from behind locked doors and bulletproof glass, cut off from the sounds, the smells, the people, the whole experience. That was my impression. Hospitality in fancy houses seemed to me little better than a sentence served in a fancy prison. It took me months to learn to see such visits as a vacation of sorts, and nearly a year to realize that I could make friends with people who lived inside such houses.[5]

---

[3] These criteria were the direct result of graduate training for fieldwork. They were developed along with the dissertation project itself, during the two years preceding my departure, in discussions with my graduate advisor and other senior scholars.

[4] The Yoruba-speaking area has long been urban, its economy based on agricultural and artisanal production as well as commerce. There is a long and abundant scholarly tradition about history, anthropology, and the arts in the Yoruba area, although little has been written about fieldwork there. Gloria Marshall, "In a World of Women: Field Work in a Yoruba Community," in Golde, ed., *Women in the Field*, 167–91; and William B. Schwab, "Comparative Field Techniques in Urban Research in Africa," in Freilich, ed., *Marginal Natives*, 73–121, described their respective experiences in Awe in the 1960s and Osogbo in the 1950s.

[5] This was a prejudice with which I arrived. I describe it now with special thanks and appreciation to Nick and Norma Robertson, and David and Helen Williams, who taught me some valuable lessons about maturity and the meaning of friendship.

My first day in Nigeria, just to escape the confines of the embassy guest house walls, I was out exploring the streets in Lagos. Walking around on that first day, although I was dressed in what I hoped would be an appropriate manner, I was painfully conscious that my feet were the center of attention. Everyone seemed to be staring at my feet. My journal entry for that first day contains a rather lengthy passage about feet and footwear, concluding with the statement that, ringworm or no ringworm, I did not want to spend the next two and a half years of my life watching people stare at my feet. This was Lesson Number One. I had learned that my shoes were somehow wrong, but it would take me the next six months and several footwear experiments to learn how to make them right.[6]

While I was actually living those first six months, a sense of constant frustration was with me. I felt I was wasting my precious grant and time, that I was accomplishing nothing, that all attempts to get any "work" done fizzled into perplexingly dismal failures. That "wasted time," the business of daily life, was full of little adventures. Looking back through the pages now, my journals of the first months in Nigeria are hilarious.

There was the lizard I found taking its bath in my coffeepot one morning, the snake I met in the kitchen on Christmas morning, the army of red ants that invaded the compound when a mango tree came down in a storm, the unknown person who literally robbed me of the roof over my head the very night after it was installed....[7] By way of consolation, a foreign neighbor would drop by to say, "Everything you ever read about in *National Geographic*, it's here," and tell me that all I had to do was survive "the first hundred days."

It took more than a hundred days, and it is good that it looks hilarious in retrospect, because those first six months were miserable, although I would never have admitted it to myself at the time. The humor means that I moved past that stage, that I eventually learned to be who I needed to be and to do what I needed to do, that I learned to appreciate Nigeria, and to make a home there. In the end, I loved it so much that I never wanted to leave.

---

[6] The specter of ringworm was reinforced by the sight of the sores on the feet of an expatriate at the guest house. I had arrived in practical, sturdy shoes, intended both to prevent ringworm and to comfortably withstand much walking. But what I considered to be practical shoes were regarded as masculine in Nigeria, and glaringly incongruous on a woman. Proper footwear was a pair of feminine, stylish sandals. A comfortable compromise between practicality and femininity was finally reached, to the benefit of my feet, when I learned that sandals could be custom-made.

[7] The lizard and snake incidents occurred while I was house-sitting for a foreign researcher, at a house which had been vacant for some time. The lizard was an object lesson in never leaving water receptacles uncovered. The snake slithered away in ineffectual frenzy on the linoleum floor, putting an end to my brief stint of house-sitting. The theft of the roof and the invasion of the ants occurred at the house I was allocated on the university campus, which had also been unoccupied for some time and was in need of repair. When I heard plunking noises overhead late one evening I thought it was only the sound of mangoes falling from the tree onto my new roof. It never entered my mind that a person could be up there, prying out each new nail with a plunk, removing the new roofing sheets. But such, I discovered in the morning, was indeed the case: the roof was gone. After the carpenter had replaced it a second time, the roof withstood the fury of the early rains, but the mango tree did not. A storm brought down a big chunk of it one night, scattering debris and mangoes all over the compound. Neighbors, friends, and even strangers passing by on the street volunteered their help, braving the angry retaliation of the ants to remove the debris, as ants swarmed over all of us. By evening, nothing remained of the disaster but our ant bites, and my growing admiration for my new Nigerian neighbors.

Rereading my early journals, I am astonished to see the sense of excitement that pervades virtually every page. Entries many pages long are packed full of incidents, observations, and bits of conversations. Every day merited long descriptions and comments. In retrospect, I am amazed at how much I was actually learning when I thought I was doing nothing. At the time, watching my life become rearranged, and a sizable chunk of my self-concept along with it, I did not know that the base foundations of my research were being laid and cemented. I was meeting people, some of whom would become deeply cherished friends. I was learning how to relate to people. I was learning how to present myself to people. I was learning how to be patient, how and when to react, how to fit myself into my new environment.

In the midst of all that, my shoes were among the least of my worries. Though it may sound simple, it took me a long time to learn to present the right physical appearance. It took about six months to get the basics, including the shoes, down pat. Afterwards, as my research advanced, my dress became more personalized, and more situationally-specific. I learned to dress the part. On campus, I would wear fine *adire* to which I could point and say, "Oh, no. This is not in the market. A friend of mine made it." When going to see dyers, I learned to wear *adire* about which I could say, "Yes, this is a simple one, but I like to wear it because a friend of mine made it." When going to see weavers, I learned to wear *adire* about which I could say, "Oh, no. I cannot weave, and have not the patience to learn, but I do know how to make *adire*, and this is one I made myself."

Wearing the proper dress when going to see someone is a mark of respect; failing to do so is an insult. By the same token, by being properly dressed, one earns respect, and establishes credibility. Dress tells people who you are and what your business is. I had to learn to make my appearance match what I said about myself. Once I had mastered that, the transformation was almost like magic: eighteen-year-old boys no longer tried to hit on me, no one questioned my status as academic university staff, and communicating with people in general became much easier.[8]

My own reactions, and relations with people, entailed more of a constant effort than did my physical appearance. Looking back, I am surprised at how open I was with how many people. I had no choice really; not having known anyone long enough to know whom to trust and whom not, I simply confided my troubles to everyone who was nice to me. As a precaution, I confided my difficulties to and asked advice of as many different people as possible. So I asked drivers how to deal with vice chancellors, asked stewards how to deal with professors, asked typists how to deal with students, and so on.

In those first six months, dealing with frustration was a constant challenge. Housing, money, details of the grant, immigration, even my status at the university, all of these issues had to be sorted out. My journals are full of people saying, "Come back this afternoon," or "Come back tomorrow," and dutifully I always

---

[8] People routinely lopped ten years or more off my age until I learned to compensate by dressing older, at which point the unwanted attentions of boys and young men ceased. Proper dress included moderately long skirts or dresses, and a scarf to cover tightly braided hair. Custom-made, research-expressive clothes helped, and only very gradually did I acquire the confidence to personalize my dress and sometimes even to venture outside of the house wearing slacks.

did. At the same time, I had ample opportunity to observe other visiting scholars getting angry, and to assess the results. Clearly it would not do to show anger, frustration, or impatience.[9] This required constant self-vigilance. In the end, I was forced to develop some positive changes in my own personality and ways of coping. I had to learn how to relax and be patient, and get things done anyway.

There were days in those first few months when I would find myself feeling so annoyed or frustrated that I just did not want to see anyone at all. When I felt my state of mind becoming negative, I set myself the task of going to buy peanuts. These are sold on practically every street corner in snack-size bags by small children. My purpose in buying peanuts was to give myself a set goal, a task to accomplish, off campus, and away from the difficulties. I would walk or take buses or taxis or all three just to get a fifty-kobo bag of peanuts, because I knew that somewhere along the way someone would do or say something to make me smile and laugh and make the world seem a wonderful place. In this I was never disappointed. The people I met on my peanut expeditions got me through the toughest days.

Housing, I believed, was the single largest problem. Once I had a place of my own, once I could settle in and cook for myself, I was sure things would get much easier. I was right in the sense that I am very much the sort of person who needs to feel settled in order to be productive. I was wrong in the sense that I had no idea that the acquisition of housing would create a whole new set of difficulties, many of which were far more challenging to my basic sense of self.

Cooking was a big one. Once I had the house, I expected to be able to cook. Instead, I found I had to learn how to cook all over again: to manage an unfamiliar set of ingredients on a kerosene stove and to learn a new set of food preparation and preservation techniques in the absence of a fridge. It was when I realized that I didn't really know how to cook anymore that I also realized how very dependent I was on others. Someone had to teach me. I had to ask people questions about things I had taken for granted as mastered since childhood. It was as if my whole status as a self-sufficient adult was thrown into doubt by the cooking question, and I resisted that idea as stubbornly as possible.

Having my own house also meant doing my own housework, to which I was also looking forward, if for no other reason than the satisfaction of having my clothes and surroundings be properly clean.[10] The reality, however, was another big shock. Housework in Nigeria is truly hard labor, and lots of it. Carrying water, boiling water, battling the harmattan dust and the rainy season mildew . . . even the simplest tasks required much more labor than I had expected. This, I knew, was the daily reality for Nigerian women, and I was determined to do as they did. To my dismay, as hard as I worked, it seemed somehow that I just could not keep up with the spotless perfection which seems to be the norm of Nigerian households.

A place of my own, doing my own cooking, doing my own housework; these all raised major dependency issues for me. These and many other things I thought any normally capable person should have learned how to do by the age of about twelve, I had to learn all over again. I was nearly mortified with embarrassment at

---

[9] These can be serious affronts, and not quickly forgotten.

[10] I am no great lover of housework. This was but another manifestation of a wish for some sense of control over my environment, which ranged from the more personal aspects of space and hygiene to the amount of vegetables in my diet.

what seemed to me a childish sort of helplessness, yet no one I asked for help ever acted as if they thought it was silly. In the process of spending what I perceived to be an inordinate amount of time on things I thought should have been non-issues, I was really learning very important lessons. I was learning about cooperation, authority, men's and women's roles, the functioning of households, and much more, as friends and neighbors pitched in at my house and invited me to their houses for cooking lessons.

In the midst of this process I began to realize that by doing what I was doing I was challenging all sorts of stereotypes. This became clear in numerous little ways: I was not doing what people expected visiting researchers to do, although I was doing what many Nigerians routinely did. As I worked on my campus house, students passing by would stop and stare. One young woman was so persistent that I asked her if she had never seen her mother clean house. When she didn't respond, I asked her if her mother had neglected to teach her to answer when addressed by her seniors. Thereafter, she and her friends were polite. Definitely, I was learning much more than housekeeping.

At the time, I was angry at myself for not having enough energy. Looking at my journals, I am appalled at how hard I pushed myself. I walked miles a day, cleared the bush, carried the water, haggled and negotiated with people. I remember my first malaria as a one-day illness, a mild indisposition. In my journal, it is patently obvious that I was ill for about two weeks, but only let it slow me down for about one day.

The second malaria was not so easy.[11] It was a turning point for me in every possible way. It changed my outlook on everything I was doing, on where I was living, and on many people I knew. It also forced me to just sit and try to think, as I was unable to do more than that for about three months. Most importantly, it forced me to evaluate and accept the fact that I was, and would remain, much more dependent on other people than my pre-malaria self could ever have accepted. In the future, I would be much more selective about who I was dependent on, and what form that dependency took.

So I moved out of the sophisticated university environment, and moved away from invisible neighbors, silent telephones, immobile cars, and long walks in the sun to reach public transport.[12] I moved to the quintessential urban environment: eroded dirt roads, goats, sheep, chickens, children playing in the streets, and neighbors galore. There were no phones in my new neighborhood, and few people had cars, but never again would I be isolated. In such a neighborhood, help would never be more than a shout away, and no shout would ever be ignored. That I

---

[11] Resistant forms of *falciparum* malaria, including multi-drug resistant forms and cerebral malaria, have been on the increase in recent years and are currently endemic to Nigeria. At the time, the university was undergoing a closure, Christian and Muslim holidays coincided, and Ibadan was in the midst of a severe gas shortage. The net effect was several days of complete isolation, during which the only available treatment was self-treatment, until qualified medical help could be reached. Recovery was a slow process, and for Dr. Gupta's superb medical care as well as her support and encouragement, I remain immensely grateful.

[12] I am speaking of course not of the normal university environment, but of the one I encountered in the highly unusual set of circumstances mentioned above. I remain grateful to the many university staff members and neighbors who helped and supported me in so many different ways, but the second malaria taught me that the risk of isolation, however improbable, was a risk I could not afford to take a second time.

knew. What I didn't know was that in escaping the isolation, I was gaining privacy.[13] Never again would I worry about my roof or my laundry being stolen, never again would I have total strangers knocking on my door to ask for money or favors. Oke-Itunu, appropriately, means Peace-of-Mind-Hill, and for me it truly was.

That was when I finally realized that I had already met the main people that I needed to meet for my research. At the same time, I realized that I had to rethink and reformulate my whole research plan based on the realities that I could see all around me. In addition to reorganizing my living situation, I rewrote my dissertation proposal.[14] As a result, I became a curiosity to everyone I knew at the university, but I and my research began to make sense to myself. The peanut expeditions became unnecessary, because funny, warm, friendly, ordinary people were all around me. Similarly, I didn't need to travel to distant towns to meet textile artists either, as I already knew them.

My odyssey became discovering the people I already knew, and my new neighbors. Among my new neighbors were the woodcarver, the dyer, the weavers, and the old woman down the street who always had the time and patience to wait for me to formulate the right answer in Yoruba, without resorting to English. All the dramas and intrigues of daily life in a small part of the big city were there, each one a revelation in some way. It was by getting to know my own neighborhood that I began to understand what I had been reading in archives.[15]

It took time to carve myself a niche in the neighborhood, to become accepted there. But by the time I arrived there, I had the basic necessary repertoire of social skills with which to do it. It was with satisfaction that I saw my house become as neat as anyone else's. It was with even more satisfaction that I watched the area in which I was simply a neighbor and not *oyinbo* (European) widen.[16] That was something to which I clung fiercely and into which I put a constant daily effort. I wanted to be treated like a normal person doing normal things, not as an object of curiosity. Nothing made me happier than new accomplishments in that direction.

---

[13] Strangers were routinely queried by neighbors/residents before entering the compound. This screening was by no means conducted for my personal benefit; it was a normal fact of life in a small part of the big city.

[14] The previous dissertation proposal had been designed to recover evidence about women's history by focusing on a women's art. It was based on the false assumptions that artistic production was organized by a sexual division of labor, and that *adire* was a narrowly defined type of fabric produced only by women. The new proposal took into account that *adire* included a broad range of fabrics produced by men as well as women. It enlarged the time period and geographical area studied to document the absence of a sexual division of labor and to place *adire* in a larger context of textile history and social history. Instead of production, it focused on the social uses of textiles as evidence for rapidly changing gender roles and relationships.

[15] Abstract questions produced abstract, normative answers. This was particularly important for women's history because questions about textiles prompted people to discuss marriage, morality, and economics in normative terms. Although I had accepted this connection in principle, the specifics were not always easy for me to grasp. As one example, normative explanations about men's roles in a polygynous society left me mystified at the existence in archives of women's complaints about male infidelity. Male infidelity in this context seemed an oxymoron, until the day a neighbor stood in the street publicly accusing her husband of it, to a large and loudly sympathetic crowd of both sexes. Most neighborhood dramas were not so spectacular, but they did produce detailed narrative explanations, which I could more easily understand. It was the texture of daily life with its punctuation marks that made the pieces fall into place.

[16] While Yoruba culture places a high premium on respectful, polite behavior, a foreigner is not automatically assumed to know, or care, about proper behavior.

When those things started to happen, they somehow seemed magically easy. Whenever I sat and thought about it, I never was able to decide exactly what had changed or how. Apparently, somehow, I had changed, something about me, to the point where even total strangers could tell that I lived there. This manifested itself in different ways. Part of it was strangers taking for granted that I could understand and speak Yoruba. Part of it was a change in how neighbors and strangers addressed me. I went from "Iyawo" (wife) to "Iyawo Nigeria" to "Iyawo Ijebu" and finally to "Iyawo wa" (our wife).[17] All of it had something to do with fitting into situations and relating to people.

Having a pretty good command of the basics, I set myself to working on more subtle things. Part of this was dress, but much more of it was speech and manner. I learned to expect a modicum of respect. For situations where that was not forthcoming, I had to learn the verbal art of self-defense. This consisted basically of a few proverbs and pointed questions about seniority and polite behavior, which worked delightfully well. A good proverb could dissolve tension in gales of laughter, and earn me innumerable points in the process. Friends gleefully provided me with stores of such verbal ammunition, and I began to eagerly await the right opportunity to try out these new proverbs or comments. No longer a struggle, fitting myself to new situations had become just plain fun, and I was learning how to play with it.

The more at ease I became with my surroundings, and the more command I developed of situations and language, the better my research went. Initially, I understood this in terms of learning what questions to ask. Later, I understood it was also learning how to act while asking them. Because I formed friendships with people who were interested in what I was doing, I had ample opportunity to watch them explain it to other people. To explain it myself, all I had to do was repeat what I had witnessed. This not only facilitated communication, it also improved relationships.

In addition to acquiring ordinary daily skills and vocabulary, I also acquired technical skills and vocabulary. I learned how to make *adire*, and along with the skills I acquired the esoteric vocabulary of a textile artist. At the same time, I became rather deeply involved in both the family and the business aspects of textile production. On a personal level, most of this was great fun. On a practical level, the more I knew, the more information people gave me. What I learned from friends and hands-on experience taught me how to get the most out of "formal" interviews, archives, and other sources. Without that personal experience as a basis, I would never have understood what I was trying to study.

By way of a conclusion, I will simply offer that an improved quality of life and improved research results went hand in hand as the benefits of time, practice, patience, and a lot of effort. Once I began to get my part right, not only did life become much easier, but my research also became much smoother and better. Mostly, it was a matter of learning to communicate properly, in words, in attitudes, and in actions. To arrive at that point, I believe no shortcut exists. All in all, it was an experience that I would not have missed for the world, and one which I am eager to continue at the earliest possible opportunity!

---

[17] "Iyawo" is a cordial term of address for a young adult woman. To the status of adult, married woman, the qualifiers ascribed nationality, ethnicity, and social place.

Postscript

Some months before my departure, I accompanied close friends in the taxi, enroute for their departure. Gazing out the window, watching the streets of Ibadan go by, I had the uncanny feeling that I was seeing it all for the first time, as if the last two years had been erased, the sights of a familiar part of home once again rendered as a foreign swirl of confusing colors.

Nigeria then stood on the edge of a troubled part of its history. Violence was escalating in many parts of the country, and would soon reach Ibadan. Ensconced in my neighborhood, I heard the news reports as if they came from a foreign country or a distant time. Sitting in the taxi that day, watching the world pass by the window, just for an instant, I knew these disturbing changes were no dream, that it would soon be my turn to leave. My research materials were more than adequate for a dissertation; I had no excuse to stay. For just an instant, I glimpsed this reality through the window, then promptly forgot it.

Months later, when we finally left (my husband of a few weeks and I), Nigeria seemed engulfed by a rising tide of chaos.[18] The riots had since reached Ibadan, along with all the major cities in the south. All of the main roads in the south were closed, as well as the land borders and the embassies. The current round of rioting had continued for days. Although the airport was still open, we had no way of reaching it, most airlines had canceled their flights, and the evening news made the scene there look like the fall of Saigon. I was sure we wouldn't be going yet, so sure I saw no reason to make the rounds of saying good-bye. In the midst of this, the arrival of the driver early one morning was surreal. When he said to pack the car, I did so in disbelief. When he said the road to Lagos was open, I didn't believe it, not even when we were on it. When he parked the car at the airport, said good-bye, and told me to go in, that it was open, I did so in disbelief. Even sitting on the plane, I didn't believe it. Arrived in London, I thought I was in Lagos. In time, I adjusted.

This postscript is not about repatriation stress, nor even about recent events in Nigeria. It is not about the letters that came from friends in Nigeria, telling me that all was not right in my absence, warning that someone had come to make trouble for me, or about how I disbelieved these letters and forgot them, as one forgets a bad joke. It is about going home, and about having a home to go to. It is about relationships and connections once formed that last, continuing to grow and change long after one has left. It is about being absent but not forgotten.

I write this postscript, knowing that in a few short weeks I will once again be in Nigeria, but not in the place I knew and considered home. Whatever the effects of subsequent political events may have been, it is not these events which prevent me from returning to Ibadan, but the actions of a single individual. These actions metastasized, intruding themselves into my life and taking on a life of their own, affecting relationships with people who knew me well and involving me in "rela-

---

[18] The troubles referred to here were among the symptoms caused by the unsustainability of, and growing popular dissatisfaction with, policies of the government then in power. In a precipitating move, the currency was suddenly and severely devalued in early 1992, causing immediate and widespread economic hardship. With the abortion of the transition to democracy in 1993, the situation has continued to deteriorate.

tionships" with people I had never met. Events subsequent to the award of a new grant brought this emphatically to my attention. Several months and innumerable courier services and telephone calls later, my husband returned to Nigeria in an attempt to straighten out the mess. Because his good family name had been implicated, this proved impossible, as the gossip had only served to exacerbate existing tensions. At this writing, grant officials have agreed to allow me to return to Nigeria, but not to Ibadan, and thus not to family and friends.[19]

Looking back, pausing here, and looking ahead, it is clear that fieldwork is a continuing process. It does not simply stop when the researcher leaves the field. It is not merely a planned trip to a particular place. It is an ongoing journey, one in which there may be multiple routes, but no shortcuts. Like the life and learning with which it is entwined, fieldwork is not without difficulties but also not without renewal and growth. The destination may not be known in advance, but much joy may be found along the way. In this I count myself among the very fortunate indeed. At its best, fieldwork rewards with lasting relationships and with a sense of home, however long the journey home.

---

[19] A foreign researcher had sought an expedient means to get research results by inventing comparisons to my own work. I am deeply indebted to friends and colleagues, new and old, who rallied to our support and helped us to unravel and sort through the tangled threads of this Gordian knot. First in more than alphabetical order, a big note of thanks goes to Professor Babatunde Agiri. Thanks also to Ruth Bittorf who went hundreds of extra miles literally as well as figuratively, and to Patricia Byrd, Funke Ejemai, Curt Huff, Nick Robertson, and Nancy Searles, without whose efforts we would not be going back. This next chapter is just beginning, and although the end is not yet in sight, with the support of such good friends, and with the Otunba himself, it will all turn out right in the end.

2

Fieldwork Among Neighbors: An African's View of Another African Country

Tefetso Henry Mothibe

For a long time, only European and American graduate students pursuing doctoral degrees undertook fieldwork in Africa, and were thus exposed to various experiences in different African countries. For African graduate students pursuing similar degrees, the obvious place for fieldwork remained their home countries except where adverse political situations made going back impossible. Their reasons were primarily practical and economic: it was practical to return to one's own country when much remained unresearched there, and it was usually more economical to do research at home. As one of the few who had the opportunity to do fieldwork in a neighboring African country, this paper reflects my experiences among neighbors.[1]

The Political and Socioeconomic Background

On July 25, 1990, Zimbabwe's twenty-five-year-old state of emergency finally lapsed, following a government decision not to renew it as had been done every six months

---

[1] The fieldwork resulted in a dissertation entitled "Organized African Labor and Nationalism in Colonial Zimbabwe 1945–1971" (University of Wisconsin–Madison, 1993) and in my articles listed in the Bibliography. Funding for the fieldwork was provided by the International Development and Research Center and in part by the National University of Lesotho. The assistance of Professor Ngwabi Bhebe of the University of Zimbabwe has been particularly important for the success of my research. Research in the field (1990–1992) consisted of both work in the National Archives of Zimbabwe and oral interviews. Archival research was absolutely critical to this research project.

since independence in 1980. From April through July of the same year, Zimbabwe experienced the lengthiest labor strikes in its post-independence history. The nurses' strike paralyzed the health services for nearly three weeks in April. In June, the state resorted to emergency powers regulations to force the teachers back to the classrooms after a strike which had dragged on for two and a half weeks. Even this coercive measure proved inadequate; the one thousand teachers who defied the ultimatum to end the strike were later suspended, or less euphemistically, fired. In June and July, commercial bank workers and Air Zimbabwe staff also struck but for shorter periods. In three of these strikes, cabinet ministers were asked to intervene to resolve the deadlocks between workers and employers; in one case, the president had to mediate between a government ministry and civil servants. While the specific causes of the strikes varied, there was a common core of grievances relating to poor wages and working conditions.

These strikes took place ten years after independence. Significantly, they occurred soon after the second post-independence elections provided the first opportunity for Zimbabweans to elect the country's president.[2] During the election campaign in February and March of 1990, the president shrewdly organized meetings with the labor movement.[3] These campaign meetings provided a rare opportunity for representatives of organized labor to address their concerns directly to the president. In most instances, the president promised to attend to their specific concerns and the organizations more or less endorsed the president's election. It was in this context of electoral politics that the impression was given to the nurses and teachers that their salaries and conditions of service would be significantly improved immediately following the elections. In addition, workers, including public servants, were experiencing the severe impact of the spiraling cost of living, of the housing and urban transport crises, and of the declining value of the Zimbabwean dollar. All of the latter were the results of the structural adjustment program imposed by the IMF/World Bank on the government of Zimbabwe.

This was the background against which, in September of 1990, I began eighteen months of fieldwork. Although the country was experiencing industrial unrest, its problems were familiar ones to which I could directly relate, coming as I did from a neighboring country which was also suffering, although perhaps to a lesser extent, under an IMF/World Bank–imposed structural adjustment program. Three years earlier, I had visited Zimbabwe to attend a conference and was very impressed by its economic success: business was buoyant, life was vibrant, food was abundant and cheap, and its people were charming and friendly. Its most important achievement was, perhaps, the reconciliation that was evident between blacks and whites. In 1990, the economic problems notwithstanding, Zimbabweans had not changed. It was a great pleasure and honor for me to be back in Zimbabwe on an extended visit.

---

[2] Robert Mugabe, chief executive of Zimbabwe since 1980 (prime minister 1980–1987), became Zimbabwe's first executive president in 1987 by parliamentary election following constitutional changes. Following additional constitutional changes in 1990, he was re-elected by popular ballot.

[3] This included meetings with various commercial and professional associations such as the Commercial Farmers' Union (CFU), the Confederation of Zimbabwe Industry (CZI), the Zimbabwe Nurses Association (ZINA), the Zimbabwe Teachers Association (ZIMTA), and the Zimbabwe Congress of Trade Unions (ZCTU).

The Research

For much of the period of my research I lived in Harare and Bulawayo, respectively the first and second main national cities. I was seeking information on the history of African trade unions from World War II to independence. My research relied mainly on archival sources and oral evidence. The archival work was carried out at the Zimbabwe National Archives in Harare, at the Bulawayo Public Library, and at the Bulawayo branch of the National Archives. The material was abundant and required three months of daily trips to the archives for detailed note-taking as well as photocopying. The archives were well organized and the staff friendly, cooperative and professional.

My work at the archives was eased by the personal introductions made by the then-chairman of the History Department and the Zimbabwean graduate students who were also doing research there. It turned out that most of the archives staff were graduates of the History Department at the University of Zimbabwe. We became good friends and they literally went out of their way to look for materials that would have a bearing on my research and to connect me to informants. The archives also had a young but very useful collection of oral traditions. This was a mine of information of taped interviews with both living and past Zimbabweans. More archival material was obtained in Bulawayo, where again I was well received as a result of an introduction that preceded me from Harare. The Bulawayo Public Library had particularly useful boxes containing material on trade unions. The librarian who worked there was very helpful, at times going an extra mile to give me time to finish whatever I had to finish after official closing time.

A major feature of the fieldwork entailed gathering oral statements. This turned out to be the most exciting and challenging part of the research, requiring much time and patience. My experiences confirm the observation that "talking with informants in the field lies at the methodological heart of Africanist history."[4] Talking with informants entailed not only visits to various provincial towns but also exposure to different lifestyles and environments.

Interviews were conducted with the former leaders of trade unions as well as with the workers. The former mediated conflicts between the workers, settler state, and management, a role providing first-hand experience with both management and workers. They were also nationalists who had firsthand experience with the settler state; most, if not all, had been either detained or exiled at one time or another for their political activities. Most of these men were highly educated and boasted of doctoral and masters degrees from American and European universities, earned in exile. They now occupied influential positions in society. Others, although less educated, continued to play an active role in the labor movement. They resided in "low density" suburbs among other "chefs," as the rich and politically powerful are cynically called in Zimbabwe.

My interaction with these influential men was that of equals. Armed with appropriate introductions from the History Department as well as prior communication through letters and contacts, I was usually well received and lavishly entertained either in their offices or in their homes. Interviews were held mostly during working hours and rarely in the evenings. All the interviewees without exception

---

[4] Paul Thompson, *The Voice of the Past* (Oxford, 1988), 5.

expressed great pleasure to see an African researcher from within the region coming to Zimbabwe for research. I was always told that I was the first from within the region, outside South Africa, to do fieldwork in Zimbabwe.

As a result, they treated me as a brother and as one of them. As such I was privileged to ask any question without worrying that it might cause offense. They were very open about their different roles and activities in the trade unions at different times. Most of these roles and activities were corroborated in the written sources. Their stories and statements reflected in large measure the acceptance and trust that they had given me. Their frankness was also a result, I think, of the fact that my research topic posed no danger to their current positions; more importantly, although one of them, I was from outside Zimbabwe, and could therefore deal with any aspect of the topic without threat. Our interviews were almost all conducted in English, not by my choice but the informants' choice. They always insisted that we were all comfortable in English and therefore had no need to use other languages.

My experiences with the rank and file workers were different. They resided in the "high density" areas and were part and parcel of the *povo*, as the ordinary people are cynically described. Life, although greatly improved since independence, was still tough. They were hard hit by the economic pressures brought about by ESAP, the acronym of the hated IMF/World Bank economic program. They were victims of long lines at the bus stops, shortages of bread and cooking oil, ever-increasing prices, and falling wages. My interviews were held in the evenings or on weekends at their homes. It was an enormous sacrifice on their part to find time to sit with me and answer my many questions. They gladly did because they believed that I would attempt to honestly put across their stories and experiences.

Although we had very open, friendly, and informative talks, our interactions were unequal. Whenever I arrived at a worker's house, I was accorded too much respect and this usually embarrassed me. I was led to the house or part of the house reserved for visitors. When I protested, I was gently reminded that as an educated African child, I was a source of great pride to other Africans and so deserved special status. That, however, did not mean that I was more important than other African adults. Education accorded one special status but did not imply superiority over one's elders; good education meant respect for one's elders. Zimbabwean hospitality and courtesy resembled my own Sesotho hospitality and the apparent inequality of social relations was offset by sharing similar cultural traits and common languages. This was the case in spite of the much talked about "tribal differences" between the Ndebele and the Shona. I found out that a large percentage of my informants spoke both Sindebele and Shona fluently and I easily got along with my Zulu proficiency. This was especially true in Bulawayo and all Ndebele-speaking areas.

All in all, the oral part of the fieldwork proved most challenging and rewarding. This was largely a result of the generally warm and welcoming Zimbabwean community. It was also a result of my being virtually the first black non-Zimbabwean from *esan*zi, as all the countries below the Limpopo are known, to undertake research in Zimbabwe. I cannot recall any instance of overt hostility at all, only some degree of reluctance to talk in the initial stages of contact as the following examples from interviews with older workers indicate:

The Research

—You're black: Why can't you speak Shona? Are you too proud to do so?
—Okay: you're non-Shona. Have you finished studying the history of your own country? Why did you choose Zimbabwe?
—You are young: we can't tell you everything. Some secrets are traditionally reserved only for the ears of the elders.
—You want to record our voices? Are you not a spy?

Contacts had been facilitated by the fact that I lived on the main campus of the University of Zimbabwe, in the capital city of Harare, for the first months of my sojourn. There I was able to mix with fairly senior people in the university and government, including deans of faculties and permanent secretaries. I also attended evening lectures in the company of such people, went to the nightclubs that they patronized, and was treated with much greater respect than I think an average research student normally received. I normally saw the staff members during the week, and on weekends interacted more with the students whom I met at my lodgings in a graduate student hostel. I had my meals and drinks with the university staff in the senior common room.

I also established good relations with the trade unionists at the Zimbabwe Congress of Trade Unions (ZCTU) headquarters in Harare. During the period when I worked in the archives, I began taking trips to familiarize myself with the ZCTU regional offices in Gweru, Bulawayo, and Umtali, equipped with letters of introduction from ZCTU officers in Harare as well as from the chairman of the History Department. On these trips, I traveled with some of my graduate student friends and stayed at their homes. They not only provided free accommodation but also helped me to find informants in their areas. As a result, I was easily accepted by informants. I believed that people trusted me and so they did. This smoothed relationships between fieldworker and informants.

As an African in the midst of an African majority, I was just one in a crowd and part of the people. This helped to successfully establish cordial and trusting relationships with my informants. The following vignette from my fieldwork illustrates how I was just one in a crowd. One early Monday morning, I traveled from Mutare (former Umtali) to Bulawayo by bus. It was full to capacity and I was sitting in a seat meant to accommodate three people but we were five. Next to me were a man and a woman. A few miles into the trip, the man commenced a conversation in Shona and I was able to understand here and there. I immediately responded with an apology that my Shona was not that good, but would he mind if we could converse in Zulu. "Yes, of course, *shamwari* (friend), although you are an African, I can tell that you are from *esanzi* from your accent." When I asked how he had detected my accent so fast, he replied, "Because I spent a long time in South Africa."

In Zimbabwe, as in many countries, contacts are very important if things are to be done and done quickly. Key personalities whom I knew smoothed my way considerably. The chairman of the History Department, a well-known Zimbabwean historian, was particularly crucial in connecting me to most informants. The fact that I knew a number of Zimbabweans, then highly placed in government, from our own undergraduate days at the University of Botswana, Lesotho, and Swaziland (as it was then called) at Roma was critical. I had also visited Zimbabwe on a number of occasions before.

The tricky aspect of the research was getting access to informants, including the former trade union leaders. Most of them held high office and had very busy schedules; it took time to get to see them, let alone hold long interviews. As a result, it took a while before I got the information. It was the same difficulty with those who were employed and self-employed; time was not usually available and patience was the key thing. In addition, a shortage of funds tended to restrict my travel.

There was also the problem of evaluating information, especially from some former trade union leaders. The information was not always very original. Some of them appeared to have been exposed to the published sources, whether through their own reading or through having talked with previous researchers. At times they were merely repeating to me what we had both read in published accounts.

It must be underlined that although I was warmly welcomed most of the time at most places, I was regularly faced with two rather irritating but expected questions from both former trade unionists and workers: Have you finished studying the history of your own country? Why did you choose our country?

What exactly did fieldwork do for my research? It seems to me that I would not have been able to write my dissertation if I had not been able to go for fieldwork. Most of the archival material is available only in the Zimbabwe National Archives where it is jealously guarded against pilfering. More importantly, the interviews provided a medium through which individual members of the working class could be heard, thus offering fresh perspectives on their lives. Their life stories provided me with a window into the qualitative substance of the data, as distinct from the merely statistical and quantitative data that one finds in documentary material. In short, their remembered life experiences provided significant insights about what life was like for them during the period under study. This enabled me to produce a balanced picture in which the statements of the government and the trade union headquarters were juxtaposed with the voices, both apathetic and militant, of the rank and file.

The experience of fieldwork not only exposes the researcher to the environment in which the research is undertaken but also brings one closer to the issues being studied and the people involved. In the process, one develops sympathy, and this is manifested in the thesis. This should not be surprising because after all, "all history depends ultimately upon its social purpose."[5] The more one learns about the realities of the subject through interviews and casual talk, the more one feels drawn to the source.

To the extent that fieldwork overturned earlier viewpoints about the activities and roles of the workers in colonial Zimbabwe during the period under review, it was crucial. My personal experiences and interests elsewhere, however, had already drawn me to labor history.

Many historians have done fieldwork in Zimbabwe before and since independence and many more are currently in the country. Nevertheless, as a generalization, most otherwise good studies on Zimbabwean labor history suffer from a lack of oral evidence. Recently, Phimister produced what has been described as the first comprehensive early-twentieth-century history of the land and peoples of Zimbabwe.[6] This marked a culmination of Phimister's historical work dating back to the

---

[5] Donald Moore and Richard Roberts, "Listening for Silences," *History in Africa*, 17/19 (1990/91), 319.

[6] I. R. Phimister, *An Economic and Social History of Zimbabwe, 1890–1948: Capital Accumulation and Class Struggle* (London, 1988).

1970s. Its weakness, however, lies in its scarcity of real voices of the African people. This is a result of the author's lack of interviews. For example, no attempt was made to interview participants in the 1948 General Strike although many are still alive. Bhebe, on the other hand, has produced the first comprehensive study of one of those labor leaders and history-makers normally condemned to silence by "backwardness."[7] This work is informed by personal experiences as well as by interviews done by the author and students at the History Department of the University of Zimbabwe, from which it draws its strength.

What can be said, in conclusion, to have been the lessons learned about fieldwork in another African country? I learned that in order for a researcher to successfully gain acceptance and trust from informants, the ground must be extensively prepared beforehand. The fieldworker must make contacts and be willing to negotiate. When on the ground, the fieldworker has to be patient. Perhaps most importantly, an African researcher should be outgoing and adventurous. One should not hesitate to talk to people even if you do not know them and ask questions. One can meet many people naturally through using local recreations and facilities. In short, be just one in a crowd. In this manner an African researcher will also solve two other main problems: loneliness and financial constraints. The latter tends to feature most prominently in these times of general economic crisis in most African countries.

---

[7] Ngwabe Bhebe, *B. Burombo: African Politics in Zimbabwe, 1947–1958* (Harare, 1989).

3

Both Sides of the Border: The Impact of the Political Milieu on Field Research in Burundi and Tanzania*

Michele D. Wagner

From the perspective of a historian of precolonial Africa, Buha in western Tanzania and Buragane in southern Burundi are subregions of the same place. In the mid-nineteenth century the people who made their home along the hills flanking these two opposite banks of the Malagarassi River spoke essentially the same language.[1] They shared similar concepts of family and community; they held common religious ideals and nurtured congruent views of social responsibility and justice. Spanning the river, households and families traded together, gathered in friendship and mutual aid, and united in marriage, thereby bequeathing bonds of solidarity to future generations. The histories of Buha and Buragane resonate together from the earliest memories recoverable in oral history into the twentieth century.

---

* The Burundian research was carried out in 1985–1987 with the assistance of a Fulbright doctoral dissertation grant (Department of Education) and a Fulbright research grant (IIE). The Tanzanian research was carried out in 1991–1993 with post-doctoral assistance from the J. D. MacArthur Chair and the Vilas Fund at the University of Wisconsin–Madison. The author would like to express her appreciation to these programs and individuals, and to all of those who assisted her. Results of this reserach can be found in "Environment, Community, and History: Nature in the Mind in 19th and Early 20th Century Buha," in G. Maddox, J. Giblin, and I. Kimambo, eds., *Custodians of the Land* (London, 1996), and "Whose History is History? A History of the Baragane People, Southern Burundi, 1850–1932" (Ph.D. thesis, University of Wisconsin–Madison).

[1] The southern dialects of the Kirundi language (sometimes called Kiragane and Kimosso) show strong resemblance to neighboring dialects of the Kiha language (for example, Kiragane resembles Kiha dialects spoken in Manyovu and Heru).

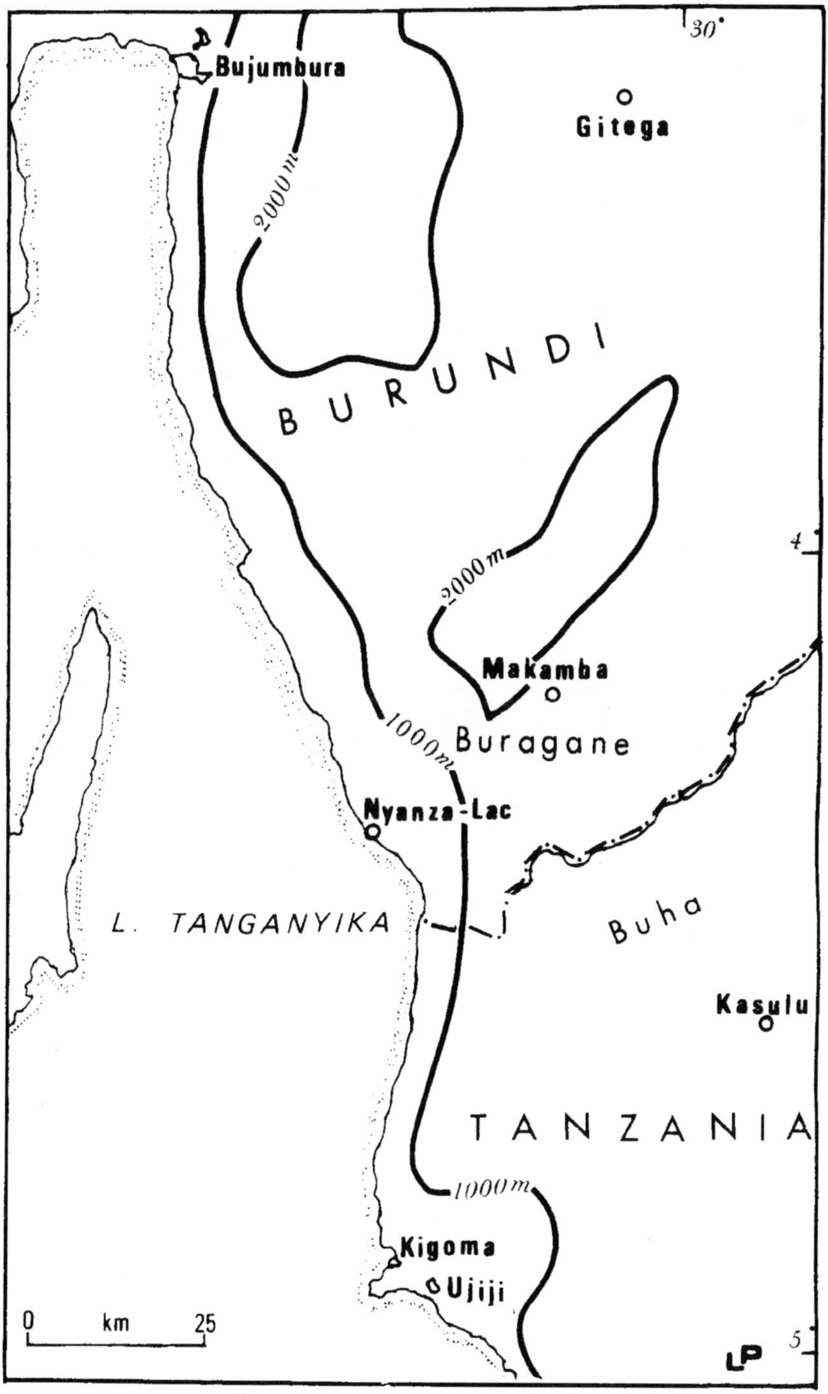
30°
Bujumbura
Gitega
2000m
BURUNDI
2000m
4
Makamba
1000m
Buragane
Nyanza-Lac
L. TANGANYIKA
Buha
Kasulu
TANZANIA
1000m
Kigoma
Ujiji
0 km 25
5
LP

Yet the border between the two regions divides the study of their history into completely separate, discordant endeavors.

Part of the difference lies in their colonial experiences. After the First World War, Buha and Buragane were partitioned into different colonies. Buragane was administered as part of the Belgian Congo: linguistically francophone, institutionally structured by the Belgian colonial regime, and geographically considered Central Africa. Buha was administered by the British: officially anglophone, institutionally overlaid with British bureaucratic culture, and geographically East Africa.

Another part of the difference lies in their postcolonial experiences. Buragane is a peripheral farming region of the tiny nation-state of Burundi, a state roughly based on the late-nineteenth-century borders of one precolonial kingdom. Modern Burundi is governed by the military, itself controlled by a minority ethnic group which dominates the majority.[2] Buha is a peripheral and underdeveloped region of the much larger nation-state of Tanzania, a state that incorporates so many precolonial political structures, languages, and ethnic groups that Buha's internal differences are overwhelmed by the burgeoning nation's collective need to develop. Many of Buha's colonial-era elites have left the region and moved to Dar es Salaam. The up-and-coming groups of the independent period tend to be self-motivated businesspeople, like the fishmonger who became a millionaire, or money-minded clerics who have gained power through mission contacts abroad.

What significance does the Ha fishmonger or the Burundian soldier have for the student of precolonial history? After all, the historian is absorbed by the past. Passing day after day in the company of elders, the historian becomes engulfed in a view from a different era. The elders lived in another world, one filled with possibilities, both wonderful and tragic, that are difficult to imagine in the world of today.

Intent upon the world of the elders, a historian can literally wander about with a mind wedged in the nineteenth century. The day-to-day experience of contemporary issues can slide right by. That truck with foreign license plates can rumble past, covering the historian, absorbed with reviewing the verbal tenses of research questions, in a cloud of dust. The historian, busily collecting the vocabulary of medicinal plants at the side of the town's most elderly woman, may never hear the rumor that the truck was loaded with weapons. Time and money are limited. Foreign trucks from the twentieth century are not part of the research design. Nor are the refugees jammed into a makeshift camp on the edge of town.

A historian can literally become an expert on a country whose present situation he or she knows little about. After all, the present is not the historian's domain; it belongs to the political scientist. But my experiences, drawn from Buragane, southern Burundi, in 1985–1987, and from Buha, western Tanzania, in 1991–1993, have led me to question this conventional, detached approach of the historical researcher to politics. The political milieu imposes itself at every step of historical research whether the historian wants to admit it or not. Thus, the time period when

---

[2] Until 1993, successive regimes of independent Burundi have been controlled by the minority Tutsi-controlled military who dominate the Hutu majority. The political events of 1993–1996 have not significantly shifted the ethnic balance of power.

Bujumbura, Burundi

Research on Burundi began for me in Madison, Wisconsin, in graduate seminars and the post–seminar discussions that took place in the nearby Rathskeller. In these sessions, students of African studies, both African and American, shared ideas about politics, culture, the redefinition of African history by colonizers, and the importance of rewriting histories distorted by colonial notions of tribe. My dissertation topic developed from this ongoing forum. I proposed to write a history of the concept and actualization of community from a Burundian point of view. The plan was to live in rural Buragane and to learn from elders how they saw and experienced community life.

Touching down in the capital city of Bujumbura in September 1985, I was filled with boundless optimism. Years of all-night reading sessions fueled by instant coffee and months of tedious word-by-word translations of historical texts written in French had culminated in this moment: I was standing on Burundian soil. In this joyous, unquestioning frame of mind, I was greeted at the customs counter by a familiar face, a Burundian whom I had known in the United States. As he and his driver delivered me to the American Cultural Center, I bubbled with enthusiasm and fatigue.

My first introduction to the diplomat heading the American Cultural Center was a collision with the then-current American perspective on Burundi. He received my enthusiasm with an air of bemused sarcasm, informing me that my airport welcoming committee was a deputation from the Burundian security police and that my research clearance, which I had been instructed to pick up in Bujumbura, would never materialize. Enthusiasm shattered and choked with doubts, I collected myself with the thought that this man and his attitude were exactly what I had been challenging in antigovernment demonstrations back at the University of Wisconsin. My eyes had been opened by African friends and classmates: I would see a different Burundi. I would get my clearance and set to work to combat such neocolonial attitudes.

What was the context for this inhospitable greeting?

At that time, relations between the Burundian government and foreign governments were dismal, particularly in matters concerning the Roman Catholic Church. The Church and the Burundian government were locked in a protracted struggle, which had led to a push by Burundi to curtail the Church's activities. The Burundian government found the Church's criticism of Burundian human rights abuses subversive. It contended that the Church had overstepped its religious bounds and was trying to influence national politics; an effort, it pointed out, that was distinctly neocolonial since it was being perpetrated by an institution guilty of having worked hand in hand with the Belgian administration during the colonial era. The government, launching a campaign for tighter control, had arrested Burundian priests, ousted foreign missionaries, and nationalized church property. The American government, getting in on the action, defended the right of religious freedom for all denominations. The Americans denounced Burundi's actions against the Catholic Church, and went a step further, upholding the right to religious freedom for Jehovah's Witnesses, Seventh-Day Adventists, and other groups that the Burundian government regarded as covers for subversive activities. It was in this context that I set out to gain research clearance, while my official American connection, the cultural officer, sneered at its impossibility.

Then I found a new problem: what, indeed, was research clearance? To whom did I apply? I had thought that clearance was automatic, since the university and the government had participated in the decision to invite me. But there I was, with what Burundians regarded as a United States government scholarship (a Fulbright) at a time when intergovernmental relations were strained, waiting for an undefined event to occur that my *patron*, the cultural officer, promised would never happen.[3] How did one apply for clearance? Nobody seemed to know. At the time, there was no standard procedure for seeking permission to conduct research. In response to my queries, those officially charged with my case, on both the Burundian and the American sides, shrugged their shoulders. One person in the chain of command over me suggested that the minister of interior should be the granting authority, whereupon I set out for his office twice a day, morning and afternoon, to follow up my documents. This continued for weeks. Optimistically at first, then tensely or miserably, depending on the day, I sat in the waiting room trying to read the facial expressions of his clerical workers. Did he have my dossier? Did anyone have inside information on what the answer would be?

During this time, a sympathetic acquaintance arranged to borrow a car and accompany me to the town of Makamba, my proposed site of research. Just to see Makamba, to be able to have an image of the place, seemed a wonderful opportunity. We set out southwards on the Nyanza Lac road which follows the shoreline of Lake Tanganyika. The road is breathtaking: it hugs the bases of steep mountains that plunge into the lake. Streams of people, women clad in yards of iridescent cloth, bearing all manner of goods, poured along the roadside. At Nyanza Lac, the road turns inland and passes over the mountains, which descend in green velvet ripples. When we reached Makamba, I delighted in seeing the dusty, tree-lined town square. Shopkeepers, lounging on their storefront verandas, eyed me and I smiled back. They were to be my new neighbors.

Back in Bujumbura that evening, tired but happy, I left my traveling companions and called it a wonderful day, whereupon they were promptly apprehended by the security police. During the night's proceedings, of which I still know next to nothing, they were instructed to convey to me the message that I was not to try to go upcountry again.

I was stuck in Bujumbura, a liability to those who had helped me. Helping me further was not worth the risk. Soon, university professors were not available to see me. My official *patrons* were occupied: couldn't I just relax and go to the beach? My situation became so bad that others found it potentially profit-

---

[3] In Burundi, the term *patron* designates the person who gives access.

able. Two people offered to help me if I paid them first by rendering intimate services. When it got to that point, I knew my case wasn't going anywhere soon. So I buried myself in the National Archives to make some use of being in the "field."

Although disinterested in the political situation, I was subject to it. It affected my access to language training, housing, and colleagues. The main language school, run by missionary priests, had been closed because the priests were being deported. Housing was difficult because there were informal but strict zoning laws about where a foreigner could live. Who could associate with me and in which settings, what could be said: none of these were spontaneous choices. They were influenced, if not dictated, by politics. Politics also dictated whom I received as guests, for I had to entertain the security police who imposed themselves now and then to check me out and demand free beer.

The process of living in Bujumbura in 1985–1986 was one of gradually internalizing fear. Foreigners were afraid because many among them, particularly Catholic priests and Indian businessmen, were being deported. Some were given twenty-four hours' notice to leave. Others, having lived in Burundi for years, were refused the renewal of their residence permits. Lives and businesses were destroyed literally overnight. Burundians were even more afraid. There seemed to be soldiers on every streetcorner checking identity cards and passes. Everyone was required to carry an identity card at all times, and anyone with an official residence elsewhere had to produce a pass to show he had permission to be in Bujumbura. Buses were halted and people whose documents were found inadequate were pulled off and dragged away. Several kinds of police, from military to road police, from municipal to security police, apprehended people for all manner of alleged wrongdoing. The line between legal and illegal was hair-thin. Potentially anything could induce suspicion and just being in the wrong place could be grounds for arrest. Public displays of patriotism jostled with public displays of violence; schoolchildren marched and sang government slogans, and children were clubbed to the ground as a form of crowd control. Such were the commonplace in the anxiety-ridden, mixed-up atmosphere of Bujumbura.

Learning to take the quiet road, I stopped pushing for clearance. I worked in the archives and the university library. I took the university's newly created Kirundi lessons for foreigners, which culminated in the ability to inquire "Those fish are good, how much do they cost?" I made friends with Burundians brave enough to befriend me in that atmosphere. I learned how to live in the Burundi of the late 1980s.

Through external events, one year later, research clearance materialized. It came in the form of a black Mercedes that appeared and collected me one day.

Makamba

As much as I had learned to fear the government, I also learned to appreciate and respect ordinary people, particularly rural people. These two attitudes, in which people and government were sharply separated, were not at all incompatible. In fact, they were quite normal, as the events of one afternoon out in the hills serve to demonstrate. I had spent the afternoon at Kayogoro, the site of an old Swedish mission, chatting with the elderly Burundian pastor about the impact of Christian conversion on community institutions. As I navigated a borrowed bicycle down the rocky hillside, a sharp stone pierced the tire. The tire went flat. Makamba was far away. The only thing I could think to do was to push the bike to a nearby homestead, a traditional *rugo*.

The family inside was quite surprised to find me coming down their path, but I explained my dilemma, and we collectively decided that the best course of action was for me to leave the bicycle at their house and return to Makamba before dark. Then I would return to fetch it on an appointed day.

The day I returned, the family received me like royalty. Food had been cooked. A place to receive me had been prepared. Children brought me bouquets of grass. And the father of the family presented me with the bicycle, which he had repaired. He had walked all the way to Mabanda, about eight kilometers away, procured a patch by his own means, and repaired the inner tube himself.

The thoughtfulness this family had shown was deeply moving. Although I was an uninvited stranger who had chanced upon their path, they treated me like an honored guest. To demonstrate appreciation, I stayed for a long time, ignoring the ominous rain clouds that were filling the sky. Minutes after we said good-bye, the clouds opened up and released torrents of rain. I pushed and slid the bicycle down the mud-sloppy hill road to the main road below. To my good fortune, a car was coming. When it stopped and a window rolled down, I recognized the passengers as government people from Makamba and greeted them heartily. In return, a passenger fired questions at me: "Why are you here? What do you think you're doing? How long have you been here?"

Since these people knew who I was (not long before, I had presented all my papers to the governor of Makamba himself), I was thrown off balance by this barrage of questions in the pouring rain. And more questions followed: "Exactly who have you been visiting? What did you want from them? Who else was present?" I shivered miserably by the side of the road as these questions came forth from the vehicle's dry interior. When somehow the appropriate level of satisfaction was attained, the window rolled shut and the car skidded away, kicking up mud in every direction.

I was left on the road in the rain, pushing the bicycle to Makamba. My only satisfaction was that I had misled the officials in order to protect the family who had helped me.

The political environment of Makamba strongly influenced my fieldwork, both in context and in content. Politics profoundly affected the degrees of trust and levels of anxiety I encountered from local people, as well as those I carried within myself. And these emotions determined the quality of information I could gather.

It took a long time for Makamba residents to develop even a modicum of trust for me. Initially, it was clear that many people didn't trust me at all, but neither did they feel free to refuse me. In many cases, elders made any kind of statement in order to satisfy the stranger and entice her to leave. It became increasingly clear that the level of tension or familiarity during an interview mattered a great deal. If the import of a question or a situation was in any way threatening, the information transmitted could not be considered reliable. As a result, most of the initial data I collected had to be considered suspect, and could not be taken literally unless substantiated by later material.

Consistent with the political climate of Burundi, I was pursued by Makamba's chief security agent. Everyone in town knew that he was watching me: that was the point. The security man made theatrical scenes in the town square, to publicly announce that I was his. "You certainly get around, Michele!" he joked loudly in front of his entourage. He always had an entourage. He drove around conspicuously in a flashy car, the entourage packed inside. When I was conducting a public interview at a lower-level government office, the familiar vehicle pulled up in front and out hopped the security man. Barging into the meeting, he stalked up and down among the rows of elders, hands clasped behind his back. After a few perfunctory questions, he left. Needless to say, so did the elders. At other times his harassment was more private, as when he followed me across the town square at night, cruising slowly in his car, headlights turned off. When people cooperated with me in spite of all this attention, they did so with a high degree of personal anxiety and courage; some claimed it didn't matter because they were accustomed to living with anxiety. Attempting to counterbalance his influence, I interviewed local government officials from Buragane, called public meetings with local officials as invited guests, invited neighbors to home interviews with elders, and generally did everything possible to demonstrate that I had nothing to hide. I preferred to have witnesses present at initial or controversial interviews, until a bond of trust had been built and the neighbors were no longer curious.

The political climate also impaired the logistics of research. To work in more remote regions it was necessary to spend the night away from home. All overnight visitors who came from outside the cell (the set of households which formed the most local level of administration) had to be reported to the cell leader. This discouraged families or local mission stations from inviting me to stay because it drew official attention which most families wished to avoid. Taking the responsibility of hosting me and reporting this to the government posed a high risk, since I was controversial enough to attract the security agent.

As a further constraint imposed by the political environment, private ceremonies and cultural events were for the most part off-limits. The central government was gradually abolishing these events. It regarded these gatherings as occasions for wasting labor and resources, and opportunities for subversion. Since most rural people were uncertain as to what was illegal and what was not, they performed these ceremonies less frequently in public. Perhaps a family could pass off a ceremony as nothing but an informal beer-drinking session, but to invite me would draw attention and create a special risk. Without official permission, I did not attend. As a result, I missed an important facet of community life and failed to witness many of the contexts in which social values were publicly expressed.

As yet another constraint imposed by the situation, I was pressured to keep as a research assistant an individual whom others identified as a security agent. To transcribe tapes of interviews, I hired secondary school students home on vacation who, as the elite of Makamba youth, were few in number. A week of flaunted arrogance and little output on the part of one of the students told me that something was amiss. After visiting the student at his home where he boldly lectured me on politics, I suspected that he was linked to the youth branch of the security system. These doubts were soon confirmed but I was warned not to fire him, for this would bring security problems upon myself as well as the other students.

In this environment, the study that I had proposed to conduct, a community history, was impossible. The civil war of 1972 had created such turmoil in the region that the sense of community was disrupted. Encouraging elders to discuss community, even historically, was very difficult. So many people had died or fled in 1972 that a community census, even a family genealogy, could not be accomplished. Genealogies reopened painful wounds and evoked terror for families who believed that acknowledging many missing people carried political implications.

The most important category of identity existing in Burundi at the time of the research, ethnic identity, was taboo. In Bujumbura, I was warned in no uncertain terms never to use the words "Hutu" or "Tutsi," and this avoidance carried through to Makamba. Having internalized the fear of uttering these words, I avoided them and became anxious when others used them in my presence, fearing that I was being baited by someone seeking to entrap me. The words signaled danger, but they were necessary for colonial history. This dilemma imposed itself frequently. Its resolution came late in the research, when individual elders and I began to know each other well. Only then could the labels surface.

Many specific events of the colonial period, especially abuses committed by subchiefs or their agents, were totally off-limits in conversation for the reason that these individuals were still alive and were often prominent members of the community. The abuses, although they came from another political era, had percolated below the surface of daily life where they simmered, I sensed, in a collective rage. The strategy I developed for dealing with this was to maintain a loose format in talking about the colonial era. Elders took the conversation where they wanted. When the conversation stumbled across a traumatic event, I waited for the elder to set the terms by which it was to be discussed and followed along carefully. If an elder got stuck on a traumatic issue, I offered a way out by nudging the conversation in another direction. In certain cases, it was not necessary to name names in colonial-era history, and this reduced an elder's anxiety. If the discussion moved toward a certain subchief whom the elder feared to name, we could leave it at "subchief." After a year's work in the archives, I had the names, and I could verify them with my notes later.

These techniques became conventions in conducting historical research in such a fear-ridden and threatening environment as the one that existed in Burundi in 1985–1987. They were not merely "research techniques" but survival strategies, mutually forged by Burundian elders and myself in order to find a way to connect, across not only cultures but also considerable political barriers. They developed out of basic and mutual human respect, a sentiment that was strongly discouraged by the government at that time. Life was heavy. It is difficult to describe the feeling we lived with; it was just heavy. Anxiety and fear remained below the surface, but their impact on daily life was so profound that even a historian of the nineteenth century couldn't help but notice.

Kasulu, Tanzania

It was with considerable apprehension that I went back to the field in 1991, to Kasulu, Tanzania. Kasulu is much more distant from the capital city and from national politics than Makamba. Although Kasulu residents listen to Radio Tanzania, the capital city of Dar es Salaam is far away, geographically, culturally, and psychologically. Many, if not most, Kasulu residents harbor no expectation of ever seeing it. Like Iowa farmers who complain that the politicians are too far away to understand, Kasulu residents in 1991 expressed the view that the Dar es Salaam politicians lived in another world.

Sometimes the worlds intersected. During my first days in Kasulu, the president came to tour the region. He visited Kasulu and stopped to deliver a speech. This was my first opportunity to see national politics played out on the local scene. After the experience of attending political ceremonies in Burundi, I was a bit frightened. I waited for columns of armed soldiers to ride by on trucks, for my cell leader to instruct me to present myself to cheer. But nothing happened. A few police stood along the road, complaining that the president was late and the sun was too hot. A tiny crew of townspeople rallied at a semi-abandoned skeleton of a bridge, vigorously gathering and passing stones along a human chain in order to affect the appearance of "building the nation." When the president finally arrived, his modest cortege moved to the football field of the Teachers Training College, where townspeople sauntered about freely, applauded occasionally, and chatted lackadaisically.

The president's visit established the pace for this new research. Relaxed. Low-key. Participants spoke or canceled the interview as they wished, assuming that they were free to call the shots. Often the most intense part of an interview was trying to reach the site. Travel on Kasulu District's notorious roads was no mean feat. Once arrived, however, I encountered communities accustomed to town-meeting-style gatherings. Public expression of opinion, often presented in the form of a joke, was lively and vivid. Public discussion worked best when men and women had separate fora, but expression of opinion was not a problem.

Initially, I wondered at the casual attitude of elders, at the interest in history expressed by local officials, and at my freedom to move about. The astonishment was not lost on Kasulu residents, who knew by my accent and self-account that I had lived in Burundi. They offered explanations of the difference: "We may not be wealthy like the Burundians, but we are wealthy in peace"; "We have bad roads, but good neighbors"; "We simple people may not have been important in the past, but it is we who have lived to see the present." Hearing these formulas, I recalled the words of Tanzanian graduate students at Wisconsin. Lacking the resources of their oil-rich Nigerian or land-rich Kenyan counterparts, Tanzanian students had a habit of standing up for themselves by saying: "We Tanzanians may not be rich, but at least we own our country," or "We may dress shabbily, but at least we know who we are." At the time, this was attributed to "Ujamaa mentality" and we called our materially humble but self-consciously proud classmates "the people of Ujamaa." Did this consciousness we joked about actually exist? Was I encountering a form of "Ujamaa mentality" in Kasulu?

The question presented itself at every point of contrast with Burundi. In Kasulu, I found that village chairmen, with few exceptions, adopted a demeanor of respect, rather than haughtiness, toward elders. The elders, in return, organized and controlled public "history gatherings" themselves. Were these traces of Ujamaa? Many of the village chairmen, as well as some of the prominent elders, described themselves as retired teachers. I had not encountered this in Burundi where leadership was most closely linked to the social position of one's family, and traces of mass education, beyond agricultural extension and women's needlework, were not apparent. In Tanzania, the village chairman was often literate; in many cases he (or she) asked historical questions, sought clarifications, and took notes. Literate involvement by local leaders had occurred only infrequently in Burundi, and note-taking had usually served to heighten tension. My research team, too, developed questions, participated in interviews, and planned their participation in a fledgling historical society founded by a local schoolteacher. This adoption of the project as their own, this interposing of their own questions during interviews, was unprecedented in Burundi where assistants handled the historical material for me, the *patron*, but not for themselves.

The issue of ethnicity, which had struck a chord of fear in Burundians, was just one more subject for discussion in Tanzania. Certainly, ethnic differences existed, and there were people who identified as Hutu and Tutsi, but it was not a source of divisiveness in the same way that it had been in Burundi. Indeed, ethnicity, and its development, became a major topic of discussion for the research team as they considered various elders' explanations of ethnicity and developed their own.

Was the Tanzanian research aided by traces of Ujamaa? Only further research will tell. But the contrast between the Kasulu and Makamba research makes clear that the larger picture of national politics enters into historical research in a variety of ways. As historians, we do not give enough attention to this. We debate the pros and cons of oral history, the relationship of the present to the past: Are oral narratives "true" accounts of the past, or are they so rooted in the present that their historical value is minimal? Are oral narratives historical or are they simply elaborate justifications for what exists presently? These arguments deadlock seminars (I can remember quite a few during my graduate studies), and they have contributed to the current trend of post-modernism whereby "facts" cease to exist as anything more than the malleable material of mental constructs, wherein historical data and history itself dissolve in fluid reinterpretation.

Instead of annihilating the possibility of "history," we need to develop a more acute contextual awareness. In place of dismissing oral history and fieldwork on the basis of their untidy subjectivity, we should take a closer look at the character of the human milieu in which historical research is carried out. This will be difficult so long as scholars strive to be paragons of that spurious objectivity which consists of studied avoidance of that human milieu. This is particularly true in countries where political awareness is a morally painful burden and studied avoidance is a convenient reprieve.

Politics are unavoidable, practically and also morally. As historians, we must burden ourselves with political awareness. We must take into account the larger context in which we and those whom we encounter have no choice but to operate.

4

Women's Work in Kano[*]

Beverly B. Mack

When I arrived in Nigeria to commence research on Hausa women poets, a Hausa man at the university in Kano took me aside and confided, "Hausa women don't write poetry." He meant to convey a confidence that no one else had thought important enough to tell me during the whole long process of grant-applications and field preparations; that Hausa women neither wrote nor performed—indeed, they in no way produced—Hausa poetry. He thought he was doing me a favor. But I had arrived armed with several years of Hausa language practice and field research training, along with funding to support an extended period of residence in Kano. Imagine my dismay. There are two "first things" you learn in Nigeria: things never go as planned, and yet things always happen as they should. Patient acceptance is a virtue highly esteemed among the Hausa.[1]

I had visited Kano briefly in 1977. I went back there to live and do research in 1979, funded by a Fulbright doctoral dissertation grant, and aiming to collect women's poetic works—songs, oral poetry, and written poetry. My initial fieldwork period lasted for eighteen months, after which I returned to Madison for a year to write up. I then returned to Kano in 1982, Ph.D. in hand, to teach at the university there while doing post-doctoral work. For the second period of research I stayed another eighteen months.

---

[*] Several people have read and commented on this essay. I am especially grateful to old friends and colleagues Janet Beik and Catherine Coles for their lengthy and constructive critiques, as well, of course, to the editors of this volume for their input, interest, and patience.

[1] Hausa social structure is often described as hierarchical, ranging from a base level at which blacksmiths and entertainers are found, to royalty at the top. Most individuals who now identify themselves as Hausa are urban-dwellers, English-speaking, educated, and Muslims. Hausa-speakers are concentrated in northern Nigerian cities such as Kano, where there has been considerable mixing of Hausa and Fulani peoples, largely as a result of the nineteenth century jihad led by Shehu Usman 'dan Fodio. The jihad, through which the shehu sought to reform Islamic practices in the region, involved the replacement of all Hausa kings with Fulani emirs, who have since then served as traditional rulers of the Hausa-Fulani populations. The most important influence in Hausa culture is that of Islam, introduced to the area in the fifteenth century, perhaps earlier. Because of Islam and its focus on the family, Hausa culture has long adhered to customs that include gender-specific socioreligious obligations. Islam, flourishing in urban areas, also carries with it a focus on literacy, and Hausa culture has long enjoyed a rich tradition of poetic productivity.

Prior to fieldwork, my aim was to study Hausa women praise singers attached to the palaces in Kano and Katsina. I was fortunate to be introduced by royal women to other women who produced written works in the Arabic poetic mode. Their poetic works were more compelling to me than the praise songs, focused as they were on topics of more universal concern than flattery for monetary gain and the perpetuation of the status quo. Therefore, my presence in the palace, and the chance encounters with women who could direct me to authors of written poetry outside the palace, led to the redirection of my research following fieldwork according to *ikon Allah* ("God's will"). Such redirection led eventually to the publication of the complete works of a major nineteenth-century woman scholar, Nana Asma'u, daughter of Shehu Usman 'dan Fodio, on whose scholarship the subjects of my twentieth-century field research modeled their work.[2] Therefore, my fieldwork rendered material which then needed a context I could find only through further research in greater historical depth. (*Ikon Allah* again.) In this situation archival research of the standard kind was not relevant to my study. The archives important to me were the cardboard boxes in which my poets kept their written works.

During each of the two eighteen month periods mentioned, I was privileged to have a close association with the women of the emir's palace. I am grateful for the freedom I was given in visiting there regularly; I cannot remember ever being treated in a less than gracious manner. From Hajiya Abba Bayero, third wife of His Royal Highness Alhaji Ado Bayero, I learned a great deal about women's roles, rights, and obligations in Hausa culture. In addition, she provided introductions for me to many of the poets with whom I worked. Certainly my being centered in the royal palace means that my views on Hausa culture are biased from this perspective, which is one that includes Islam and Hausa traditions as its hallmarks.

My associations with Hausa culture outside the palace included the women poets and performers with whom I worked, trips to the Old City market, and visits to villages and markets outside Kano. The women poets and performers were from a wide range of social strata: those who wrote their works were educated, devout Muslim women of middle- to upper middle-class; extemporaneous performers were of lower social classes, regardless of the amount of wealth they might have amassed as a result of their talents. Trips to the Old City market gave me the chance to establish acquaintance with market stall owners and sellers. Later in my period of residence, when I did a cost-benefit study for the World Bank, the incomes of these people were the focus of my attention. Outside Kano, I sought women singers in their home villages for interviews—in Funtuwa, I found only Maimuna Coge's husband at home, attending to the children while she was "on tour"; in Dambatta, Hajiya 'Yar Shehu proudly gave me a tour of the mosque she had built for her town; and I took Hauwa Gwaram to Gwaram village to visit her father during his last illness. Late in my second period of residence I visited counterparts of Kano's royal women in the "palaces" of smaller emirates—and found their lives to be in striking contrast to the

---

[2] Jean Boyd and Beverly Mack, *The Collected Works of Nana Asma'u, 1793–1864* (East Lansing, Mich., forthcoming).

conviviality of women's conditions in the Kano palace. I also acted as interpreter for an expatriate researcher investigating the iron-working peoples in the hills of northwestern Nigeria; through this, I learned a great deal about rural Hausa life and the extent of Islamic influence there, even in a region known for its pre-Islamic roots, and maintenance of non-Islamic customs in contemporary times.

Through such a variety of experiences, one thread remained constant—the importance of Islam in northern Nigeria. From the exemplary circumstances of the royal palace, to the most basic rural conditions, Islamic tenets are the foci of Hausa life. Without a clear understanding of the ways in which Islam influences values and customs, and the ways that these are expressed through the Hausa language itself, the validity and merit of research on Hausa culture is questionable.

Arrival in Kano

I arrived in Kano, Nigeria, in January 1979 at dawn. The harmattan was well underway, with dust clouding the sky well into the day. My trunks were somewhere between New York and Kano. No one met me. The taxi drivers converged like hungry piranhas. They found it hard to believe I intended to sit down and wait for daylight before venturing into the city. It was a ploy; I had no idea what to do, and needed time to plan my strategy.

One thing I learned from the start is that Allah provides; in this case intervention came in the form of a graduate school colleague who was by then teaching at Bayero University in Kano. Eventually, I found my way to his flat. He was surprised to see me delivered to his doorstep at breakfast time, but living in Kano makes one expect the unexpected. Through his generosity I had temporary housing.

I pleaded for my lost baggage at KLM without much hope of it turning up—especially since I had not arrived on a KLM flight. Miraculously, the two trunks appeared at the door one day a week later, with all my tapes and equipment in them. Now all I needed was a place to unpack them. A short while later, through an American woman who knew Kano well, I found a place to rent within the walls of the original Old City. It turned out that this compound had been used by a series of other researchers of Hausa culture, whose publications I was using as references. That was a happy antidote to an inauspicious beginning.

Becoming a Neighbor

My compound in the Old City was a traditional urban dwelling; the high walls were open to the sky except for several sleeping rooms, toilet, and kitchen, and there was a delightful courtyard garden full of scarlet hibiscus blossoms. Yet living in a Muslim society on my own presented other problems. In a family-oriented religion like Islam, men and women each have specific domestic roles to play. Here in Kano, traditionally girls are given in marriage at adolescence, and there is no social place for the unmarried. In such an urban Muslim setting, men and women populate different spaces. Men move freely in public, doing the family's marketing, and working outside the home. Since the nineteenth century jihad, women have been increasingly restricted to the home.[3] As guardians of the domestic realm, they observe the practice of seclusion, remaining for the most part in the women's quarters of traditional homes, where garden courtyards and private rooms are all sheltered behind high protective walls.[4] A woman who goes about in public freely and lives alone is not a traditional Hausa woman. Indeed, the presumption is that the only women who live alone are prostitutes.[5] Therefore, when I first established myself in the compound, I took time to introduce myself to the *malam* and his students who studied the Qur'an under a tree near my door. I explained that I was studying history, a subject much revered among the Hausa/Fulani, and far better understood than the more esoteric study of women's poetry. I knew they would spread the word. Such a tactic proved extremely important to my physical welfare when a drunken stranger pounded on my door one Saturday midnight. Fortunately the door was metal, and withstood his blows; his pounding was so severe that the door was jammed shut where he dented it, and I was "in seclusion" for the weekend, until we could get a locksmith to extract me. When I failed to show up in the women's quarters of the emir's palace on that Sunday morning, according to my routine, Hajiya Abba Bayero sent her son out to check on me. Through the only (barred) window to the outside I was able to explain the situation. He returned in a few hours carrying dinner for me from Hajiya. Another time, when a strange man knocked on my door seeking favors, he was run off on my behalf by the neighbors. In each case, the men who came to my door were not Hausa, and although they may have been living in Kano, they were not part of the neighborhood. Rather, they were businessmen who lived in the metropolitan district of Kano, outside its Old City walls. The outcomes of these incidents reassured me that my house had become my home, and I had been accepted in the community.

Part of getting along in the neighborhood depended on dressing and behaving as much like a Hausa woman as possible. Because I spent a great deal of time with the women of the emir's palace, I had the advantage of receiving the very best in lessons of comportment. I am embarrassed to admit that the first time I visited Hajiya in the palace I wore a sundress with a cross-cut back and no sleeves. I must have seemed naked to everyone there. After that, I always wore traditional Hausa women's attire: an ankle-length wrapper, a matching top (with sleeves!), and a head-tie to cover my hair. No one ever mentioned what I had worn on that first visit, but after I got to know the palace women fairly well, someone suggested that I should not "go about naked"; this time

---

[3] Shehu Usman 'dan Fodio and his followers did not advocate the seclusion of women; this came in successive generations as traditional patriarchal organization was used to suppress women's participation in society outside the home.

[4] With their husbands' permission, women go out of the home to attend naming ceremonies and wedding celebrations at other homes, to the clinics to give birth, to evening adult education classes, or to their birth homes to visit their families.

[5] Exceptions to this became clear as I got to know women who were widowed or divorced. Some chose to maintain a single lifestyle, but their reputations as devout Muslims and respectable women precluded their being subject to criticism.

she was referring to my naked eyes, and suggested I start lining them with kohl, because "even small girls know that one is not dressed without it." At celebratory times, of course, fancy dress was expected. I followed the cue of the women with whom I spent time, and although I could never match the opulence of palace wardrobes, I made sure to dress respectably.

Comporting oneself appropriately involved separate sets of rules depending on my environment. In the palace I needed to behave myself suitably, averting my gaze, if not bowing in submission, when the emir passed by. I learned to speak in the royal third person rather than addressing the emir directly. On the few occasions when I interviewed him privately, the lack of an audience allowed for direct exchange, in a less formal atmosphere. What was important was to maintain self-respect, in order to be respected. Therefore I made sure to accommodate Hausa custom as far as possible without abandoning my own values; no one expected me to prostrate myself before the emir, but a bend of the knee and averted gaze were appreciated in public settings, for form's sake. In the privacy of Hajiya's compound, the emir would shake my hand in greeting and I had to respond, even though my hand—which was not supposed to shake a Hausa man's hand—tingled in embarrassed response. He was meeting me halfway to my culture when circumstances allowed.

Research

For my initial forays into my intended research on Hausa women poets I (fortunately) did not need to rely on the discouraging perspective offered by my Hausa contact at the university. I had already met Hajiya in the palace two years earlier, while visiting Kano in the summer of 1977. I took his advice to her and her cohorts, and watched with delight their polite self-control as they disagreed strongly with him. It was my good fortune that they sent me on my way to the very women he had promised did not exist: Hausa women who ran the gamut from literate, devout Muslim authors of Hausa verse in the Arabic poetic style, to illiterate performers of extemporaneous, often bawdy, oral poetry. In retrospect I can understand his perspective. The authors of written poems were so private about their work that it remained for the most part within the women's community. It was widely distributed for educational purposes, but among women who were less educated and more strictly secluded than the poet/teachers. The extemporaneous performers entertained in what were often less than respectable circumstances. Neither type of poet would be familiar to a Hausa university professor, or even to his wife. But these were indeed the women poets of the Hausa, and between them they served a wide range of clients. Nevertheless, the professor's perspective was apparently widespread: I never did receive a research clearance for my work. Then again, my research pursuits were never hindered.

To be fair, it must be said that another Hausa man, a professor at a nearby university, had quite the opposite attitude. Less conservative (or better informed), this man not only was interested in my work, but also provided a local research affiliation for me when it became clear that none was forthcoming from Kano or the Lagos university offices.

I was asked several times by officials whether I was doing research on prostitutes. When they heard an emphatic "no," they were satisfied and promised to pass my research clearance application along. The presumption was that I was welcome to waste my time chasing chimeras, as long as I was not going to expose an unsavory aspect of the culture. Being ignored by Nigerian officialdom was as important to my research as choosing to disassociate myself from the expatriate community in Kano (see "Daily Associations," below). It left me free not only to make my own mistakes, but also to make my own choices and friendships; the last more than compensated for the first.

Research among Hausa women in the region had rarely been done by a foreign woman researcher. Several American and British "research wives" had collected materials on Hausa customs and women's biographies, but the idea of an "outsider woman" focusing research on Hausa women was a new concept in Kano, even in the late 1970s. Part of the reason for this was the sense of privacy promoted by this Muslim society in which life roles are mandated by religious obligation.[6] A man works in the public sector, and attends to commerce for the family, doing the marketing and seeing to errands around town. Women are obliged to see to the domestic scene. They are responsible for households that are often quite large in number, and must attend to the feeding and social development of all those who live there. Households often have several co-wives to share these responsibilities, and many homes have extended family relatives living with them, for whom the wife or wives are responsible as well. The custom in Kano is for traditional Muslim women to remain in seclusion during their child-bearing years; from the time they marry (usually in late adolescence) until they are past child-bearing, they remain in their married home compound, going out only occasionally for obligatory visits or to the clinic. For the most part they focus their energies on the family: raising the children, and running the household. Occasionally during the 1960s and 1970s they were visited by itinerant teachers (women who acted more as social workers than instructors in literacy). In the 1980s, an incipient adult education program for women was having great success with night-school classes for women whose education had been interrupted by marriage and its expectation of seclusion.

I was an anomaly in this environment. As a woman clearly in the middle of potential child-bearing years, it was unusual for me to be "going about" freely in Kano. Although it helped tremendously to speak Hausa, my single status was a constant handicap. With neither husband nor children, I had not yet achieved adult status. At first when people greeted me with "How are the children?" I would explain patiently (and naively) that I had no children. Finally a female friend took me aside and suggested that I simply reply politely, "They are all fine." Another friend, a very respectable, devout woman, and an accomplished poet, gave me a simple gold band and suggested it might be prudent to wear it. Ultimately one is

---

[6] Once while I was sitting with Hajiya in the palace, a report came to us of a foreign woman in conference with the emir, who was railing against his "keeping his wives locked up in purdah." Such blatant disregard for and lack of understanding of the cultural context would end such an individual's research efforts before she had begun. I saw how the visitor was received, and I know how little real information about the culture such an approach would get. The point here is that there is merit in knowing the local language, spending a sufficient amount of time in the field, and being willing to suspend fixation on one's own cultural expectations.

judged by one's actions rather than appearance, but initially (without a track record) my friends sought to protect me from potential criticism. That I was treated so kindly despite my ambiguous status is testimony to the generosity of the people among whom I lived in Kano.

Some, however, were understandably suspicious of me. The husband of one of the women with whom I spent a great deal of time was an extremely conservative man who was wary of the many hours I spent with his wife, and my potentially unsavory influence. One day he confronted me about converting to Islam, commenting that I was doomed to burn in hell if I did not at least marry. When I asked him to bring me the Qur'an and show me where it said so (my patience was running low that day), he became enraged at my audacity in challenging him. Later I learned that this reaction covered his defensiveness about his illiteracy; he could not have cited the appropriate passage, even if there were one.

Research is not done in a vacuum, but is as much about personalities as intellectual pursuits. For instance, one of the poets with whom I worked extensively was herself working for Nigerian Airways. Whenever I begrudged the trips through circuitous, dusty streets to meet with her at her home, I had to remind myself that I was intruding on her time. Similarly, the emir's praise singer, Mai Zargadi—a great, massive woman with a booming voice—suffered from an undiagnosed pain in her legs. Nevertheless, she always welcomed me cheerfully, and talked freely with me, even as I saw her pain revealed in her eyes. Hajiya Paji taught me to play the one-stringed lute in lessons conducted during the heat of the day. And a woman in the palace put aside her pasta-making to talk with me about her life. Without successful interaction between these women and me, no research would have been accomplished.

Further, research can be viewed as "things learned while trying to cope." I contracted typhoid after visiting a friend outside Kano, and there was no one back in my home to help me. I was able to drive myself to the university clinic during the early morning hours when the fever broke, but it took three days of treatment for malaria before the right diagnosis was made. During that time I wondered whether I would survive to turn the experience into an anecdote. My lack of contact with the resident expatriate community also meant that I had no idea I was supposed to hold a residence pass card. I had to summon all the humility I could muster to face the prospect of going to police headquarters to ask for one, after already having lived there for thirteen months. The experience proved as frightening as I had anticipated, and understandably so, considering how suspect I must have appeared in such circumstances. Nevertheless, with very few exceptions, people in Hausaland were far more generous with their time and resources than was reasonable to expect. I doubt I would have been as gracious to someone intruding into my life for their research.

Daily Associations

I had heard of other Fulbright recipients who had been hosted by United States government officials, and at first I was upset that no such connections existed to help me with mail or illness. I was not only unconnected to any United States government presence, but completely ignorant of it until I was about to leave. This proved to be a useful disassociation. Nor did I remain closely connected with the Bayero University crowd after finding my own place in town. It was comforting to know that there were several colleagues from the University of Wisconsin at Bayero University, including my former Hausa teacher; we began referring to Kano as "Madison East." It was good to have a community of United States scholars with whom to talk while I was getting settled, but after moving to my own place I saw the expatriate community far less than the Hausa people among whom I lived, and with whom I spent my working days.

I felt I should begin my research as soon as I arrived—not wait to get settled—so I walked to the university gates, got a taxi into town, and arrived at the front gate of the emir's palace on that first day. There I asked a guard to deliver a note in Hausa to one of the emir's wives in the women's quarters: "Dear Hajiya, We met two years ago when I visited Kano in the summer. You told me then that if I came back for research on women praise singers I should come to see you. I have just arrived and would like to visit. Yours, Binta." The guard returned and led me through the labyrinthine path that was to become my regular route into the royal harem.

My field research focused on collecting oral poetry from Hausa women. To complement and deepen my research experience, I intended to live in the Old City, and learn as much as I could about the Hausa; research on women poets and praise singers was my vehicle for experiencing Hausa culture. Of course, this was not a conscious decision. At first I thought my sole task was to find, collect, and analyze Hausa women's royal praise songs, but linguistics got in the way. In the Hausa language "praise song," or *wa'ka*, is defined broadly as anything in the realm of song or poetry. Therefore, Hajiya's leads were not only to the praise singers who performed solely for the emir, but also to women in the city, not connected to the royal family, who wrote Arabic-style Hausa poetry. Eventually, my interest in women performers led me to other extemporaneous performers who worked for political campaigns, and recorded for the radio and television. Eventually I was dealing with women across a wide spectrum of socioeconomic statuses, and in several different walks of Hausa culture. These included mostly women of middle-income level, although I apprenticed myself for a time to a performer who was of lower-class status. Thus I became as interested in the cultural web in which they were enmeshed, as I was in the praise songs I intended to record.

Each day involved a set of visits to women connected with the palace and poetry. The royal women's quarters became the hub of all my activities. I visited Hajiya almost daily, learning which times of the day and year were the best and the worst for a sit-down conversation. During the second eighteen-month period of my research I had fallen into the habit of being a piece of the adobe wall, just sitting around and observing. By then I had become familiar enough that people went about their daily activities without feeling they were slighting me. I was there so much that they had no choice but to carry on, or nothing would have gotten done at all. This was the period in which I observed the quotidian aspects of women's lives: who was a regular member of Hajiya's quarters besides her children; which other children came to play, and from what other parts of the palace; which women paid regular visits from outside the palace; which old women of the palace were connected to Hajiya (made evident through her sending news and gifts to them); when the children went to Qur'anic classes and secular school; which market items were distributed among the palace wives for sale; who cooked for whom and how often; where the gardens were and who oversaw them; what were the regular tasks of the concubines and servants connected with Hajiya; what kinds of problems were brought for Hajiya's advice from both within and outside the palace; and so on. Of course, celebratory times had their own special foods, entertainments, attire, and schedules, and I was privileged to experience several Sallah[7] festivals inside the palace.

In addition to observing the rhythm of daily life in the women's quarters, I was able to learn a great deal about the history of the palace from the women's perspectives. Former royal wives can spend the duration of their lives in the palace after their husbands' deaths. Several who still lived there told fascinating stories about such things as their experiences during the arrival of the British in 1903, or about the colonial era, and one had an Arab father who came to Kano as a trader and stayed on. Eventually they also offered opinions on their own lives, explaining conditions more frankly than I ever expected.

Layered on to these histories were the perspectives of Hajiya, my contemporary, and those of her daughters and foster daughters, the next generation. The younger the woman, the more openly she spoke, but the older the woman, the more insight she expressed. Thus, my affiliations provided perspectives from at least three generations of Hausa women. I was interested in their own definitions of their lives, and the daily contact I enjoyed with them helped me to broach an inside vision of their lives.

This ever-expanding circle of connections led to my interviewing women in other emirates in northern Nigeria, too. Wives, concubines, and servants in other palaces had experiences that contrasted sharply with those of the women in the Kano palace. My status as an envoy of the emir of Kano was the best entrée I could have; I was always treated with the graciousness characteristic of the Hausa.

Thus, over two eighteen-month periods of residence, my research started out with perfect focus and expanded into a great, blurred bulk of fascinating and dubiously connected material. In graduate school I had heard that if during fieldwork all the pieces of a culture seemed to fit together well, then a researcher's perspective on that culture was woefully misguided. Considering the jumbled state of my research, I wagered cheerfully that I was right on the mark.

Social Boundaries: Life in a Fishbowl

As a guest among the Hausa, I could cross social lines, visiting in the private women's quarters of the palace, observing a public celebration like Sallah outside the palace walls, or attending a nocturnal spirit possession ceremony (*bori*) nearby. Nevertheless, no matter where I went I knew that my behavior and conversations

---

[7] Sallah is the annual parade and festivities celebrating the end of a month of fasting (Ramadan).

were being monitored. In three years of almost daily visits to Hajiya in the center of the palace, I surprised her only once. Otherwise, a messenger always reached her with news of my arrival before I did.[8] It was several months into my first period of residence in Kano before I realized how little privacy I had; Hajiya asked me about a conversation I had had with a market stall keeper earlier in the day. Hajiya did not often leave the palace,[9] and were she to do so, she would never go to the market. It became clear that where I went, how I got there, what I wore, and how I behaved were all subject to scrutiny. My connection to the palace required respectable public behavior, but even without such a tie, my behavior would have been noticed in Kano more than I knew. I was an anomaly. First, I was unusual in my status as a foreigner who was given license to frequent the palace. Second, I clearly did not fit the behavioral pattern for a traditional Hausa woman; I was a grown woman who dressed like a Hausa woman and spoke the language, but I moved around town with the freedom of a man. I held a non-specific role in Hausa society as a guest, and an exception to the rules. Neither wife nor mother, and very much in the public realm, I could only be classed as ambiguous—neither male nor female, but able to cross social lines imposed for each.

Another indication of my dubious female status was my failed attempt to cook for my friends in the palace. When I ate at home, it was usually an omelet or soup, along with fruit, or snack food from the street markets. What I enjoyed most was the spicy stews and standard Hausa fare my friends shared with me constantly (berating what they saw as my inadequate attempt to nourish myself) during the time that I lived in Kano. I returned to my compound at night, but especially during my post-doctoral fieldwork I nearly lived at the palace. One dish I like especially well is *moi-moi* (bean pudding). Because someone had told me the recipe, I decided to make this as a surprise, trying to reciprocate for all the delectables I had been fed. The process is labor-intensive, and involves a virtue of Hausa culture that I admit I have always lacked: patience. I failed to let the beans soak long enough to soften them, and when my hosts took their first taste I was amazed to see women of unusual decorum and control literally rolling on the ground in laughter. As they wiped their eyes, they told me, "This is like eating road gravel. Binta, you stick to your writing, and we will do the cooking. Please promise you will never again cook for us!" These women accepted me with all my faults and disabilities: a grown woman who wore no makeup, could not cook, and had to have her Hausa corrected—no wonder I was not married! Still, they were among the most generous, patient, and kindest friends I have known.

While child-care duties are shared by co-wives and concubines in the palace, only women of slave/servant status could go outside the palace to do errands. Respectability involves seclusion, and there is a great deal of social pressure not to go out if you can have someone else do the errands for you. My ambiguous status allowed me advantages, because I could go where Hajiya, secluded in the palace,

---

[8] The one time I surprised her I shrouded my head and upper body in a veil as a woman in mourning would do, and let my wrapper hang extra long to cover my telltale white ankles. Also, I crept into the palace on this occasion from the back, and during siesta time. Nearly all the gatekeepers were dozing in the heat.

[9] She has traveled abroad (to England and Mecca), and goes to the clinic in Kano.

could never go. At some point I became Hajiya's alter ego, ferrying women poets who lived elsewhere in Kano, or delivering packages on her behalf. Also, since I had become their "auntie," I could take the children places Hajiya could not. Six of us went to the Kano zoo for a day's outing. I took some of her daughters with a few of her servants to a naming ceremony across town, and to their paternal grandmother's home nearby. One time Hajiya even entrusted me with four of her children for a weekend visit to her family home in Katsina.

The Old City market is a fascinating place but, unlike markets in southern Nigeria, it is not a place for women sellers or buyers. But I had neither husband nor servants to make purchases for me, so I went to the market often. I enjoyed being able to chat at leisure with the vendors, examine leatherwork, stumble upon rows of cow hooves for sale, and haggle over enamel pots. When I went to the market, I could swaddle Hajiya's youngest on my back, and take her four-year-old daughter with me; by the time she reached adolescence she would be promised in marriage and too easily recognized to be allowed to wander around the market. Interestingly, I was recognized at the market, but she was not. When we got home, she cocked her head haughtily and said to her mother, "They all wondered what a Fulani girl was doing with this white woman, but I didn't say anything. I just let them talk!"

An advantage of having become a known member of the palace community became clear the day I had a car accident on the road ringing the palace. Kano traffic makes New York City at rush hour look rural. Road accidents in Kano can be lethal, even when no one is hurt, depending on how high tensions are running for the particular political period and weather; during tough economic times, or in the hot season, tempers sometimes flare, a crowd forms, and a car can be burned. This is why we were advised not to stop, even for one's own road accident. One day a bicyclist and I collided—neither one of us was paying sufficient attention— and I started to get out of the car to see if he was hurt. He was fine, with especially healthy vocal chords, hurling admonitions at me, understandably upset. Someone walking along intervened and immediately defused the situation by saying that I lived in the palace. Shaken, I arrived in the serenity of the women's quarters understanding better the occasional advantage of being served and kept secure in seclusion. On that day I would gladly have considered trading my freedom for some peace.

Before I went to Nigeria I had been a runner for ten years. Needless to say, it was out of the question for me to put on shorts and take to the streets for exercise in Kano; the only people running down the streets were thieves being pursued and madmen. But I found the agricultural station two miles outside the city, and went there just before sunset to run the perimeter of the field in full sweats—as covered as possible. This worked out fine until the day I learned that the adjacent field was a burial ground. That day's procession of men bearing a corpse did not end my daily activity, but it certainly caused me to look around carefully before setting out on the trail. More than once the exercise was cut short as I made a quick—and I hoped, anonymous—exit.

During the month of Ramadan people fast from sunup until sundown. It was not fair, I thought, to expect people to work responding to questions when they were fasting, unless I knew firsthand what they were feeling. So I fasted too. I thought that if I could still work during this time, then I could expect it of others. It took only the first day of my fasting to realize that Ramadan turns life around. And no one ever complained. The women worked through the heat of the day without food or water to cook for the evening meal that would break the fast. Otherwise, not much of anything got done. The last fifteen minutes before the evening call to worship and breaking of the fast was the longest for me. Like a child who works up to the full thirty days little by little each year, I was proud of "doing five" days. (The rest of the time I laid low, and ate only in private during the day.) Although mine was a meager attempt, it was not lost on my Hausa friends, who bragged about it to others as if it were their own child's accomplishment.

Finally, I knew I had been accepted the day the gruffest guard at the palace (who had been quizzing me with Hausa riddles from the start and been disgusted with my ignorance of them) greeted me with a riddle I answered appropriately. His smile was broad as he said, "Good, Hajiya." Prior to this I noticed that people in the neighborhood had moved from calling me "Malama" (teacher, scholar) to "Hajiya," a title for a Muslim woman who has been to Mecca. I was puzzled (taking everything literally), because I knew that they knew that I was not Muslim. In the palace Hajiya explained it was meant as an honorific. When the guard who was my toughest critic called me "Hajiya," I knew that Kano had become home.

Conclusion: What I Learned

There was very little of United States life that I missed, other than closer contact with family and friends. And although I endured a bout of typhoid alone, suffered with everyone else the debilitating harmattan dust storms, and worried occasionally about the prospect of an anonymous car accident outside Kano, the positive aspects of life there far outweighed the negative. I was healthier than ever, with sunshine, good basic food, and a day divided equally between night and day. In addition, I shall always be grateful for having the good fortune to have studied the language for three years before needing it for research. Relying on translators means that you cannot really do your own research. In addition, among the Hausa, speaking the language is the highest complement one can offer, and the best indication of a sincere interest in the culture.

In Kano I learned what may seem to be a lesson in perversity, but it is really about adjusting one's expectations: first, you need to have a list of things that need doing; second, you must plan on accomplishing none of them; and third, you will be delighted with whatever gets done. I learned that sincerity and good intentions are not lost on people, who will respond generously to kindness; but I also heard quite often that one's "reward is in heaven." I never intended my research to unfold the way it did, and certainly never expected to become so involved with the community of women in the palace. When I went there, all I had was an idea of a beginning. But Allah provides, and where it will go from here, only He knows.

5

Learning the Dance, Initiating Relationships *

Sheryl McCurdy

That first Saturday evening in February 1993, emotionally and physically drained, I virtually collapsed onto my kapok mattress. But I wasn't ready to sleep. Instead of blowing out the candle, I reached over to the pile of folders on the floor next to me and pulled out one with a list of Kigoma Province TANU women leaders inside.[1] "It's about time to start seriously searching for some of these women," I thought and gazed up at the list. I was simultaneously thrilled and shocked to see the name of the Kigoma TANU Provincial women's leader, Bi Amina Hassan.[2] I had just spent the entire day with her and many before that negotiating my entry into the female initiation ceremony, *unyago*. Bi Amina Hassan was now my *somo* (instructor) and I was her *mwali* (initiate), with all the ties and responsibilities that such a relationship entailed.

This was my fourth stay in Tanzania.[3] I had come this time to Ujiji, in the urban Kigoma area,[4] to study how individuals and groups manipulated notions of

---

* I am grateful to the Social Science Research Council who funded both my pre-dissertation and dissertation research. I conducted this study in Tanzania and England from 1992 to 1993.

[1] Many thanks to Susan Geiger for sharing this list with me, and to her, Dorothy Hodgson, Pier Larson, Amy Stambach, and the editors for extensive comments on earlier drafts of this essay. TANU refers to the Tanganyikan African National Union, the nationalist organization formed in the 1950s which was active across Tanzania.

[2] Note: Names given to the women cited in this chapter are pseudonyms.

[3] In 1981 I had first traveled across northern Tanzania from Kilimanjaro to Lake Victoria, staying for four months as I conducted an independent research project and visited friends. From 1984 through 1986 I was a master's student at the University of Dar es Salaam; this opportunity was provided by the University of Minnesota's Reciprocal Exchange Program Scholarship, 1984–1985. In the summer of 1989, under the auspices of an SSRC pre-dissertation fellowship, I returned again.

[4] Before the influx of Burundian refugees in October 1993, urban Kigoma was home to roughly 150,000 inhabitants. For the purposes of this essay the area includes Kigoma town, Bangwe village, Mwanga, Gungu, and Ujiji. These towns have grown so extensively that today they flow into each other. Although Ha and Tongwe are spoken by peoples northeast and south of Kigoma, many of the long-term residents of Ujiji speak only Swahili.

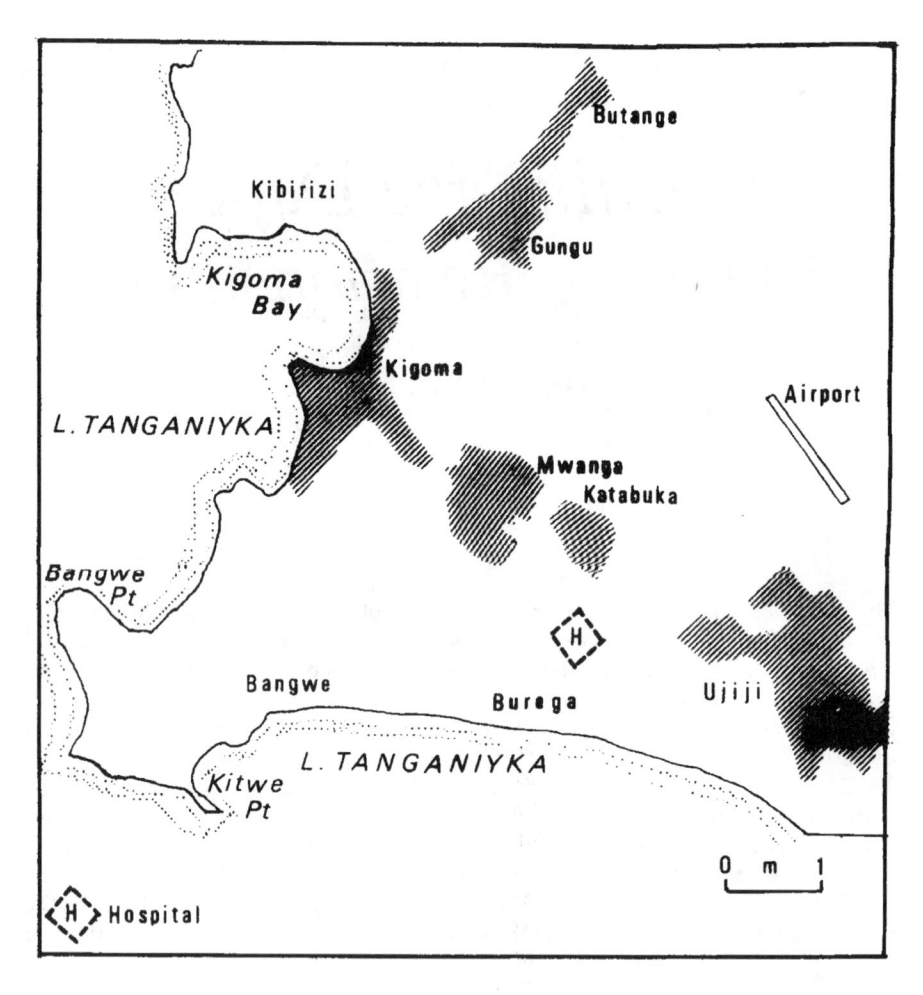

Map 3, Kigoma

disease and medical practices within the changing boundaries of their social, economic, and political environment. By focusing on complaints of infertility and high infant mortality since World War II, I wanted to examine the roles played by individuals, women's associations, and healers in negotiating and managing the changing realities of people's lives. I hoped to learn how different traditions, ideas, and practices were being negotiated and transformed.[5]

---

[5] My master's research had been a study of women's childbirth practices in the Iringa region of southwestern Tanzania. Sheryl McCurdy, "The Position of Women in Tanzania and Their Ability to Make Reproductive Choices" (M.A. thesis in Development Studies, University of Dar es Salaam, 1987). UNICEF had a maternal and child health project in the area and provided financial support and equipment for my research. This experience led me to several decisions regarding my doctoral research. I chose to avoid affiliation with a project this time because my previous connection with UNICEF had led informants to

Ujiji, home to a multiethnic population, is situated on the shores of beautiful Lake Tanganyika. But this urban area is not really a destination for pleasure trips. More often than not it is a beginning, middle, or end point for a myriad of traders and travelers from Burundi, Zaïre, Zambia, and Tanzania. Bypassed by both German and British colonialists in favor of the European colonial town of Kigoma, Ujiji's inhabitants hail primarily from all around the lake and from the interior forest area of eastern Zaïre, and together they share a history dating back through the nineteenth century. Adjacent to the town of Ujiji proper is the more recent settlement of Mwanga, initially inhabited by railway workers and migrants. In the early twentieth century, factional differences and social conflicts among this mixed population had been expressed in dance competitions between women's associations. Although these groups and their competitions have since disappeared, a female initiation association, *unyago*, and some of the many spirit possession cults still survive. It was this history of changing identities and social conflicts within a diverse population which had drawn me to choose this border town as a research site.[6]

My decision to be initiated to *unyago* grew from a desire to learn how women's concerns, beliefs, and practices were expressed, ritualized, and passed on. Equipped with the special knowledge contained within the rituals and functions of *unyago* I expected to ask better and more informed questions. I hoped in this way to establish relationships with women and their families, and to discover what health beliefs and practices were taught in the ceremonies. By learning about the differences and similarities between the tradition of *unyago* and the various spirit possession performances, I wanted to better understand the history of the social factions of Ujiji. I wondered whether these former factions and their associations had particular healing beliefs and/or practices, and what had happened to these ideas and practices once the groups and their competitions dissolved in the mid-twentieth century.[7]

---

manipulate information in attempts to improve their access to health services. I wanted Swahili to be the primary language in the area so that disputes, jokes, and offhand comments would all be accessible to me rather than filtered through interpreters, and I wanted the continuity and long-term view of staying in one area that I had missed by moving between different areas.

[6] Relations between resident and immigrant (Manyema) groups in Ujiji had been strained since at least the mid-nineteenth century. The interested reader will find more historical background on the region and its peoples in Beverly Brown, "Ujiji: The History of a Lakeside Town, c. 1800–1914" (Ph.D. dissertation, Boston University, 1973); and Deogratius Bimanyu, "The Waungwana of Eastern Zaïre, 1880–1900" (Ph.D. dissertation, School of Oriental and African Studies, University of London, 1976) and Sheryl McCurdy, "The 1932 'War' Between Rival Ujiji Associations: Understanding Women's Motivations for Inciting Political Unrest," *Canadian Journal of African Studies*, 30, 1 (1996).

[7] Supraethnic political and religious associations had operated among and between many ethnic groups of the Manyema region as well as in western Tanzania. These are described in: Bimanyu, "Waungwana," 27–32; Jan Vansina, *Paths in the Rainforests: Toward a History of Political Tradition in Equatorial Africa* (Madison, 1990), 180–91, 188–89; and J. Abemba, "Pouvoir politique traditionnel et Islam au Congo Oriental," *Cahiers du Centre d'Etude et de Documentation Africaines*, Serie 1: Sociologie (Brussels, 1971), 1–42. The differences and hostilities between the Manyema and the longer-term Ujiji residents crystallized around female dance competitions in which both factions expressed their animosities towards each other through songs. See McCurdy, "The 1932 War." Different from dance competitions and spirit possession is a female association called *unyago*. It is an initiation ceremony for girls. The term *unyago* denotes the association itself as well as the ceremony and the initiation.

Would initiation give me privileged and open access to the historical knowledge of my instructor? I hoped Bi Amina would teach me about Ujiji's past, the dance competitions, the two factions which performed them, women's lives in the 1950s, her role in TANU, and her own life history. But the pursuit of research on a particular topic is not a one-sided affair directed by the researcher. Conducting fieldwork is like a dance in which both partners, the researcher and the researched, must learn new steps and negotiate the path on which they will embark. Fieldwork relationships may have multiple meanings for the different parties concerned, while moral and ethical issues flow from the sharing of information, as I was to discover.

The Story

I wanted to see an *unyago* initiation ceremony. But there was a catch. According to local women, such ceremonies were only seen by the initiated. To see the ceremony, I would have to be initiated. Neither of my two initial hosts, both young women, had been initiated. So I began to search out avenues of opportunity through both them and older women I had met. For two months I was repeatedly told it was not possible, no European had ever been initiated. In other words: forget it, we are not interested. My inquiries were informal. For example, when during a short visit over tea, my hosts' relatives began to discuss the most recent *msondo*,[8] I would request to join them the next time. They would laugh good-naturedly and tell me it wasn't possible; only initiates could attend.

One late January afternoon I went on one of many visits to Khadija, a friend who suffered from frequent bouts of malaria. I had often confided to her my desire to witness *unyago*, and on this day she told me she thought her *somo* might agree to initiate me.[9] She often told me she would introduce me to new informants: a wonderful historian, a hospital medic, a distinguished local healer. She seldom got around to it. I enjoyed her company and decided that these unfulfilled promises didn't matter. She was a wonderful storyteller herself. One day Khadija surprised me with the information that the next day we were to visit her *somo* to discuss initiating me, but I had to promise to keep my information secret.

During the last week of January, Khadija and I plodded through the red rain-soaked streets of the old Ujiji ward, Kitongoni, to visit Bi Amina Hassan. Located just below the main market, her home is one of those old whitewashed Ujiji houses with high ceilings, a cement base, and an extended cement platform where children play and women often sit talking, breastfeeding, weaving mats, and preparing meals. We circled around to the back of the house and found several women and children in the courtyard and a meal cooking on the outside kitchen fire. After quick greetings we were whisked inside to a long dark hallway and ushered through the middle left door. In an equally dark and starkly empty room we found Bi Amina sitting alone. There were old, tattered

---

[8] This is the word most frequently used in Ujiji to denote the female initiation ceremony.

[9] The term *somo* refers to an individual who has passed through certain ranks in the initiation cult and has the right to initiate another individual in a *msondo* ceremony.

mats on the floor, and a cord drawn across the far side of the room where clothes were hung. Bi Amina wore old *khanga*s[10] and sat on a mat with her back to the wall, feet outstretched. We approached her with our heads and knees bent, shoulders stooped, and hands cupped one over the other clapping until we reached her. She put her right hand on Khadija's head and then mine, and approvingly nodded for us to sit. Her mother had died some weeks earlier and she was in mourning, confined to the house for forty days.[11]

As we three sat in a triangle on the floor, Bi Amina in her dignified and well-spoken manner requested my explanation for seeking initiation. I tried to articulate as best I could my interest in learning more about the culture of women's lives. I explained that I was a student of history and public health. Since this ritual was such an important facet of women's lives, then I felt obligated to learn and participate as fully as possible.

This interview represented a crucial, perhaps final, chance for me to enter into this realm of women's lives. With great trepidation I ended my difficult appeal and watched what seemed to me the agonizingly slow process of her decision-making. Bi Amina nodded when I finished, then continued to chew on her tobacco. She slowly pulled out a small glass jar from behind her and proceeded to spit into it. She looked at me and confirmed Khadija's earlier pleas of the necessity for secrecy about the ceremony. After explaining with whom the ceremony could and could not be discussed, Bi Amina asked if I was prepared to abide by these restrictions.

I had invested too much to back out. Bi Amina was informing me that yes, I could attend the "dance," but I must be silent about what went on there. I decided that although my study could not focus on the specifics of the ceremony, what I would learn could inform and enhance my research. I would be able to ask better-informed questions about women's concerns and lives by participating in this important ritual. I resigned myself to not using directly the information provided in the ceremony and told Bi Amina and Khadija that I would keep the secrets.

My acceptance presented me with the ethical and moral responsibility of respecting the wishes of my informants and reevaluating my research plans. I began to understand that the research process meant negotiating a path of inquiry in which I would learn more about women's lives, but they would choose how and what information to divulge. The respect I granted their requests would not only reflect my own integrity, but also expose their trust in me to a broader public. It would continue to determine the path and the nature of my ongoing relationships with these women.

After a period of silent reflection Bi Amina turned to Khadija and asked her what she thought of all this, if she believed I could be relied upon to keep my word. Khadija put her reputation on the line. Our relationship had been short, but she vouched for me as a trustworthy and honest person. She believed that secret knowledge could be imparted to this *mzungu* (European) without repercussions. After Khadija's endorsement Bi Amina looked each of us over

---

[10] A pair of matching rectangular designed cloths with Swahili sayings across the center bottom. In Ujiji women wear one of them tied around their waist and the other over their head or shoulders, or tied to carry an infant on their back.

[11] Older Manyema women with some social standing and means are most likely to follow this practice in Ujiji. Men do not engage in this practice.

and advised us she would meet with some other women to discuss the request. She told Khadija to come back later to see her. A few days later Khadija informed me that arrangements were in progress and that additional meetings were being held at Bi Amina's.

Only after the *somo* elders' joint decision to trust me did we begin to discuss the logistics of my initiation. We assembled a list of the necessary cash, gifts, and objects for the ceremony, and negotiated options. Dates for the event were offered, agreed upon, and canceled three times before the initiation actually occurred. Since Bi Amina was in mourning during this period and restricted to in-house activities, the ceremony was designed to be held inside her home. Spatial limits, my financial constraints, and consideration for my privacy led to restricted participation. In order to reduce the number of women involved, secrecy marked the occasion.[12] Bi Amina only informed a handful of close friends and family members when the event would take place and she warned me that sorcery might be attempted to thwart our activities.[13]

After living only two months in Ujiji I became a *mwali*.[14] Bi Amina and Bi Fatuma, the women who had achieved the highest status in this ritual for Kigoma area, were good friends and decided that first week in February I should not only be initiated, but progress through all possible steps to become a full-fledged *somo*. They did not want to stop halfway.[15] Already these women, about whom I had read in archives at Dar es Salaam, were making decisions about how extensive my knowledge of women's lives should be. So the morning after my discovery that

---

[12] A recent trend towards streamlined *unyago* ceremonies with more exclusive participation in both inside and outside performance of the ritual is noted by Marja Liisa Swantz in *Blood, Milk, and Death: Body Symbols and the Power of Regeneration Among the Zaramo of Tanzania* (Westport, 1995), 128. The *unyago* ceremony has been performed inside in the past as well. See Margaret Strobel, *Muslim Women in Mombasa, 1890–1975* (New Haven, 1979), 204; Sarah Mirza and Margaret Strobel, *Three Swahili Women: Life Histories from Mombasa* (Bloomington, 1989); and Laura Fair, "Women's Popular Culture and the Creation of a National Identity in Zanzibar, 1890 to 1930," a paper presented at the meetings of the Arts Council of the African Studies Association, New York, April, 1995, 19–20. According to Fair, freeborn Zanzibari women received their instruction inside during the nineteenth century.

[13] Both Bi Amina and Khadija warned me that sorcery might be attempted. At their insistence, Khadija and I obtained charms from a healer which we were to wear hidden in our clothing throughout the ceremony. This protection was to provide us with safe delivery from whatever sorcery might be sent our direction.

[14] This short time period was the direct result of previous stays and contacts in Tanzania. In Ujiji I was living with the extended family of my friend and colleague Zubeida Tumbo-Masabo. Twaha Masabo, her husband, who is Manyema, had arranged with Zubeida for me to stay with his family. My friend Hawa Abdallah had introduced Khadija to me. Later, I discovered that Khadija had been a childhood friend of Twaha Masabo. I feel it was because of these connections that I was so quickly accepted and trusted. I thank Zubeida, Twaha, and the family of the late Juma Hassan for their support and assistance during my last two visits to Tanzania. I also want to thank my friends Laura Fair and Kpepwa Tambila for suggesting I ride the train second-class to Kigoma. It was this forty-eight-hour period and the ensuing events ensued that sealed my relationship with Hawa Abdalla.

[15] Khadija was embarrassed that she had not progressed beyond the first stage. She felt that by the age of thirty-something a respectable woman should have progressed to the stage of being able to initiate a young girl. To her it was a question of status in the community and also the ability to gain financially. A woman who is a *somo* and has already initiated one young girl is entitled to keep the gifts from the initiate's family. Bi Amina was interested in having me progress to the stage of initiator because her status would improve by leading a *mzungu* through this stage. Also, everything I received during the first initiation I performed was to be given to her.

my *somo* was a TANU leader, I stopped by Khadija's and together we went off to Bi Amina's to begin the next stage of rituals.

Everyone was late that morning. When I arrived at Khadija's she hadn't finished feeding her children. I remained at her house until we departed at 10 A.M. I couldn't relax and was preoccupied as I talked to her youngest son, while her youngest daughter alternately played with my hair and rolled around on the double bed. Khadija kept saying, "Oh! don' t worry, these women are never ready on time, they didn't really mean for us to be there at 9 A.M."

True to her prediction, we discovered upon our arrival (well after 10 A.M.) that the party we were to depart with was still in the process of organizing itself. In the meantime we went to visit Bi Amina who, due to her confinement in mourning, could not leave her house. After we greeted her, she explained that other obligations were slowing things down. She anticipated that another step in the program would have to take place the following morning instead of that same day.

Shortly thereafter Bi Fatuma arrived and took us on our way. Along the path we met two of the women who had been around the day before and another joined us as we descended the sloping paths of Kitongoni ward for another ritual by the shores of Lake Tanganyika. This event did not capture the attention of as many women as the initiation rite the day before, and only a few of us were together this afternoon.

Bi Fatuma and Bi Amina decided that early the next morning (Bi Fatuma placed a great emphasis on *early* and gave Khadija and some of the other women a stern glance), we would go to the bush and complete my training. There was some haggling over money, objects, and food for the next day, along with Bi Amina's threats to discontinue the entire proceedings. After considerable negotiations these problems were resolved.

The next day we all managed to arrive by 8 A.M. at Bi Amina's and then we took a taxi to a place nearby the designated area. We collected our things from the car and started walking into the bush. After a short time the leaders announced that they had found a suitable place and told Khadija and me to wait in the distance. Until this weekend Khadija had only been through the beginning stage of initiation. Part of the reason she had helped strike the bargain for my initiation was to improve her own status and position by rising in expertise within the initiation association.

I bided my time walking around picking wildflowers and wondering what was going to happen next. Suddenly, I heard hands clapping behind me. Two young women from Mwanga had arrived. They had received word of where we were and had searched for us. They were greeted appropriately but reservedly by our *somo*s. The younger of the two was a *mwali* who had not progressed to this stage of initiation. The Ujiji women were upset that she now knew where a section of upcoming rituals would take place. They were also worried that she might see or hear something she should not, and angrily complained among themselves about this intrusion. The visitor apologized profusely for upsetting her elders and promised that her *mwali* would sit far away, deaf, dumb, and blind to the proceedings.

Mildly placated, my *somo*s returned to their activities on one side of the tree in the center of the field and assigned the new arrival a duty at the nearby yet separate site. First, however, she led her young charge to a suitable distance away from our gathering. I listened to the others mumbling among themselves: "Why had this young women appeared?" They were obviously surprised and disappointed to see her there. When I inquired about it, they told me she had been sent to spy on us and see what the Ujiji women were telling the *mzungu*. I was startled and dismayed. When we had sought protection in the form of charms, I had not anticipated the extent of the controversy that my initiation would spark.

In my fascination and dread of what this intrigue could mean, I turned to see what the spy was doing. Just as I looked in the direction where she had left her young *mwali*, I saw her walk further to the west of us and throw a plucked chicken in the air between the two sites where the Ujiji women were working. I naively asked the woman working near me if this were part of the ritual. She looked at me quizzically and asked me to repeat myself. She quickly called over Bi Fatuma who asked me again. I told them, "She just threw a plucked chicken, over there! Let's go look!" "No, we won't look," Bi Fatuma assured me, *"Ni hatari! Usiende kule, ni uchawi!"* (This is dangerous [business]! Don't go near there, it is witchcraft!)[16]

By this time the spy had moved to her designated site, a short distance from us, and Bi Fatuma instructed us to pretend that we had already finished the ceremony. She had the women collect what they were doing and told them we would return to her house to finish the ceremony there. In hushed yet anxious whispering tones the women hurriedly gathered their belongings and we all walked over to the spy. Bi Fatuma announced, "Too bad you've arrived so late, everything's been completed! Give our greetings to the Mwanga people when you return home!" Shortly afterwards we left. I wanted desperately to look at the chicken and see if it had fetishes attached to it or had been ritually cut, but I was instructed to move away from the site quickly, without looking back.[17]

Unfortunately, we had told the taxi to meet us at a designated place and time. Some of us waited for the taxi; others loaded bundles on their heads and walked home to begin preparations at Bi Fatuma's. Waiting for the taxi seemed endless, partially because of my undying urge to look back over my shoulder (I knew I was being watched and couldn't), but mostly because of our conversations. My *somos* started to complain about those interfering Mwanga women who wanted to find out if, indeed, Bi Amina and Bi Fatuma had initiated the *mzungu*. And if it were true, what exactly was the European being told, all the secrets of *unyago*?

Khadija kept me off to the side of the women and told me not to ask too many questions. "We'll talk later, I'll explain later," she kept repeating to me. I found that very frustrating, but felt I had no choice other than to follow her lead. Soon

---

[16] I never learned whether this was meant to harm one of us individually or if it was simply intended to subvert our actions. From the discussions and actions I witnessed, I got the impression that the Ujiji women believed the Mwanga women wanted to wreak havoc on our activities.

[17] During a ritual I had previously witnessed to end a *degedege* episode (febrile convulsions in infants and toddlers) and to prevent another, the healer killed a chicken during a *zindiko* (a spell to cast off disease) and then instructed us to leave the bush without looking back. The idea is that you have left the disease or cast off the spell in this particular place and now you are free of it; the next person who happens along will catch it. So in this case, by following their instructions I was respecting my elders and showing deference to their wishes. I was also avoiding endangering myself or my companions. They viewed my wish to explore and investigate as mere ignorance, and felt they needed not only to educate me but also to protect me. If I had looked, it would have meant I had no respect for them or understanding of the situation and in their eyes I would have put us in danger.

the taxi arrived, we rode over to Bi Fatuma's, and after some more silent waiting, the ritual began.

Late that afternoon as we prepared to return home, Bi Fatuma warned me, "Don' t listen to those Mwanga women! We did what we desired and now it's complete. There's nothing they can do about it!" I found this proclamation a bit odd and troubling, and I turned to Khadija as we walked home together and finally asked about it. Khadija told me that there were jealous women in Mwanga who didn't want to see Bi Amina and Bi Fatuma initiate me, but that I shouldn't care. "Bi Fatuma is the leading *somo* in Kigoma region. No one can stop her from doing what she wants," Khadija pronounced.

I did not know many people in urban Kigoma beyond the family I lived with in Ujiji, my informants, and a few Europeans I had recently met. I had not told anyone that I was being initiated. I was stunned therefore when women along the paths of Ujiji, Mwanga, and Gungu began to point at me and hiss, "That's the *mzungu* that Bi Amina initiated!" It was clear from their tone that they were not pleased that I was now a *mwali*.

These events occurred in early February. I had arrived in Ujiji in mid-November, and shortly thereafter my husband came to stay with me and my host family through December. I had been in Ujiji about six weeks after his departure, without much contact outside my host family, neighbors, and a few informants. The mail service in Ujiji was miserable and around this time I quit writing anyone because the replies rarely arrived, or if they did, they were generally two to four months late. Feeling isolated, the hostility which had been generated through my initiation weighed heavily on me.

A week after our trip to the peri-urban bush and the encounter with witchcraft, I visited Bi Amina and Bi Fatuma with Khadija. All the women who had participated in my initiation were Manyema. To me this fact was a consolation prize. I had come to Kigoma urban area primarily because of my interest in the Manyema ethnic identity. I had desired the opportunity to build relationships with precisely these women living in the old quarter of Ujiji. Bi Fatuma sat cross-legged on the old worn mat in Bi Amina's mourning room. Both she and Bi Amina sat in their *khanga*s, with one piece veiled over their heads, methodically chewing their tobacco. Bi Fatuma's *buibui* (black over-robe) lay folded on the multicolored mat beneath them.

Bi Fatuma is a short, wiry, and opinionated Manyema woman. That day she was even more animated than usual. Rocking back and forth, gesturing with her hands as she laughed, she repeated again and again the details of a recent council meeting the influential *somo*s from Ujiji had conducted with the leading *somo*s from Mwanga. At the end of her recitation, Bi Fatuma leaned forward, smiled triumphantly and in hushed tones announced, "They told us we were fools for initiating you!" Lifting her head back confidently she continued her diatribe, "They said we've initiated Arabs before, but not *mzungu*s. And you are not just any *mzungu*, you are a researcher! They say a researcher is here to do one thing and one thing only." She paused, smiled, and spit into her little uncorked bottle. Cocking her head to the side and looking deep into my eyes, her raspy voice echoed the worries of the Mwanga *somo*s, "Researchers look for secrets and they write about secrets! They are afraid you will return home, write about *msondo* (the initiation ceremony), and the people of Ujiji and Mwanga/Kigoma will look like fools!"

This information and its delivery profoundly disturbed me. Bi Amina was silent as Bi Fatuma delivered her tale. Bi Fatuma continued laughing and repeating little tidbits insinuating how distrustful and provincial the Mwanga women were. She trusted me, she claimed, and announced that she believed in me so much that she wanted me to initiate her granddaughter before I left Tanzania. I was overwhelmed. I felt honored, yet apprehensive. By continuing to move up the ranks in Ujiji, would I further anger and alienate women in Mwanga? Khadija, on the other hand, was thrilled. She tapped my knee and blurted, "Isn't this great! Bi Fatuma's granddaughter! What an honor!" I nodded my head and mumbled thanks.[18]

Throughout the remainder of February we frequently visited Bi Amina and Bi Fatuma, and the ongoing tales of the joint Mwanga–Ujiji council meetings provided a forum for continuing entertainment. Sometimes Bi Amina and Bi Fatuma wanted to know more about the difference between "researcher" and "student." Sometimes they wanted more details about my research project. But they always ended laughing and clucking over "those backward women in Mwanga." Bi Fatuma furthered her proclamations of support and her wish to take me to ceremonies in Dar es Salaam when I traveled there to continue archival research.

In time it was no longer merely along the paths that women pointed me out. It was in the market in Kigoma, at the train station, and on the bus, and it was not only women. On the bus, I overheard men pointing me out to each other as the "*mzungu mwali.*" Men generally were surprised and thought this was hilariously funny. Women were not amused and there was no element of surprise when they pointed me out. Rather it was just a nod of understanding, "Aah! That *mzungu.*" As the only *mzungu* living in Ujiji it was impossible to be anonymous. Now I feared I was infamous. I rode the bus daily around the urban area, collecting oral traditions, oral histories, and interviewing local healers. I didn't want or need negative publicity prior to my arrival upon someone's doorstep.

I didn't know the women and men who pointed me out to each other. My notoriety was an advertisement for Bi Amina and Bi Fatuma and for the rift between the women in the neighboring towns of Mwanga and Ujiji. I was walking proof that Bi Amina and Bi Fatuma had successfully completed my initiation in spite of, or perhaps to spite, the Mwanga women. My initiation probably also irked those who could not afford to pay for the ceremony. My research assistants and young neighbors lamented that they or their families could not afford to initiate them.

---

[18] I think Bi Fatuma wanted to inflame the relationship with the Mwanga women as much as possible and offering to have me initiate her granddaughter was an effective route to that end. This initiation was never carried out, I think, because the relationship between Bi Amina and Bi Fatuma became increasingly strained after my initiation. Bi Fatuma and Hawa Abdallah (her *mwali* and my initial informant and friend in Ujiji) believed that Bi Amina was jealous of my relationship with Bi Fatuma. They encouraged me to visit Bi Fatuma only secretly during my last couple of months in urban Kigoma. This was extremely difficult to accomplish since Bi Amina and Bi Fatuma lived on adjoining streets and all the neighbors knew me and their children called out to me. The one formal interview I conducted with her ended abruptly for she feared that Bi Amina had appeared on the premises. Hawa and Bi Fatuma believed that **Khadija** and Bi Amina had schemed to have me initiate Khadija's daughter so that they could keep the **money** and gifts that would accrue.

I was an outsider in an urban area with a long history of factional conflicts and intrigues. Although I had been told repeatedly by informants and acquaintances that it was impossible for a *mzungu* to be initiated, I had naively miscalculated these statements. It was not impossible for me to be initiated, but it did offend their sensibilities. The Mwanga women, relatives of one of my informants, had hoped to sidestep my requests to observe an initiation. Not only were they unwilling to assist me to that end, they did not want to see me initiated at all.

Needless to say, I felt distressed about the situation I found myself in. I wanted to focus my research more on women's concerns, complaints, and actions. Suddenly I was feeling that I might be one of their concerns or complaints and wondered what sort of collective action they might take against me! Would they refuse to let me interview them? Would they purposely mislead me? Would I be completely ostracized after I had already been silenced on one potential topic, *unyago*? These were my preoccupations at night as I sat in the courtyard playing with my host's one-year-old daughter. Somehow her first steps, her first words, *"Toka hapa!"* (Get out of here!) blurted indiscriminately to chickens or anyone bothering her, cheered me up and brought some levity to the situation.

As time passed, I encountered fewer and less hostile comments from women about my status as *mwali* as I traveled about the Kigoma area conducting interviews. By mid-March, what had once been hissing evolved into a more subtle nodding of heads. "That's the *mzungu*," people murmured. By May, my *mwali* status was generally known, and I no longer overheard negative comments about it. Instead, if the subject of my initiation arose during interviews, my informants were generally pleased that I had undertaken such an effort to learn about their culture.[19] Many were even more impressed that Bi Amina was my *somo*. Through my association with her I felt I gained privileged access to information about the Ujiji factions and their former dance competitions, but by June I had reached an impasse. More and more of my interviewees kept asking me why I was asking them these questions. Everyone knew that Bi Amina was the expert on these subjects.

I explained that it was necessary to collect versions of history from many different sources. But finally I was asked point-blank, "Have you interviewed Bi Amina, and if not, why not?" The answer was no. I had been told that it would be impolite and improper to request an interview with her while she was in mourning. So instead, during February, I visited her often, began to know her, her family and friends, as a good *mwali* should. I also contributed to and attended the *musbah*, the fortieth day of prayers and a feast following the death of her mother. After greeting the separately seated groups of female relatives, friends, and neighbors in the courtyard, Khadija and I were ushered into the mourning room to sit with Bi Amina, Bi Fatuma, and others for the duration of the ceremony.

The *musbah* marked the end of Bi Amina's confinement. I let a week pass to allow Bi Amina the chance to move freely outside for the first time since I had known her, then tried to arrange an interview. She could not oblige me, she said: the family had another funeral she needed to attend. This was at the beginning of Ramadan. During most of Ramadan I found informants tired, hungry, and less in-

---

[19] I have no explanation for these shifts in the reactions to my initiation. I believe it was beyond my control, and that once people had a chance to observe me and my actions, they felt less threatened by me.

terested in talking. Few healers and no spirit possession cults were active during this period. Shortly after 'Id al-Fitr, I traveled to Dar es Salaam for the month of April to meet my husband, Pier, and to conduct archival research. We returned in May and moved into a house in Kigoma town. Soon after settling in, we received word that Bi Amina's granddaughter had died of yellow fever. Again Bi Amina confined herself in mourning for forty days. Again I could not consider interviewing her.

I discovered an intensely sorrowful woman and her equally sad daughter-in-law when I next visited Bi Amina. Her favorite granddaughter had contracted yellow fever and had died very suddenly. She left three small children. The motherless children were sprawled out on the mats fast asleep in the mourning room. The two women angrily and bitterly described how the lack of access to essential drugs and adequate health care were responsible for the senseless death of their loved one. They were right. It was all deeply disturbing and depressing. I felt numb with the hopelessness they expressed and sat transfixed as they began to weep. My thoughts wandered a thousand different paths as we sat silently in the dark.

In moments like these a researcher's concerns and interests are suddenly set into perspective. My interest in these women's lives had led me to experiences that were lined with pain and joy. Although they informed me in new and important ways, these relationships also pulled me into women's lives in a way that required me to gain some distance so that I could still function as a researcher.

The *musbah* for Bi Amina's granddaughter was performed at the end of June. Bi Amina completed her formal mourning period and again involved herself in community affairs. In early July the young granddaughter of her extended family was to become a *mwali*. It was a huge affair. Bi Amina expressed her desire that I attend every day of the event which was to last ten days. She wanted me to observe every detail of this elaborate function so that I could be better prepared when I initiated Khadija's daughter in July.[20] I was commencing a pregnancy history survey in Ujiji and Mwanga and was in the early stages of meeting with local ward secretaries who would be facilitating my interactions with local ten-cell leaders and the women who lived in their areas.[21] I could not cancel appointments with local leaders without fear of repercussions, and had to negotiate this with my attendance at the *msondo*.

At the end of the second day of the more private indoor part of the *mwali* initiation ceremony, as the women were leaving, one of my *somo* elders rushed into the room where I stooped putting on my sandals and said, "Your husband has come for you!" I panicked, knowing that he must have bad news.[22] Arriving in the

---

[20] At an elementary level there are several stages through which individuals can pass in the association. The first stage makes one a *mwali*, while each successive step increases an individual's rank.

[21] A ten-cell group is the smallest Tanzanian political unit and ten-cell leaders are responsible to the ward level. In urban Kigoma some ten-cell leaders could have as many as thirty or more households under their wing. These individuals were to assist me with introductions and the selection of households for the pregnancy history survey.

[22] I was initially concerned about the possibility of a transgression, but no one seemed curious or concerned about the presence of the men. Since the day's events were completed and most of the women had gone on their way, we made quick introductions and left. Had there been any suspicion of the men seeing something they should not, the case could have been very different. One of my informants had been caught observing as a child, and his punishment was to be initiated.

courtyard I saw both Pier and Shabani, one of my research assistants, standing there. "Mama Mkubwa *amefariki*" (the eldest wife [head of the household where we had lived] has died), they told me. We immediately proceeded to her home to find funeral preparations underway. Pier and I contributed as we could, giving our condolences and bringing market supplies, then arranged to return the next day for the burial.

We spent the entire next day at the *musbah*, Pier with the men outside and I with the women in the courtyard. I sent word to my *somo*s that I could not attend the *msondo* because of a death in my host family. When I arrived late in the afternoon the next day for part of the ceremony, I found a very annoyed *somo*. Bi Amina was outraged that I had missed an important part of the ceremony the day before. She wasn't impressed that I had outside obligations and concerns. This *msondo* was a priority. I needed to prepare to initiate Khadija's daughter at the end of the month, Bi Amina argued. She wanted me to observe some rituals which were not performed or were conducted differently during my initiation. She was concerned that I might have trouble performing some of my duties when I initiated my *mwali*, which would reflect poorly upon her skills as my *somo*. My research priorities and growing obligations to extended family networks in Ujiji were beginning to pull me in alternate directions.

Now that I lived in Kigoma I had to leave the ceremony before the last bus. An early departure meant eating early with the women from Mwanga who also needed to catch the last bus. I was not thrilled about sharing a meal with women who had so vehemently opposed my initiation. My partner that night on the bus was the very woman who had been the most opposed to my initiation. She leaned over and asked me tauntingly, "Do you have enough information to write about *msondo* now?" My eyes felt like they almost popped out of my head, every nerve in my body was on alert. I couldn't believe my ears. I sat bolt upright and informed her in a caustic tone, "I have no intention of writing a description of *msondo* now or ever." "But you are a researcher, are you not?" she chided me. "My work is to study the history of healing practices in this urban area. I do not believe *msondo* falls in this category," I replied. "Well," she continued, "then, why do you keep coming to the ceremonies?" I smiled and told her disarmingly, "I like the drumming and I love to dance." She looked at me in a manner that signified, "Sure you do," then dropped the subject. It was only after repeated interaction and my paying bus fares for her and another senior *somo* on a couple of other occasions that she switched from plying me with questions to telling me stories and inviting me to other *msondo* ceremonies.

It was about this time that my experiences on the paths in Ujiji and Mwanga changed for the last time. When children who were not familiar with me or who just liked to scream out that there was a European around started shouting, "*Tsungutsungu*" (*mzungu, mzungu*), women would come out of their houses, see me and say, "That's no *mzungu*. That's our *mwali*." I felt I had reached a new plateau, elevated from a detested and threatening foreign researcher to a trusted individual with some redeeming qualities. No matter that some of these qualities may have been my imagined or real ability to bring someone status, monetary advantage, or some other unknown.

By late July I was busy preparing to undertake my survey and anticipating the arrival of my initiate and other visitors. I had high hopes to begin at last formal tape-recorded interviews with Bi Amina Hassan. I made special pilgrimages to her home in Kitongoni ward to request interviews. Dates were set and I would arrive to find no Bi Amina. Every time I arrived she was away attending a funeral. This was not unusual. In one week, out of eight arranged interviews, six were canceled due to funerals or wakes. Had I been studying death or funerals, I would have been in the right place. However, after the third time that Bi Amina failed to meet with me, I realized I faced a significant challenge.

I finally found the courage and the privacy to confront Bi Amina and ask her why she avoided my interviews. I knew she could leave some of these wakes for an hour or so. She informed me that it would be good for us to go visit the son of her extended family. She would feel more comfortable if he approved this interview process. As luck would have it, the son of her extended family, a professor, was home from the United States for the summer. We had already met and spoken on a couple of occasions. Together Bi Amina and I went to visit him. In Swahili, I explained to him my research project, the oral traditions and histories that I had been collecting, and why I felt Bi Amina's contribution was important. She sat silently listening to our conversation. We had a friendly conversation about research, attempts to contribute something new to the field, and the differences between life in the United States and Ujiji. At the end of our discussion, I was dismissed. He informed me that they would stay together and discuss the uses and implications of oral histories in the research process. I should return the next day to see what she would agree to, but not to worry.

It was the second time I had poured out my heart to Bi Amina in my attempts to gain access to important arenas of information and knowledge. It was the second time that I was to wait to hear her verdict. With great apprehension I arrived at her house two days later. She was not home, but left word that I should return at 3 P.M. the following Monday for an interview. Monday arrived and I did not find her at home. A close friend had died. Bi Amina however send profuse apologies and had arranged for an alternative interview that actually took place. We arranged for another meeting the following week.

My time was limited now. My visitors were on their way home, my husband Pier had returned to teach in the United States, I was relocated into a temporary house-sitting situation, and the pregnancy history survey was nearing completion. My intended initiate had returned to secondary school in Dar es Salaam uninitiated. The ceremony was never performed because her mother brought her from Dar es Salaam after the proposed date, the somos refused to agree on a new date at short notice, and I had other obligations before her return to school.[23] With only two days left in Kigoma I completed my second and final interview with Bi Amina.

---

[23] I do believe they truly intended for me to initiate Khadija's daughter. All of us would have benefited from such a plan. Khadija would have received gifts from me and would have become formally tied to me in this new relationship I would have with her daughter. The daughter would have had a notorious if not prestigious *somo*, along with the status and gifts that would follow. Bi Amina would have received all of the gifts that normally go to the initiator, since it was my first initiation and I was therefore obligated to give my gifts to her; or I could have given her monetary compensation as Khadija advocated. She claimed that she wanted to keep my gifts as mementos of the event. Others believed that she and Bi Amina had a scheme to benefit financially from this enterprise. For my part, I lacked the time, money, and motivation to further advance my status in the association.

Reflections

Secrecy and the fear of exposure were the main concerns of the women in Mwanga when they discussed my initiation. In contrast, the women in Ujiji merely informed me that secrecy was essential and accepted my vow backed up by that of my friend. Perhaps the fact that a local person vouched for me or would be around to scapegoat if I did not keep my promise was enough consolation for the Ujiji women, but I do not believe so. Rather, I think the Ujiji women, especially Bi Amina and Bi Fatuma, saw my initiation as a feather in their cap. Now they had initiated and instructed not only most of their children and some Arabs, but also a foreign *mzungu*.

Being a *mzungu* had its advantages and disadvantages. Sometimes others believed that by association with me they would gain status. Almost everyone also expected somehow to gain materially. Through the rumor mill, I heard that my initiation was one of the most expensive affairs Ujiji had recently seen. While I know this was false (since I saw much more elaborate *msondo*s), this rumor was believed by most in urban Kigoma. This promoted Bi Amina's status considerably. Not only had she had the nerve and power to initiate an outsider, but she had gained materially.

Khadija, who contracted this affair, also gained from it. It was she who advocated that we continue through to higher stages of the ritual. She convinced me (which was not very difficult) to pay for the two of us to continue on past the initial ceremony. Bi Amina and Bi Fatuma found this interesting, since after the initial ceremony, and its surrounding controversy, they could only gain materially and personally. The more advanced I became, the more money I spent and the more benefits they reaped.

Bi Amina and Bi Fatuma knew that my initiation would cause a stir. I think they relished the chance to assert their authority and lord it over the women in Mwanga. The rivalry there was old. In the 1950s, the most frequent dance competitions had been between the women of Ujiji and Mwanga. Many of my interviewees from both areas enjoyed detailing and reveling in how different the populations of the two towns were. Today, spirit possession, initiation ceremonies, and healers of many kinds continue practicing more openly in Ujiji than in Mwanga.

The council fight between the women in Ujiji and Mwanga over my initiation was another round in their rivalry. The Mwanga faction was outraged at not having been consulted prior to my initiation and brought the detested urban Kigoma word "researcher" into the debate. Up to this point, I had found it more expedient to describe myself as a student when I explained my project. A student conducting her practical was a more readily understood and respected concept than that of researcher. I do not know what experiences the urban Kigoma population had with researchers in the past, but the word has come to be associated with interference, deceit, and great monetary gain. Lack of cooperation and/or considerable negotiation over demands for a substantial financial reward for an interview were the norm if my informants considered me a researcher. Those who considered me a researcher did not believe that I wanted only to understand more about their lives and chosen professions. They saw this as a ruse to trick them into teaching me about healing so I could return home and become a wealthy healer in the United States.

The interjection of the term "researcher" into the *somo*s Ujiji–Mwanga council meetings mildly alarmed my *somo*s. I learned from Khadija that while I simply called myself a student, she had intentionally misled them and denied that I was a researcher. She told them I was studying medicine. I felt this was deceitful and agonized over it. I was not a medical student, but a student of history interested in medicine. When I confronted her, she claimed it was unimportant: "You are not going to write about it so what difference does it make if they call you student or researcher?" She had a point. What difference did it make?

To me, the difference was not only semantic, but moral. By agreeing to keep secrets I have accepted certain responsibilities. I have a vested interest in respecting the wishes of those who placed their trust in me. Morally, my own ideas about whether or not it is important to keep secret the practices of *unyago* are secondary to those for whom it matters most. Ethically, my decision to respect their wishes not only reflects the integrity of the research process, but also has wider implications. Divulging the secrets of *unyago* would destroy the association, for its secrets are the reason for its existence. Betraying the secrets would be a betrayal of the individuals who trusted me; it would alter relationships in the community, hinder a future researcher's efforts, and affect my own continued research in the area. When I presented Michele Wagner's gift of pictures to one historian/healer, his obvious delight facilitated our interviews. What reaction might I have encountered if a previous researcher had disappointed him? Closed doors, I suspect.

Ujiji is a difficult area in which to conduct research. People are suspicious of outsiders and reluctant to discuss the past. The factional conflicts of the past continue to influence the present. The contest over my initiation only intensified a long and heated struggle over status and authority. My initiation in itself did not change the balance of power, but it could if I disclosed the secrets. The women of Mwanga would be vindicated in their initial decision to distrust me, and this might increase their standing temporarily. Ultimately, however, all would be losers.

The women of Mwanga feared a betrayal would expose them as fools. Were I to betray them, the women who trusted me would indeed appear as fools, for not protecting their initiation rituals from an outsider who could not or would not respect them. For the women of urban Kigoma, *unyago* would lose its power. Women involved in *unyago* possess a position of status, power, and authority in their communities. If the secrets were known, all that would be lost. Young girls would not respect and fear them. Without respect and the networks which sustain them, what status would women have in the wider community?

I would never knowingly insult or betray the trust and generosity of my informants by exposing their secrets. I feel that my agreement to keep their secrets can provide one step toward building trust between researchers and researched, between outsiders and insiders, and between women of vastly different backgrounds.

6

Suspected of Sorcery

Z. S. STROTHER

How a Picnic Led to a Trial

The problem with real life is there's no musical score. In movies, you know you're in danger because there's an ominous chord underlying the scene, a dissonant melodic line that warns of sharks in the water and boogermen behind the door. Real life is dead quiet, so you're never quite sure if there's trouble coming up.

–Sue Grafton[1]

On November 4, 1988, I was at the point of wrapping up two years of research on the arts of the Eastern Pende of Zaïre before crossing over to do comparative fieldwork with the Pende in a neighboring province.[2] The Pende are a rural population settled on the bush savanna of southwestern Zaïre. Noted for their vibrant masquerades, they also produce architectural sculpture and exquisite staffs. One project I was concluding involved the men's fraternity (*mukanda*), which serves as patron to a large class of masks.

In their initiation to the fraternity, boys learn a considerable corpus of songs, many of which are very beautiful encapsulations of oral history. One theme in particular kept surfacing: nostalgia for "Manda," the sheltered site where Pende first built and began to prosper in the region. It was the site of notable victories by the

---

[1] Sue Grafton, *"H" is for Homicide* (New York, 1991), 133.

[2] This essay draws on events experienced during thirty-two months of fieldwork conducted in Zaïre, January 1987–August 1989, with the aid of a Fulbright-Hays dissertation grant with two extensions. I dedicate it to my fellow sojourners at Manda: Chief Nzambi (Kibunda a Kilonda), Nzomba Kakema Dugo, and Gisagi Kidiongo. Field research centered on the history and institutional development of masquerading and sculpture among the Pende peoples. Archival work in Zaïre and six months of preliminary archival research in Belgium (supported by the Belgian–American Foundation) provided questions as well as necessary benchmarks to evaluate oral history. This research is discussed in my dissertation, "Inventing Masks: Structures of Artistic Innovation Among the Central Pende of Zaïre" (Yale University, 1992); my forthcoming book, *Masked Evidence* (Chicago), and several articles, including "Pende Constructions of Secrecy," in Mary H. Nooter, ed., *Secrecy: African Art that Conceals and Reveals* (New York, 1993).

great chief Kombo[3] over his rival Kisanga and the powerful Maï Munene. Manda was abandoned under the pressure of Chokwe invasions in the late 1880s and 1890s, when people fled north towards the Kasaï River. The region was only fully repopulated and rebuilt during the Belgian occupation in 1934. At this time, Manda was deemed too secluded; everyone was obliged to build along the road for better surveillance.

The fabled Manda piqued my interest and before leaving the region I wished to check out the archaeological possibilities of the site. First of all, it would be an opportunity to see where and how people had chosen to build before the mandates of the colonial system. People spoke with regret of the beauty and healthfulness of Manda, located on a high, vast plateau, surrounded on all sides by forest and hills, wafted by a continual breeze. Nearby streams provided the clay used to smelt iron and the site was littered with *inganga*, the remains from that process. They also waxed eloquent about the forest of tall and long-lived *kamba* trees still in place on the plateau, planted by successive chiefs as part of the veranda for their ritual houses and which have endured for decades as memorials.[4]

Best yet, the site was defensible, as access to the plateau could be controlled through a narrow neck. During conflicts, the inhabitants would build a stockade-like barrier across this neck to impede the enemy while they knocked them off with bows and arrows. This strategy worked well until the Chokwe came with guns. As I had never heard before of the Pende building stockades, this was yet another reason to investigate the site, especially as part of the fortification used against the Chokwe was said to survive.

Yes, a trip to Manda was in order. Deciding to make the day something of a holiday, I invited Chief Nzambi, one of my most brilliant exegetes, and two other friends who were history buffs. To make a picnic, I bought a tin of corned beef (Nzambi's favorite) and we took along some manioc bread and a sauce of manioc leaves. I also borrowed a hoe from my hostess in case we found the stockade overgrown with vegetation.

It was a two-and-a-half-hour hike, so we left early to avoid the afternoon heat. On the path, we surprised the Pende pastor of a local church. He was out early, too, on his way to deforest his manioc fields. We paused briefly to say "hello," and then continued on to Manda without seeing anyone else.

---

[3] Readers may find the profusion of "Kombos" in this story confusing. The Eastern Pende have positional succession, so each successive holder of a title takes the name of the title and is in some sense equally exchangeable. The paramount chief for the Bakwa Samba, the largest Pende clan, holds the title "Kombo-Kiboto," usually abbreviated as "Kombo." Personal names are used only to distinguish among holders of this title. The title of Kombo's rival, the leader of a splinter group in the same clan, is "Kombo-Kabenga," or "red Kombo." The man who served for years as adjunct to the elderly and ailing Kombo (Mukanzo Mbelenge) has come to be known as "Kombo-Kakese," or "little Kombo."

[4] Lt. Hans Mueller, adjunct of the German explorer Hermann Wissmann, gave a vivid account of his visit to "the great village of Kombo" in 1884–1885. He also was struck by the "beautiful situation under high oil palms." Mueller's description of his difficult negotiations with the chief, "blind, an old man, weary of life," dovetails perfectly with Pende depictions of the blind Matshiobo-a-Nguanya, who was too old and tired to flee with the others when the Chokwe attacked a few years later. Hermann Wissmann et al., *Im Innern Afrikas: Die Erforschung der Kassai während der Jahre 1883, 1884 und 1885* (Nendeln, 1974), 106, 108. I am grateful to Joseph Servey and Angelika Krüger for helping to speed up completion of my dissertation by translating important sections of the Wissman text.

Manda's situation turned out to be all that had been promised. One could not choose a more secluded spot and the continuous breeze was delightful. Although the hundreds of palm trees planted during the site's occupation had finally died out, the enormous *kamba* trees remained as monuments to the past.

Once arrived, however, I was disappointed to find the site entirely turned over to women's peanut fields. This is not unusual, as abandoned village sites make richer farm land, but Nzambi was as surprised as I was. "Who was farming the land?" we asked. The women present responded that they came from Kombo-Kabenga, the village of a rival clan. Disappointed that years of farming would destroy any archaeological value in the site, we asked some of the women who were hoeing about the fortifications, but they seemed not to understand the question.

I then amused myself for a while walking up and down the troughs in the fields, on the lookout for potsherds and smelting remains. There was quite a lot scattered about and sometimes I would use the hoe to dislodge a piece for better examination. I pocketed some of the larger or more fanciful samples, including part of the bowl of a pipe. Finally, we adjourned to find shade in a nearby strip of forest, ate our picnic, and returned home.

Very early the next morning, as I was heading off for the spring, an acquaintance arrived breathlessly to ask if I knew that Kombo-Kabenga, the chief who technically owned the peanut fields comprising Manda, had left at the crack of dawn to file suit with the paramount chief at Ndjindji. He was charging that I had gone to Manda, equipped with a shovel, to dig up the bones of his chiefly predecessors for my sorcery (*wanga*). I had enlisted the pastor to pray away the spirits of the dead guarding the site and had then sacrificed and eaten a chicken on the spot. The heritage of Belgian colonialism being what it is, Kombo-Kabenga did not quite dare sue me directly.[5] Instead, he named Chief Nzambi as defendant. For this serious charge, he demanded that Nzambi pay an enormous fine of seven goats. (Ndjindji is in the diamond zone and a goat sold for as much as seventy-five dollars at that period.)

In the days that followed, the rumors flew. The hapless pastor was officially accused by his church for his part in the affair and threatened with loss of his position. There were competing stories that we had gone to steal the earth or "break" the stone of Kombo. One early version that spirit guardians had led us astray when we searched for the secret cemetery lost out to the more exciting version that we had found and "chopped off" the head of Kombo.

Since the paramount chief was away, the case was put on the docket of the traditional court and Kombo-Kabenga was forced to return home to wait. In Ndjindji proper, where people knew me, this charge was greeted as a hilarious joke. Many interpreted the incident as an expression of political jealousy. Kombo-Kabenga had lost out to Kombo-Kiboto, his rival "brother," in his bid for political supremacy as the local representative of the national government. Still, my powers were not in question, merely my intentions.

---

[5] Zaïre is widely regarded to have suffered one of the most severe colonial occupations in Africa. In 1931, the Kwilu Pende rebelled in response to forced labor, the abuses of concessionary companies, and excessive taxes. Brutal reprisals following the death of a Belgian colonial agent have left older Pende circumspect in dealing with white foreigners—even after independence.

People howled all the louder a few days later when word came back from Kombo-Kabenga that his village's spring had mysteriously dried up. What did he expect, the people from Ndjindji laughed back (seeming to take pride in my prowess), that he should attack Masala's great buddy Nzambi and not feel the touch of her anger? (My local name was "Masala.") The spring drying up was interpreted as a warning on my part and many urged Kombo-Kabenga to withdraw the suit. Instead, Kombo-Kabenga grew more obdurate, he refused to retract his charges, his spring remained dry, and we all awaited Kombo's return.

Kombo-Kabenga accused me of seeking *wanga*. Here crudely translated as "sorcery," *wanga* is the ability to manipulate the material and spirit world for personal advantage: it is the power to make things happen.[6] As power may be used for benign as well as self-aggrandizing motives, it is an entirely ambivalent concept. Considered the cause of all illness (with the recent exception of malaria) and sudden death,[7] it is also associated with all talents and abilities, no matter how mundane, that surpass the ordinary. A public speaker famed for eloquence, a student who always aces exams, a hunter who never fails, even a woman who routinely produces hot, delicious meals in the blink of an eye: all will be suspected of having sought out a charm or some form of *wanga*. In particular, performers and artists are all implicated (including fine singers, musicians, dancers, masqueraders, athletes, and sculptors). While the Pende admire talent as much as anyone, they fear that egocentric ambitions can undermine the communal base of society by provoking envy.

The emphasis on personal advantage is important. Performers and artists may seek to distinguish themselves; nonetheless, they contribute something very real to society. It is the wealthy who pose the greatest threat to the communal ideal. One considers that since everyone is working hard, for one person to amass significantly more than others calls for a helping hand on the other side. The wealthy are suspected not of seeking charms but spirit workers to toil for them as slaves at night in their projects. The man who pans for diamonds, for example, seeks to have spirit workers sift the alluvial deposits at night so that he will find the diamonds on top when he comes out in the morning.

Wanga stands as the linchpin of the ethical system. It is the spur that drives redistribution of goods in the communal society for fear of arousing the resentment and envy of others. The specialist in *wanga* (the *nganga*) will always emphasize that he cannot strike without ethical cause. Even with the worst intentions in the world, his recipes will not "take" unless the victim (or the victim's family) has

---

[6] Early in my fieldwork, when I protested that Westerners had no *wanga*, I was derisively corrected: "Who sends perfume here to sell?" Perfume is a beautiful example of manipulation of the physical world for the purpose of influence over others as one deploys pleasant or sexy scents in the expectation of securing the favorable response of others. By making reference to perfume, my interlocutors were not simply illustrating a common form of *wanga*, but also pointing to the absurdity of trying to argue that Westerners have no *wanga*. Any group who lives in such luxury and who wields such power over the daily lives of so many clearly understands all too well the workings of *wanga*.

[7] Because of the consistent and sometimes spectacular response of malaria to Western drugs, it has moved into the class of natural illness. Theoretically, the death of the very old should also be classified as natural, as a "death from God." In reality, there continues to be considerable speculation about who might be responsible, although it lacks all of the passion of accusations made at the death of a younger person.

made herself or himself vulnerable through selfishness, adultery, or other moral transgressions. Sorcerers will give a wheedling prayer to God, trying to transfer responsibility for their actions: "Maweze, *you* created the leaves and objects that we use, so we are just using that which you have provided us." However, it is understood that their actions will not work unless there is cause (*kitela*). Still, human nature being what it is, most people fear that it is all too easy for the malicious to find some excuse in an individual's comportment.

The most serious ambitions, such as acquiring wealth or surpassing others in the practice of *wanga*, require gaining control over spirit(s) on the other side. Kakoko, who prides himself on his reputation as a hit man specializing in lightning strikes, pulled me aside one day to tell me that he had finally figured out why white people were so rich: we had killed Jesus Christ. In his understanding, by killing God's son, the most powerful spirit around, whites were able to force Christ to privilege them over the others of God's children, to force him to send airplanes stocked with goods over from the other side for their use.

When Kombo-Kabenga accused me of seeking to "chop off the head of Kombo," i.e., of exhuming the skull of a previous paramount chief, he was accusing me of seeking to enslave one of the most powerful spirits in the Pende world.[8] Since all Americans by definition are wealthy, my goal in such an action could only be to consolidate my powers as a sorcerer.

How did this happen? I went to Manda to investigate a possible archaeological site and hosted a picnic of corned beef. I became accused of grave-robbing and of devastating environmental damage. The usual expectations of fieldwork are that, as one spends more time in a culture, things get easier. Like a child, one learns the system: how to eat, how to bathe, how to wash clothes, where to harvest the best caterpillars. One very gradually learns to communicate. One makes friends. So how was it that after almost two years in the field, I came to be accused of a megalomaniacal quest after metaphysical power?

Home Away From Home

In 1987, I began fieldwork among the Eastern Pende unsure where to go or what to do. Mennonite missionaries graciously allowed me to fly into the territory to their station at Nyanga, but where to go from there? Following Sylvia Boone's dictum that art does not thrive in a vacuum, I asked where the major Eastern Pende centers were. People told me that there were two, Ndjindji and Kipoko, but advised me to go to Ndjindji first as there was an old and powerful chief there noted for his respect for tradition.

Why do researchers prefer one site to another? Often this has to do with our work, where we get the best information, but there is also a mysterious personal equation because where we get our best information is often where we make the best friends. Although I made extensive reconnaissance journeys in the first year of fieldwork, Ndjindji was special from the first visit.

---

[8] Images such as "digging up the bones," "stealing the earth," and "breaking" the stone of Kombo are all variants on this allegation. Incidentally, it is rare to accuse a woman of serious knowledge of *wanga* as women are excluded from public avenues of power and do not often amass significant wealth.

Who could fail to be charmed by the old widows, dressed in their best clothes, come to welcome me, bearing platters of oranges, bags of roasted pistachios, bunches of bananas, thermoses of tea, or pineapples? One frail grandmother brought a bag of rare and sought-after spice. These ladies, who had as much difficulty in judging my age as I theirs, would sigh with pity and wonder to themselves how it was that my mother had let her little girl go wandering off so far from her side.

Then the married men would arrive with invitations to dine, never to be refused or postponed, even though in the beginning these could number three to six a night! And throughout my visits, in the evening as I wound my way back to the house, invitations would resound from alongside the road to come and take a cup of palm wine. My letters to friends from that first year paint a halcyon vision of life in Ndjindji that made very real problems with the *agents de sécurité*, with giardia, and with adapting to long treks on foot in the heat and sand all seem inconsequential.[9]

I had come to study aesthetic philosophy but found that first I had to understand the contexts in which art objects are produced and the degree of regional variation. In the beginning, I began a reconnaissance where I would ask reputed chiefs to organize public meetings to explain my project and then pose very general questions about how they did things in their clan. This proved to be an excellent introduction to the community of both myself and my work. Its very public nature, where everyone was free to contribute, pleased them.

I had no difficulty explaining my project. In the extended family, most people have at least one relative who has attended the university and prepared a senior's thesis for graduation. I fitted easily into the slot of "student" and it was natural enough that I should be studying the *ima jia Apende* (ways of the Pende), as they are very proud of their culture. Many felt that the more famous their arts became, the more respect they would receive on the national level, and felt that this would in some way better help them to jockey for political power in the national arena. All initially deemed my study of masks, statuettes, and architecture a harmless preoccupation.

My notes for March 15, 1987 recount a typical session where I asked Chief Kombo at Ndjindji to suggest women to discuss the women's initiation (*kindongo*) and healing cults. Approximately 150 people came, as well as hordes of children, to watch me interview eight elderly women. At first, the women seemed ill at ease to be in the public eye, but when we asked for some songs, they really got into it, and started to dance. Following local advice, I usually arranged for palm wine to lubricate such sessions with men, but for the women I gave soap and salt.

The women were delighted with these tokens and blessed me. A number of younger women came up to shake hands with me on the way home. My impression was that as women they appreciated being on center stage for a change. Another advantage of these public meetings was that one learned very quickly to what degree a community was interested in certain subjects and who the experts were for future private consultations.

---

[9] Many thanks to Elizabeth Honig, Angelika Krüger, and Ruth Herold for later sending me copies of these letters.

After four or five months of traveling, I was glad to part company with the public forum method. I arranged with Chief Kombo to attend a boy's initiation to the men's fraternity (*mukanda*) and moved in with the family of one of his subordinates, Chief Kende, who was then hosting an initiation. At first there was some brouhaha over my being a woman. In spite of this problem, as both old Kombo and his adjunct felt that it was an important arena of Pende culture to be documented, people accepted my presence after I paid a fine of a chicken and some palm wine (the normal payment for a non-initiate man who comes into contact with the fraternity's secrets).

This was a very happy period, although exhausting as I worked steadily from 5:45 A.M. when the boys started singing to about 10:30 P.M. when they concluded their evening songs. There was masking everyday and the excitement of seeing events rather than listening to descriptions. I developed a large team of exegetes and would visit them regularly to inquire about their various interpretations about what was happening. Several others in the community who cared about the initiation started to seek me out and offer their own views.

The initiation marked a turning point as I became much less of a public persona and much more associated with Chief Kombo's Samba clan and increasingly with certain individuals in that clan. Many women started to complain that I was neglecting them, that I should be going to the fields with them, or fishing, or participating in the caterpillar harvest. I tried to accommodate them as much as possible, but a day here and a day there did not do much to calm their complaints.

Because Kombo-Kakese, the chief's adjunct, encouraged my work, the chief's titular counselor took a bitter dislike to me due to his own rivalry for influence over the high chief. As this man knew little and as his position had become more honorary than real, I did not worry that he felt slighted by my increasingly frequent visits to the adjunct.[10]

Outside of the local circle, I became increasingly associated in people's minds with Kombo. The only unpleasant incident during this period occurred when I visited a public dance held by Chief Mukunzu, who belonged to the rival Tsule clan and who was also sponsoring an initiation. Before the boys' initiations began, I had been very careful about paying roughly the same number of visits to both the Samba and Tsule clans even though I got much better information from the Samba and quickly formed many more attachments there. Once the initiation started, al-

---

[10] The rivalry between the two men reached a comedic level during the investiture of the new chief. Sanji, the official counselor, was avid to hear an entire history recital, which he knew that Kombo-Kakese was obliged to give the chief-elect during his seclusion. Many of the elders wished Kombo-Kakese to give this publicly, but he refused to do so, complaining that they often slighted him because he had no "bijoux" (i.e., official standing, symbolized by a bracelet of office). Sanji then must have put spies to watch Kombo-Kakese's every movement because for weeks Sanji would appear at his heels whenever he left his house. Kombo-Kakese was quite willing to give me the official recital, but wherever we would arrange a rendezvous (in an empty classroom, at a mutual friend's house), Sanji would appear. The first time that this happened, Kombo-Kakese had already started his recital and, to my surprise, seemed willing to continue. We paused to pour palm wine for Sanji, and I dutifully continued to record the peroration. After a while, however, it became clear that his story was disjointed and that he was deliberately obfuscating chronologies that he had previously recounted, hoping with his elfin wiles to further confuse the muddled Sanji. I do not know if Sanji realized what was happening. We all sat impassive through the performance until we took a dignified leave.

though I continued to pay courtesy visits to the Tsule paramount chief Kutshia, I was quickly immersed in Samba life.[11]

During the initiation period, older boys run masked through the village, armed with whips to threaten the uninitiated, both women and younger boys. For the Samba this privilege was played out almost like a game of tag. The women were careful, but not at all terrorized. Kombo had forbidden harassments at the spring or on the path to the fields. Among the Tsule, however, I had heard stories about how the disguise offered by the mask (and its license to strike) was being abused by a few sadists to the point where many women were frightened to leave their houses before noon for fear of ambush.

As Mukunzu's invited guest I did not foresee any difficulties at the dance, but another Tsule chief, Mutshima, sent his masked nephew to strike me at that time. Apparently, the Tsule had recently been made subordinate on the government level to Kombo, the Samba chief, and they were still smarting about this. In Mutshima's mind, my focus on the Samba initiation just rubbed salt in the wound, especially after I declined an invitation that morning to go see his dance.

When the masker circled behind me to strike, I was busy with my camera and oblivious, but someone in the crowd saw what was happening and blocked his arm. The masker then circled around to the other side behind a friend, who was helping me do some recording, and struck him with the whip, drawing blood at the tip. As it is against every rule for a masker to strike an initiate, Mutshima's action caused quite a furor that played itself out over several weeks. It was an ugly incident, but a solitary one, and on the whole I deemed the work an outstanding success.

A couple of months later, after a trip to the capital mandated by bureaucratic reasons, I found that my association with Ndjindji had become well-known. Savoring a bottle of cold soda pop, I was sitting at a tiny truck stop, waiting to flag down a truck going south. An engaging entrepreneur had taken advantage of his village's location along a major road to open a restaurant. He had bought an old kerosene-fueled refrigerator from some missionaries so that he could lure the crews of the trucks passing by with the promise of cold drinks. These trucks, even when new, looked like World War II vintage troop carriers, piled high with sacks of manioc and dozens of passengers. They lumbered past at ten kilometers per hour over the deep rut of sand that comprised the major road across the savanna.

At one point, the entrepreneur's wife entered and glanced with amusement at the pile made by my bicycle, duffel bag, water bucket, kerosene lamp, and packet of salted fish: "Ahh, I see that you're on your way to *dimbo di'etu*." *Dimbo di'etu* literally means "our village," but has more of the sense that we attribute to "home." Home? Home to Ndjindji? I laughed because that was indeed how I felt. I found that my attachment for Ndjindji was common knowledge throughout the district and I began to play with this, even introducing myself as a Mukua Samba, a member of the Samba clan, on research trips.

---

[11] Such political rivalry, as recounted in many memoirs, eventually played into my hands. Chief Kutshia actually opened his ritual house (*kibulu*) to me and my camera in large part because he learned that his rival Kombo had not done so, and he wished to impress me with his generosity. This gesture was so unexpected that I had never even hoped for the privilege, much less asked for it.

A familiar leitmotif running through narratives of fieldwork is how the researcher, who sees him- or herself as a "scholar" and therefore "above" politics, becomes ensnared by local political machinations. In longer stays, however, as one cultivates certain friends and exegetes, one becomes associated inevitably with their interests. In my case, certain alignments took shape over time. My work seemed to validate the Samba clan over the Tsule, Chief Kombo over Kombo-Kabenga, the adjunct Kombo-Kakese over his rival Sanji, even the men over the women. The very sympathy that was enriching my understanding of the culture was laying the groundwork for the accusations about Manda by alienating the rivals of my associates. The Pende warn against the consequences of *luthondo* (or favoritism).

If the incident with the Tsule masker had made me aware that not everyone was satisfied with the state of affairs, I did not care. I did not care both because I had found a group of people among whom I enjoyed living and because I sensed that I was onto "pay dirt."

Never Make Passes at Girls Who Wear Glasses

Meji yagasue muenji kumona awa wanga.

All the leaves that you see, this is *wanga*.[12]

On my return to Ndjindji, I quickly learned of the benefits and costs of my associations. Chief Kombo-Kiboto (Mukanzo Mbelenge), who had reigned since 1942, had died on September 7, 1987. As befitting a great chief, he had done everything possible from his deathbed to insure a peaceful succession. In his dying oration, he told how he had performed the chief's duty of welcoming strangers and stated that he wished this tradition to continue. He did not wish for the many Western Pende who had sheltered lately at Ndjindji under his aegis to suffer problems. At this point, he even spoke of me, saying that on my return, he desired that I be received as I was during his lifetime and that I should have access to all that I needed to finish my work, including carte blanche to follow the investiture process of his successor.

Thus, on my return, I found myself thrust into the investiture process, a long series of rituals of which I had previously had only a dim knowledge. Moreover, I was provided with detailed notes on what I had missed so far by a friend, who had closely observed my methods during the boys' initiation, and who was commissioned by the chief's adjunct, Kombo-Kakese, so that I would not miss anything important. At first, not realizing all that the investiture would entail, I commenced the project out of a sense of duty to Chief Kombo. As the months passed, however, I gradually realized that it held the key to the architecture, the statuary, the masks, and much, much more.

About this time, I hired a new assistant from another region to continue my lessons in Kipende and to help with translations and transcriptions. I became annoyed with him one day when he asked me for the third time how I could "see" who the sorcerers were when I arrived in a community.

---

[12] Chief Kombo-Kiboto (Mukanzo Mbelenge).

Impatiently, I asked why he kept pestering me with this question. He replied that the local high school principal (a Pende man of considerable prestige) had been recounting my powers in this line, offering several cases as evidence. He recounted the time that a young blacksmith had rubbed himself with a love potion and come to see me with a cohort of friends. He had bragged that they would see me fall head over heels in love with him once he had touched me under the pretext of shaking hands. When he arrived, however, he was shamed before his friends because against my custom I not only refused to shake hands with the young man, I even reproached him before his witnesses: *"Udi wabola"* (you're bad). This story apparently spread like wildfire across the community because it offered indisputable evidence that I could "see" *wanga*.

The principal also told of the time I went out on the airstrip with Kombo-Kakese, who was a self-advertising sorcerer and healer in addition to being adjunct. Airstrips and airplanes provide key imagery in the modernized folklore on sorcerers and their powers. Kombo-Kakese invited me to the airstrip with the intention of "testing" the extent of my powers, but I had taken out a mirror to show him the faces of all the sorcerers in Ndjindji. Kombo-Kakese, astonished, reportedly told others after the encounter that I was not someone with whom to trifle. (In another version, I tell him: "Don't mess with white folks.")

I was dumbfounded by these accounts and by the fact that the principal (whom I barely knew) should be spreading them about since no one would ever doubt his word. Musing over these stories, I realized that I could recognize certain incidents radically reinterpreted. In the case of the young blacksmith, I remembered that during the boys' initiation, he had brought me a present of boa meat, a treat usually reserved for men. At the time, I thought nothing of it since many people offered me gifts of food, but now I knew that young men begin courting women by offering gifts of meat (usually fish). As for calling him "bad," all I could remember was an occasion when he borrowed my bicycle without asking, a fact I discovered when I heard the drums announcing a masquerade in a distant village and was unable to get there in time. Perhaps I had been trying to scold him in my rudimentary Kipende? He disappeared shortly after this incident.

In the case of the story with Kombo-Kakese, I recalled that one day he asked me if I knew that Ndjindji had an airstrip. In great surprise, I told him that no, I had never heard of it. We strolled out to look at it and he explained that the Mennonites had once talked of opening a mission outstation in Ndjindji and that the people had cleared an airstrip as a means to show support for the proposal. Nothing had come of it but the airstrip was kept in shape in order to keep the possibility alive. As for the mirror I was supposed to show him, I began to wonder if the Papermate pen that I carried (and which was dutifully returned to me whenever I lost it) might not have dubious associations because it was topped with a mirror-like surface. Mirrors again figure prominently in folklore, empowered by medicines to reveal to specialists the faces and nocturnal activities of sorcerers.

Alerted by this conversation, I became uneasily aware of how crowds at soccer games would shout my name whenever associates of mine got the ball, assuming that their skill at the game was due to charms that I had provided; or of how strangers that I would pass hiking between villages would sometimes mutter about my *khuyi*, i.e., the ability to turn myself into an eagle once out of sight in order to fly between villages. (Would any white person actually walk kilometers and kilometers on her own two feet?)

I remembered other incidents. Because certain plants turn up again and again in rituals involving art objects, I had begun to collect samples of leaves, bark, roots, and stems in the hope of identifying some of them on my return to the United States. Once during the boys' initiation, my hostess had entered the living room with dinner and found me with a huge pile of samples from a collecting expedition in the forest, busy taping the leaves in a notebook and wrapping up a ball of inflammable tree sap. In surprise, Masa actually recoiled backwards, gasping: "You have sorcery medicines!" ("Udi nu wanga!") Her husband, seated next to me, smiled and seconded: "Mama Kisanga."

Mama Kisanga is the name in folklore of the one woman who attends the sorcerers' meetings, who cooks for them, and who, notably, keeps their mirrors. At the time, I thought that they were joking since they were so well acquainted with my project, but now I was not so sure. It was old Kombo himself who had taken my wrist with one hand during the boys' initiation and had pointed with the other at the leaves overhead, saying: "All the leaves that you see, this is *wanga*."[13]

I became aware that the people of Ndjindji were observing me as sharply as I was observing them and that I was presenting a damning array of physical evidence. In the village Kingange, Sh'a Kafutshi had given me as a present the blood-red feather from the Lady Ross's turaco (*Musophaga rossae*).[14] He knew that I was interested because hunters, surgeons, sorcerers, and anyone who has taken human life (whether or not sanctioned by authority) dress with this feather. As a lark on the way home, I stuck the feather in my own hair. Some clearly had recognized this as a joke and laughed out loud at the incongruity of seeing such a feather in the hair of a woman. Others looked unnerved at what was, after all, an admission that I had either drawn blood or killed through sorcery.

Once I asked why everyone thought that an old sculptor associate of mine was a sorcerer. "Just look at him!," my source responded. "Do you not see how he never changes his clothes, how he always wears the same old blue coat? Do you not see how he walks all hunched-over and stiff-legged?" This remark connected with an acquaintance's comment that he was going to buy a comb and always keep it in his pocket so that everyone would assume that he had charged it as a protective amulet. In this communal society, goods (including men's shirts) must circulate continuously. Something seen day after day in the hands of one person becomes both conspicuous and suspicious.

In my case, although I did change my clothes, it never failed that I appeared, day or night, wearing my glasses. Rural Zaïrians usually have excellent eyesight and are accustomed to seeing spectacles only in the form of sunglasses on the faces of soldiers. People never stopped commenting on how remarkable it was that I

---

[13] "Meji yagasue muenji kumona awa wanga." To gain their ends, sorcerers employ a range of materials with strong metaphoric associations in the culture. By far the most common of all ingredients are the leaves, bark, and roots of trees and plants. Trees hold a special beauty for the Pende as an image of perfect obedience: "A tree has ears [to hear], but not the human child" ("Mutshi udi matsui uvi muna mutsu ashiko matsui"). They admire how a slip grows where it is planted or a seed where it falls without the willfulness of human desires.

[14] Many thanks to Costa Petridis for his help in identifying the bird in question.

wore my glasses even at night. Unfortunately, vision is an important metaphor in discussions of sorcery.[15]

Sorcerers are commonly described as having "four eyes," two for this world, and two to see into the other world. It is also believed that sorcerers will risk a good deal to improve their capacities in this line. When old men develop cataracts and lose their vision, the usual explanation is that their quest for improved vision backfired and cost them their eyesight. The suspicion that my glasses sent unwelcome signals to observers was confirmed after the Manda incident, when I overheard some ladies explaining to a newcomer that my power rested in my glasses; that was why I never removed them. I also fear that when in hiking mode, I tend to adopt the same hunched-over, stiff-legged stride used by my sculptor friend.

Apart from the question of vision, it was also damning to observers that I, a woman, spent a great deal of time in private conversations with chiefs, blacksmiths, and old men in general, all of whom are classed as sorcerers. In fact, I increasingly sought out (and was sought out by) these professionals. This is because, as my comprehension of the arts deepened, I realized that I needed to understand Pende conceptions of the spirit world.

My project of studying the arts was linked only peripherally to *wanga* and I stayed away from the subject as much as possible for most of my time in Zaïre. Nonetheless, chiefs and other specialists proved my most able and enthusiastic field associates because they are professionally interested in exploring and articulating the relationship between the living and the dead that is also critical for understanding the role of the arts. Unfortunately, the Pende believe, like us, that you know a person by the company that she keeps.[16]

Repercussions

The themes of most of the stories circulating about me focused on vision and apprenticeship, not actual deeds. As I had none of the kinship ties necessary for actively bewitching someone, I hoped that not much would come of such speculations. It was not long after my assistant's revelations, however, that I became aware of how my unsavory reputation might impact upon my research.[17]

---

[15] Attempts to demonstrate my glasses' corrective function were ineffectual, as anyone with normal vision sees a blur through them strong enough to provoke a headache. If anything, such attempts made the problem worse.

[16] Readers will remember that it was precisely this point that initially provoked Laura Bohannan's reputation as a witch in *Return to Laughter*. She continued to visit an ostracized and greatly feared witch because he was giving her the best information of anyone in the community. She also accepted gifts of meat from him without realizing how they would implicate her in a chain of witches' reciprocity. (New York, 1964), 220, 224–25, 252–53.

[17] There is a great deal of critical debate about how Westerners may have exaggerated the negativity of African conceptions of sorcery. To make matters more complicated, as Christianity takes root in Pendeland, its duality of good versus evil is definitely recasting the debate and shifting the balance of understanding towards the purely negative. It is also disassociating the system from God (Maweze), so that it no longer plays a role in the ethical system. Nonetheless, even if *wanga* was never construed as "evil," there seems to have been always a weighting towards the negative. Suspicions can drive old men out of the village to

Chief Kombo's successor (Munzenze Kavuka), the new Chief Kombo, was currently undergoing the long retreat required before the formal investiture process. On November 24, the chief-elect sent a messenger to tell me that he wanted to see me alone in the afternoon. When I arrived, it was unusually quiet, and he waved me back into the inner chamber. This was the first time I had seen him alone.

Chiefs Kende and Nzambi had both recounted to me that the seclusion period is a frightening one for chiefs because they feel themselves vulnerable to the sorcery attacks of rival lineages who wish to inherit. They fear illness and death. Even more, they fear that their enemies will weaken them so that they will humiliate themselves at the coming-out ceremonies by bungling the historical recitation and the beheading of the sheep. Successful accomplishment of these acts confirm that the dead accept the new chief's candidature. Unable to go out, the chief-elect broods over the gossip reported to him on his rivals and on the coming and going of sorcerers in the region.

It is in this potent climate of fear that an important orientation seems to take place on the part of the chief. Either he seeks (and finds) an effective protective medicine for himself and the village or, despite constant daily advice against it, he turns a ready ear to one of the old men in the village who say that a mastery of sorcery is the only protection.

Kombo told me that he was frightened, that he was surrounded by enemies. He said that he had prayed to God for nine years while he lived in a Christian camp, but now he was back among the Pende and what could the Christian God do? He said that he had agreed from the start to follow his predecessor's wishes to allow me to follow his initiation. All he wanted in return from me was a protective amulet since he knew that I had great power.

One inevitable consequence of fieldwork is that one discovers the boundaries defining one's own sense of self. One discovers how far one can participate in cultural and moral relativity. At that moment, I knew in my gut that if I did not accede to Kombo's wishes that I would have nothing but problems furthermore, problems from which Kombo-Kakese, the former adjunct, would not be able to shield me. The wild thought did cross my mind of giving the new chief some peace of mind by giving him a memento and telling him that all my "power" came from that. Several anthropologists have since told me that I was foolish not to do so. I do not agree, since the supposed possession of an effective amulet encourages individuals to take risks with what they say and what they eat that they might not normally take. I do not believe that such an attitude is respectful.

However, at that moment, what was uppermost in my mind was that I would not be me if I started to hand out fake amulets. Knowing full well that he could not regard me as other than a liar and a selfish ingrate, I explained that I neither used nor made protective amulets and did not even believe in their validity. I referred him to the Psalms, familiar to him from his days in the Christian camp, where David had also felt himself surrounded by conniving enemies. He was silent when I finished. Inevitably, our relationship deteriorated from that day.

---

live alone and accusations at funerals can provoke bloodshed. Unless one can counter-demonstrate one's use to the community as an accomplished healer (in the fashion of Kombo-Kakese), a reputation as a specialist in *wanga* should not be cultivated.

After Kombo came out of seclusion on December 19, there was hardly a meeting with him not fraught with harassment. The situation was made worse by Sanji, the official "uncle-counselor" who had been ignored under the old Kombo but who had used flattery and sly insinuations to gain the ear of the new Kombo. Kombo-Kakese, the former adjunct, still held that office when the new Kombo was away, but was increasingly marginalized by his old rival's growing influence.

Still, general opinion that my research worked towards Kombo's prestige stayed the new chief's hand as I continued to follow the rituals completing his investiture. In the first part of June, a very lean month in Pendeland, Kifutshi, the mentally-deranged but loving woman who adopted me, brought me two six-inch field rats per day for fifteen days to eat with my host and assistant, an unprecedented run of luck in a protein-starved season. Kombo berated me when he saw me for not sending him some of the rats (a delicacy) even though he was levying fines right and left to provide himself with goat meat to eat. He also said that Sanji had pointed out to him that, considering the great things that he had done for me, I should at least give him a motorcycle.

On June 18, 1988, I received word that the closing ceremony in the chief's investiture was to take place: the sacrifice of a goat on the secret burial place of his predecessor in the forest. I hurried down to Kombo's house where I found him fussing with his shoes. Kombo-Kakese and the other elders had already left, except for Sanji, my nemesis. Without looking up, Kombo said that I must pay a motorcycle to arrive at *malumba* (the forest cemetery). I made a light remark about how I went on foot, honestly believing that he was joking at that moment. To my horror, he jumped up in a snit, and said that he would not allow me to go as women were never allowed at the secret cemetery and ran off with his devoted counselor.

Aghast, I stood unbelieving, realizing that he and Sanji must have deliberately told the others to go ahead. His excuse was particularly ridiculous because I had already photographed and participated in a far more secretive ceremony at the forest cemetery while he had been in seclusion. Kombo-Kakese and the others were surprised when I did not show up and also complained about the absence of the sons and grandsons of previous Kombos, who had a right to be present, but Sanji insisted that they had come too far to turn back, and besides a great crowd like that would eat too much meat. In disgust, sympathetic allies quoted a famous proverb: "The moment when the hunter gives up is the moment when the prey tires."[18] In other words, one must see a lengthy project through to its end.

Following Kombo's action, in a snit of my own, I marched home to the house, grabbed my straw hat and water bottle, and did what I had politely avoided hitherto. I marched straight down the road to the seat of Kombo's great rival, Kombo-Kabenga, who headed a splinter group of Kombo's clan and who had disputed for decades the right of Kombo-Kiboto to lead the most populous Pende clan.

Kombo-Kabenga was perfectly civil if a little suspicious at why his rival's pigeon had flown the coop. In several days of interviews, I learned that whereas the last Kombo-Kiboto had reigned for forty-five years, there had been a swift succession of title-holders on the Kabenga side. The significance of this was that whereas no one at Kombo-Kiboto had performed the closing ceremony at the secret cem-

---

[18] "Ha mahuidilo a atsu, hene ha mahuidilo a shitsu."

etery (reserved for only the highest chiefs) in forty-five years, their "brothers" at Kabenga had done so many times over in that same period. Consequently, there were many people alive who had attended several of these rites and who had a very clear memory of what should take place and why. By contrast, there were only two people alive in all of Ndjindji who had attended even one of these ceremonies, one an irascible blacksmith and sculptor whom the new Kombo had not deigned to consult, and the other a confused old man who had never held very high rank.

At Kombo-Kabenga's, they described a ritual that differed in several significant respects from what Kombo-Kiboto's crowd pieced together from foggy Ndongo's testimony. From their account, I realized that I had received an "amended" oral history, shorn of all the Kombos who had belonged to the Kabenga lineage before the split. In fact, I had been negligent not to consult Kombo-Kabenga previously as independent corroboration on many points.

Back in Ndjindji, the irascible blacksmith sent for me, seething that he had not been alerted about the trip to the cemetery. As a son of a previous Kombo, he had taken part in the closing rite at least two times, once for his father and once for the present Kombo's predecessor, who had reigned for only four years. His account tallied in every detail with Kombo-Kabenga's. His mind on the past and on trips to the forest cemetery, he also began to tell me about his father's burial, possibly the last fully traditional funeral held for a great chief in Pende territory before the Belgians achieved full control over the region.

I had heard stories that such burials once involved human sacrifice, but frankly had not believed it. All too often, metaphors get confused with fact in historical accounts in the region. However, as Ngoma Kandaku Mbuya stilled his angry hammer for the first time in my acquaintance, and looked into the fire as he recounted in graphic and haunting detail the bravery of the Luba woman chosen to be buried alive with his father, I not only believed it but understood the seriousness and regret with which the action was taken.

If I had reported the customs involving burial of great chiefs before Ngoma's testimony, I would either have "cleansed" the account of references to human sacrifice or I would have dismissed them as folklore. It was my experience of Ngoma as a man and as a witness that convinced me of the historical validity of his words and gave me the maturity with which to write about them.

Ngoma's experience with me over the past eighteen months, as well as his knowledge that I had followed the boys' initiation and had been guided by the old Kombo to follow the chief's initiation, made him feel that I knew enough to be trusted with the information. Scorned as an adviser by the new Kombo, he may also have wanted to be sure that his experience gained a respectful ear. His choleric manner frightened off many of his sons and younger relatives.

In summary, Kombo's extraordinary gesture of goodwill in directing me to his successor's investiture was a result of close rapport with key members and friends of the Samba clan at Ndjindji. Nonetheless, these very associations, when joined to a growing reputation as a practitioner of *wanga*, created a volatile situation. In the end, they cost me an eyewitness account of the investiture's closing ritual, the end to eight months' work. One begins to get a sense of how important personal relations are in the gathering of data and the construction of both ethnography and history.

Fortunately, there was a silver lining. This loss bonded me to the other individual who was shut out from the closing ritual and shook me out of a sloppy historical partisanship. It also revealed some of the ways that ritual can change and adapt to new circumstances.

Back to Manda

We had left Kombo-Kabenga with a dried up spring and a charge that Chief Nzambi had aided and abetted my illegal exhumation of his predecessors' bones for use in my *wanga*. Regretting the trouble that the unfortunate picnic had spawned for Nzambi and the local pastor, I eagerly awaited the trial, hoping that it would be the means finally to address in a public forum the reputation that I had acquired and to lay it to rest.

In the days that followed, I imagined myself in Perry Mason's courtroom, calling witness after witness to testify to our harmless intentions. I imagined the peanut farmers cross-examined about the presence of a shovel and a chicken, the merchant verifying the purchase of corned beef, and so on. When the great day finally arrived, I found myself sadly deceived.

Kombo-Kakese, the brains behind the government, showed why he is held in such respect by persuading the elders on some pretext to ban my presence at the trial. He did not want anyone able to ask me a direct question. When Kombo-Kabenga presented his charges, Kombo-Kakese then deflected the entire question by saying that it was he who had sent me to Manda on official business and assigned Chief Nzambi as my guide. This was entirely untrue, Kombo-Kakese had known nothing of the proposed trip, but it effectively deflated Kombo-Kabenga's balloon.

There was no question that Kombo-Kakese, in the paramount chief's absence, had the authority to send someone where he chose. Not only did his action entirely remove Nzambi from the line of fire, it demoted the entire question from a serious charge to a disagreement over proper protocol. Outmaneuvered, Kombo-Kabenga could only complain that he should have been consulted, or at least advised of the visit. The discussion went on for hours but in the end all that Kombo-Kabenga got was a gracious promise on Kombo-Kakese's part to alert him in writing the next time that he sent someone to Manda.

Kombo-Kakese and all my friends were jubilant at the outcome, but I was frustrated that the reason for my visit to Manda was not addressed and that my unsavory reputation was left intact. As the days passed, and Kombo-Kabenga's spring did not revive, and more springs began to dry up, hostility towards me in outlying areas remained high.[19] Most fortunately, it was time to cross the river into new

---

[19] On my next return to Kinshasa, I asked development workers if they knew any reason that might cause multiple springs to dry up in a region. They replied immediately: deforestation. This rang a bell because the previous year a Swiss ecumenical group sponsored a truck that arrived in Ndjindji and promised to visit twice a year in order to buy corn. The group had the best intentions of providing an alternative source of income for men so that they would remain at home with their families rather than leaving for the wild camps along the Kasaï River to pan for diamonds. Unfortunately, corn requires rich soil and can grow only in deforested land, and even then only for a year or two at maximum. The Pende live in bush savanna with only narrow gallery forests along streams and rivers. Middle-aged men re-

territory. Although I regretted leaving Ndjindji under a cloud, I felt that I did not have many days left. There would have been one thing or another, even if the springs had not dried up.

Could this situation have been avoided? Probably not.

My project of studying the arts, which seemed so harmless to everyone in the beginning, took on another aspect when I sought to understand their context because this involved contact with the spirit world (and the experts who act as intermediaries with that world). There were many suspicious things about me, but not even my glasses and piles of leaves would have created such a dramatic situation without this connection.

People began to view my focus on art as a mere pretext (a "politique") for aggrandizing my metaphysical powers. As one old woman told me: "No student works that hard." There was precedent in the culture for what I was perceived to be doing. People will sometimes travel to specialists in neighboring ethnic groups for protective charms whose ingredients cannot be guessed and therefore counteracted. Kakoko bragged that he had gone to study among the Chokwe to perfect his lightning-strikes. Although I lacked the kinship connections to be threatening on a personal level, I could be feared on a community level once the accusation was launched that my search for *wanga* might entail control over the dead who safeguarded the general livelihood.

One day one of my hostesses among the Western Pende returned home to tell me that she had run into a woman from near Ndjindji. My stomach tightened. This woman was startled to learn that my hostess knew me and had warned her shrilly: "Be careful! That woman blighted our crops and dried up all our springs for use in her sorcery!" To my intense relief, my hostess doubled up laughing.

Notably, when I worked for the next nine months among the Western Pende, there was not even a hint of such an accusation. This may have been because the masquerading has been entirely removed from its original ritual context and the sculpture is dead. Or it may be because I did not spend anywhere near the same amount of time in any one area. Familiarity breeds not contempt, but an insistence on conformity and norms. As time passes, it no longer suffices to dismiss the foreigner's behavior to general oddity: she or he should know better. The outsider's presence demands understanding, codification, interpretation. The initial indulgence extended to an ignorant visitor begins to wane as the person becomes, in whatever eccentric fashion, a part of the community.

Reflections

Understanding the form and pressure of, to use the dangerous word one more time, natives' inner lives is more like grasping a proverb, catching

---

sponded with great enthusiasm at Ndjindji to the Swiss group's promises and began with a will to clear as much land as possible to grow corn to sell. It would indeed be an irony if this "development" project was responsible for drying up the sources of clean water in the area, contributing to great hardship for the women, who now have to cross long distances to carry in water, and illness for everyone as the quality of water declines.

an allusion, seeing a joke—or, as I have suggested, reading a poem—than it is like achieving communion.[20]

Both the host community and the outside observer apply the same processes of understanding, codification, and interpretation in their observation of the unfamiliar. For the Westerner obliged to approach Africa through a thick haze of mythology, fieldwork can have the effects of the proverbial blast of fresh air. Yet while personal experience helps put a human face on archival data, ultimately Geertz's point is well taken: true communion with the inner lives of others is impossible within our own culture, much less abroad. We can learn to predict and sympathize, but any prolonged stay in another culture is going to result in episodes of irreconcilable difference. When someone died, I learned to ask the correct question, "Who did it?" but always felt an actor in a play. We may admire the differences we discover, or actively dislike them, or assume an air of amused detachment. Nonetheless, as historians, these experiences form part of the story we came to write, for they provide insight into the distinctive world view, institutions, and motivations that fuel historical change in a particular society.

The danger is that such experiences can result in alienation and hostility, a prolonged culture shock, that may infect scholarship. Under the cloak of seeming objectivity, there may be a failure to empathize, reducing the "subjects" of a scholar's study to mere martinets of an unappealing and rigid "tradition." It is the tone that betrays.

Because of the unique nature of fieldwork, the researcher experiences difference not as some abstract speculation, but in person, personally. It is probably honest for us to admit, like Zora Neale Hurston in *Tell My Horse*, that we like some people better than others, and that some people like *us* better than others. In my case, an easy identification with the Samba clan resulted in some wonderful material and earned me the enmity of certain neighbors. Ethically, the researcher is committed to giving the most balanced view possible, despite personal feelings. Nonetheless, for good or ill, the field experience will inflect the scholar's presentation of material. We can and should try to rise above our personal feelings, but the clues are going to be there.

---

[20] Clifford Geertz, *Local Knowledge* (New York, 1983), 70.

7

Falsehood, Truth, and Thinking Between: Histories of Affiliation and Ethnogenesis

Paul Stuart Landau

Thought has known and forgotten the reproaches of positivism a thousand times, and only through such knowing and forgetting did it first become thought.[1]

Falsehood

We had come to M.'s compound[2] in the middle of the day, without warning, and he graciously took the time to sit down with us, to answer what I called "a few last questions." M. talked in a beguiling, satisfied way, and his eyes twinkled. He explained again about the journeys to GooMoremi "very long ago." But the images he called up seemed less captivating than they had before. M. was very polite, but he seemed puzzled as to why we had come. He had already told us about GooMoremi.

---

[1] Theodor Adorno, "Keeping One's Distance" (1945), *Minima Moralia* (London, 1974), 127.

[2] I have abbreviated some names and changed others, including the name of the village in which I worked, so as not to insult the confidences of the men and women who spoke to me. I lived in Botswana for two periods totaling almost fifteen months from 1988 to 1990, and in the Tswapong Hills for about four of those months. The Institute for International Education and then the United States Department of Education funded me, with two Fulbright awards. My research focused on the history of Christianity and politics, which I found to be closely entwined in central Botswana; during my stay I conducted interviews and read archival material, about equally. Interested readers can see my book, *The Realm of the Word: Language, Gender, and Christianity in a Southern African Kingdom* (Portsmouth, NH, 1995).

He had already explained that senior men, acting on behalf of all the wards in the village of Madala, used to leave Madala in the evening. They traveled twenty miles northwest by night, arriving outside GooMoremi in the wee hours. There they sometimes met with Komana cultists.[3] They left baskets of sorghum seeds by a river, then fled, amid the sounds of the forest: trickling water, settling leaves, snapping twigs, and also, sometimes, the scolding voices of the ancestors. The next morning when the men came back to the stream and collected their baskets, the seeds in them had been blessed.

M. repeated the scenario for me, and I nodded as agreeably as I could. Yet I now doubted that what M. was describing had ever taken place. What first aroused my suspicion about these supposed trips was that the Photo-photo, the stream M. had identified as flowing by the old site of GooMoremi, actually lay by Phalapye, twelve miles west. When I had suggested to M. that he may have intended to say the Mannonye river, not the Photo-photo, he quickly and vigorously assented. But the larger problem was that no other senior man recalled any journeys to GooMoremi at all—that is, taken on behalf of Madala as a whole. Trusted men from all possible factions in Madala had explicitly denied such journeys had happened.

M. sat on a taller stump than we did, or at least I remember his form as somehow looming. I urged him further. Baruteng, my friend and assistant, helped me ask for clarifications. M. listened patiently, reclined a bit, and glanced away, frowning for a moment, as if he saw the potential for discord. My most provocative plea was: "No one else has told us anything about visiting GooMoremi before the recent drought [of the early 1980s]." M. answered that it was so, nevertheless. As he spoke, he once again grew expansive and almost radiant. And I thought: How foolish of me, pressing this old man, eighty-one years old that year, to reassure me with some forgotten and persuasive detail. M. was lying.

As I apprehended this, I did not feel affronted or think, "How dare he lie to me!" Rather, I found the new wrinkle intriguing, a puzzle to be solved simultaneously with others. After we had pleasantly thanked M. for clearing things up for us and taken our leave, I may even have stroked my chin. At this juncture I made myself out to be a sort of Hercule Poirot, with Baruteng as my assistant detective. On many of our strolls through the nameless byways of Madala, to my eye identical with one another, we pondered equally subtle variations between village oral histories. Now, looking forward to sitting at my table by my paraffin lantern, figuring things out with my pencil and notepad—an evening activity I rather liked—I thought, "How odd, how interesting." I walked faster than usual on the dusty laterite path, and I leaned to Baruteng's shoulder, and said quietly, "He is not telling the truth, don't you think?" and Baruteng said, "Yes, I think so, but I don't very well know why." Our complicity reassured me further; we would figure things out; surely this one lie, or at any rate my "recognition" of a "lie," had not undercut

---

[3] Richard P. Werbner mentions Komana in "Continuity and Policy in Southern African High God Cults," in R. P. Werbner, ed., *Regional Cults* (Kent, 1977), 183n.7, and Werbner, "Small Man Politics and the Rule of Law," *Journal of African Law*, 21, 1 (1977), 24–39. E. H. Ashton, *Medicine, Magic and Sorcery among the Southern Sotho*, School of African Studies, University of Cape Town, N.S. No. 10 (December 1943), 28–32, discusses BaKoma adepts of the Southern BaSotho. For a fuller treatment of the Tswapong cult and regional ritual and history, see my article, "When Rain Falls: Rainmaking and Community in a Tswana Village, c. 1870 to Recent Times," *International Journal of African Historical Studies*, 26, 1 (1993), 1–30.

everything M. told us. No, we were two expert hermeneuticians, and our gospel corpus was alive and kicking, able to answer questions: I had only to shift about its traces on my lined pages (my Croxley five-by-eight *manuskripboek*) to accommodate any reevaluation.

What I Thought, and What I Think I Know

In 1990, "in the field," I did my daily work more or less as an unreconstructed empiricist. I had lived in Serowe and Gaborone, I had been in Botswana for almost a year altogether, and I would work and live near Madala in the Tswapong Hills for a little over four months. Here is a sample illustrating the tenor of my thinking on the spot. It comes straight from my notebook (with necessary additions in brackets), 14 May 1990. Read it without worrying about the details:

> M.'s history of Tswapong is confirmed by other general accounts collected by [Isaac] Schapera [and others]. The fact that [M.] lists Mpeo as the principle founder of Madala—buttressed by the [name "Mpeo" of the] chief *kgotla* ["kgotla": a village ward, or, a senior men's forum at the ward's center]—and others say Mpeo was born in Malebogo [near Blauwberg in the Transvaal], makes placing Moroka [an ancestor-chief and Mpeo's "father"] a difficult task. We should not conclude that Moroka did not exist, but rather that he . . . was an elder brother of Mpeo, and not his father, which would be a not uncommon confusion. . . . Now it appears that Moroka either never ruled his own village, was contested by [Lebetswe's people], or lived a very short time. Since we know [Mpeo's son] R. was born in Madala, Mpeo was a young man when he began his rule . . .

and so on in this vein. I look back on this passage, which might easily be that of an early twentieth-century South African government ethnologist, with dismay, and I am absolutely pained by the words "a not uncommon confusion." I stress again that these were my notes to myself.

But what was this all about? Why the concern with all these names? At the time I felt that by unraveling who such-and-such "really was," I could untie the Gordian knot of lineage politics in Madala. I wanted to establish a firm baseline of "what happened," from which I would then move back to the individual accounts of my informants in order to reappraise their particular biases and evaluate their meaning. I already had more general "baselines," or environments of information, for Botswana's Tswapong region and indeed for the Ngwato kingdom as a whole. Together with that knowledge, here is what I began, in the field, to hold true, or to know with some conviction.

I knew that after the 1830s, the Ngwato kingdom increasingly dominated a broader and broader swath of arable land and pasturage to the east of its capital. I knew that it was the BaNgwato who grouped the peoples of the Tswapong Hills together, under the demeaningly prefixed label MaTswapong. Most Tswapong dwellers describe themselves as "originally" BaPedi (meaning "Pedi people"), as does Madala's chiefship, and there are also three or four other quasi-ethnicities. After 1875, Ngwato royals in charge of the major wards in the Ngwato town probably assumed official responsibility for Tswapong communities. Many Tswapong

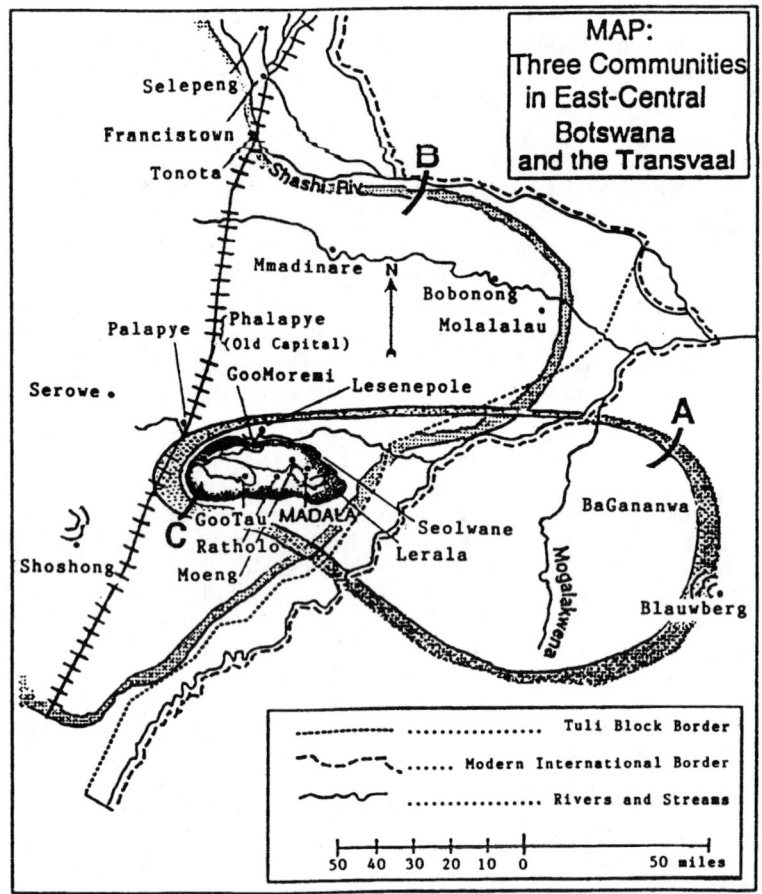

MAP: Three Communities in East-Central Botswana and the Transvaal

A Old Pedi Community B Ngwato Kingdom C New (Tswapong) Pedi Community

men herded the royals' cattle. Such a mix of political and economic servility moved a regional missionary to write that

> Matswapong are "owned" by Bangwato head-men, that is, they are their slaves. Each master owns a few of these people. If they should be successful hunting, they must give up to their master the whole produce of the hunt. . . .[4]

---

[4] Quote: Council for World Missions, London Missionary Society, Southern Africa material, housed at the School of Oriental and African Studies, University of London, Reports: Shoshong (E. Lloyd), 1/1/1887. See also John Mackenzie, *Ten Years North of the Orange River: A Story of Everyday Life and Work among the South African Tribes* (London, 1871), 366; and William C. Willoughby Papers, Selly Oaks College, Birmingham, England, File 734, W. C. Willoughby, "Notes of Tour in the Cwapong and Cweneng Hills" (1896). According to Motswaedi Dimpe, other groups living outside the capital were also placed under royals, though what this entailed is not clear; M. Dimpe, "Batswapong–Bangwato Relations: The Politics of Subordination and Exploitation, 1895–1949" (University of Botswana Student Research Essay, 1986).

In 1889 the BaNgwato shifted their capital town closer to the edge of the Tswapong Hills, to Phalapye. From this center they continued to levy sometimes onerous taxes in kind on Tswapong villages; and Tswapong people, including the villages of Madala, hoed (and later plowed) local fields for the Ngwato king.[5] This situation continued after the Ngwato capital moved a last time to Serowe. The domain of the kingdom is represented on the map as the shaded area, [B].

To the east of Tswapong lay the BaSeleka (subdued by the BaNgwato in 1887) and the chiefdoms of the Transvaal, including the BaGananwa; to the northeast, the Ndebele (or MaTebele) kingdom; and to the southeast the Boers' South African Republic. The people of Madala helped to buffer a loosely construed Ngwato frontier against the Ndebele. Ndebele regiments marched through Tswapong several times in the nineteenth century,[6] and Madala's people and other MaTswapong bore the brunt of Ndebele cattle raids as well. A praise-poem about a Madala chief lauded his killing of Ndebele, and it still, barely, lies in one old man's memory.[7]

I knew, fairly certainly, that Madala's defensive difficulties reached their height at some point in the period 1860–1875, upon which Madala's main families dispersed and fled.[8] The royal households moved toward the Transvaal and "the Land of the BaPedi," toward the lands of their ancestral origin. For reasons that need not concern us, a Madala chiefly heir named Lebetswe fell afoul of the Ngwato king, and so remained in what is now the Transvaal longer than other agnates in his extended family. The split initiated a long-lasting fracture (though not the only one by any means) in the patrilineage ruling Madala. When Lebetswe returned to Madala, probably in 1894, after the Transvaal Boers destroyed the chiefdoms in their hinterland,[9] he had to submit to the rule of his putatively junior agnate's house (see genealogy below).

I knew that back in Madala in the late 1890s, Lebetswe took charge of the rain-rites which were normally the responsibility of the chief himself. This seems to have been an unusual situation. Among other ritual duties, Lebetswe visited a cult across the border in the Transvaal, where he had grown up, and from there he

---

[5] Mackenzie, *Ten Years North of the Orange River*, 366. The plowed field, a *lesotla*, was maintained even after Khama abolished the practice in the capital; Khama III Memorial Museum, Serowe, Botswana, Khama III Papers (K III), B/10, "Verbatim Report of the Enquiry held at Lophephe, on June 19, 1907, by Captain Daniel"; Interviews: Mr. Kereeditse Sesinye, b. approx. 1908, on the road to Ratholo, 20 April 1990; Mr. L. M. and wife, 19 May 1990, GooMoremi.

[6] K III, A/2/9, H. Shippard to Khama, Kanye 7/3/1887; Neil Parsons, "Settlement in East-central Botswana circa 1800–1920," *Symposium on Settlement in Botswana* (Gaborone, 1980), 115–29; Parsons notes that in 1837 the Ndebele as a whole passed through the Hills, 117.

[7] Praise poem of R., Madala, 8/5/90.

[8] Interviews: Mr. Mathuba a Madikwe, b. 1901, Mmakgabo village, 16 June 1990; M., b. 1907, Madala, 28 March 1990; Mr. Sebele Gaborone, b. 1903, Madala, 11 June 1990; and Isaac Schapera, *Ethnic Origins of Tswana Tribes* (London, 1952), 77–78. At times, it seemed, "Madala" was part of other villages, but since the same word *motse* denotes both "village" (made of several wards) and "ward" (lying in a group of wards), this mattered little.

[9] The South African Republic conquered MmaLebogo's BaGananwa in 1894. Traditions place Dialwa's departure during Paul Kruger's war on MmaLebogo, which dwells clearly in folk memory. Many people eluded the Boers' siege; see Colin Rae, *Malaboch or Notes from my Diary on the Boer Campaign of 1894* (Cape Town, 1898), esp. 170, 180; Interviews with L. M. and M. already cited; and British War Office, Transvaal Dept. of Native Affairs, *The Native Tribes of the Transvaal* (1905), 115.

Genealogies of Actors in Madala and Ngwato Ruling Houses

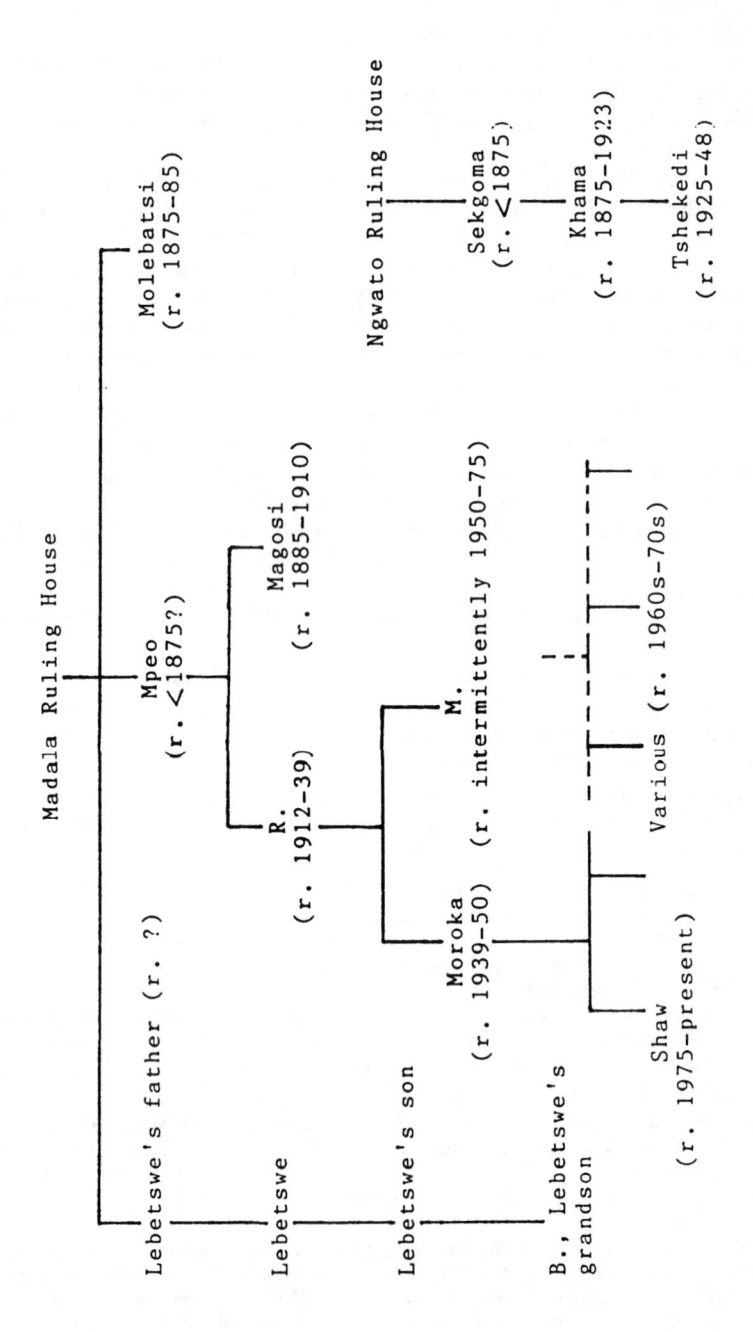

Madala Ruling House

- Lebetswe's father (r. ?)
- Lebetswe
  - Mpeo (r. <1875?)
    - R. (r. 1912-39)
    - Magosi (r. 1885-1910)
  - Molebatsi (r. 1875-85)
- Lebetswe's son
  - Moroka (r. 1939-50)
    - M. (r. intermittently 1950-75)
    - Shaw (r. 1975-present)
- B., Lebetswe's grandson
  - Various (r. 1960s-70s)

Ngwato Ruling House

- Sekgoma (r. <1875)
  - Khama (r. 1875-1923)
    - Tshekedi (r. 1925-48)

"took rain."[10] From that cultic center he recrossed the Limpopo River, walking from the east to the west, just as Tswapong ancestors had done some centuries before, and brought fertility for all Tswapong villages. Such an east-to-west vector resonates deeply with many self-called "Pedi" MaTswapong. Lebetswe's actions reflected a notion of community in contradistinction both to the authority of the Ngwato kingdom, and to the depredations of white settlers in the Transvaal. On the map, this rain-gathering community is [A].

I knew from many kinds of sources, partly because it was a focus of my research, that in the early 1900s an increasing number of people in Madala interested themselves in Christianity. Beginning with women tied to lineages that did not trace their ancestry back to the "Pedi" Transvaal, Madala developed a congregation of believers. In the 1910s the chief admitted Christian prayer and hymns into his administrative practice and into the forum of his reign, the *kgotla*. Lebetswe died and his duties were ended. These developments signaled the start of the common acceptance of Ngwato authority and for some, as I argue elsewhere, Ngwato identity in Madala. Ngwato power extended along the paths opened by Christianity.

To sum all this up more dynamically: As the Ngwato kingdom expanded, the cultic unity of the Tswapong Hill range, with the surrounding ethnically-related Transvaal countryside across the Limpopo river, retreated. In creating the kingdom, that older community had to be cut along the Bechuanaland Protectorate's borders, and part of it brought within the sphere of the Ngwato capital. Khama III ruled the Ngwato kingdom from c.1875 to 1923, and his son Tshekedi from 1925 to 1948, when the kingdom expired. In Madala, M. was chief intermittently for two decades after 1950, and the Ngwato kingdom became a memory to be put to various uses.

What M. Said

Two months before the fourth and last interview with M. described above, Baruteng and I arrived at M.'s home for our longest discussion with him. It was the morning of 8 May 1990. One of M.'s wives made us tea and after some time his form appeared on the horizon outside the village. As befit his status, M.'s farmlands lay closest to Madala, and as he gradually came closer to us we saw that he had been fetching his own firewood. His back was bent under an unwieldy bundle, but I had learned not to try to help in these situations: I was still a stranger, a white man forty miles away from the Transvaal border. Slowly, step by patient step, M. arrived. He greeted us, and sat down.

"Now, my chiefship is this," began M.

> Long ago in the years we don't remember, King Khama received Mapulana [the Tswapong ancestor], the father of my father: he, the chief who came out of the land of the BaPedi. . . . Khama then made him his helper, saying, "Mapulana, you have male children, young chiefs, and they will be strong and brave. I myself am king, and I am troubled by the MaTebele

---

[10] I discuss and analyze his movements and techniques in my article, "When Rain Falls," cited above.

and the Boers. Let those sons of yours go out and guard the country [*disa mafatshe*: herd, guard, the countries] and over there, and there. . . . [Khama, speaking to those sons:] I am sending you princes to become masters of this country on this side, to "herd" the Boers and the MaTebele.[11]

M. then described the route traveled by the most important of these princes, Mpeo (M.'s grandfather), as he moved all through the Tswapong Hills. I later realized that Mpeo's route served discursively to bind Tswapong's villages together, all under the hegemonic protection of the Ngwato state. Through his own lineage, M. seemed to be asserting, there was a harmony between the two notions of community, the kingdom's and Tswapong's. Moreover, every oral tradition about genealogical quarrels that I heard contained an appeal to "Khama" of the BaNgwato for arbitration. Several of them have the same structure, in which a question of succession arises; a conflict escalates in three repetitive stages; and Khama then decrees a solution, or if he has already, enforces a solution. The result is invariably the status quo.

But I did not believe that only peace and harmony had reigned between Ngwato statebuilding and local interests. The Ngwato king, Khama, did not really respect the MaTswapong. What sort of community was it, I wondered, that M. was imagining as having lived in Tswapong? According to his own words, the Ngwato presence "preceded" the Pedi presence. If the BaPedi in Tswapong had maintained their ethnic, ancestral unity, there must, I felt, have been problems, given the Christian Ngwato kingdom's known habit of smashing "heathen" activity. And indeed, despite giving precedence to Ngwato claims on the land, M. did show that he knew there had been a period of conflict, in which the Ngwato kingdom at least repressed Tswapong cultic unity. After the tape recorder was turned off, M. said:

> Mapulana [the Tswapong ancestor] was attacked by a regiment of Khama. When they arrived, Mapulana had already fled since he had been forewarned by his ancestors. This happened again [etc.; two more repetitions]. Finally the regiment came and heard the voices of the ancestors and were afraid. Khama then considered that Mapulana, with his powerful ancestors, could help in protecting his borders by being forewarned of [Boer or Ndebele] attacks.[12]

This was the stereotype of Ngwato legitimation in another one of its guises, but here Khama attacked Mapulana, the paradigmatic Pedi Tswapong ancestor. So I asked directly: "Did Khama hinder the ways of the ancestors?" M. replied uneasily,

> They [sic] used to hinder them . . . when Khama, ah, Mapulana—it was done that, then a black ox [*kgomo*], he [Mapulana] issued a black ox going to request rain, a black one. Now, yes, people prevented this work. They said there is nothing in it. No one can say there is a God. They refused that people should go there. And the drums of the *dikomana* [rain and fertility cultists of Komana], [the BaNgwato] refused that they cry out.

Such an enigmatic reply got me thinking. Did a secret, subversive tradition survive the reign of Khama and Tshekedi, a kind of Tswapong Albigensian heresy? I have

---

[11] Second formal interview with M., 8 May 1990, 22, transcribed in my "Notebook G." M.'s term "my chiefship" (*bogosi jwame*) conveys also the meaning "the history of my and my heirs' claim to rule here."

[12] Ibid. This is from my notes only, and not precisely verbatim.

in my notes my immediate next question (in SeTswana): Did Ngwato repression come "by force, or just by asking?" M. replied,

> They didn't ask, if they were doing this they didn't make a request, they just put a stop to it. If they heard of it being done, those people would be arrested.[13]

See how I prodded M. to tell me about the intervention of the Ngwato king in local affairs, sending clues about the sort of things I wished to hear.

Who was Mapulana? Earlier I had found that Mapulana was the putative chiefly ancestor of GooMoremi village, lying in the north of the Tswapong range, and long considered the most senior village in those Hills. Mapulana is widely seen as the "first" settler in Tswapong, and many villages (though *not* Madala) have chiefships which purportedly grew straight from GooMoremi's. It is GooMoremi that has the agricultural, rain, and healing cult called Komana. In 1983, during a serious drought, the initiates of this cult called on Madala (and in Madala, "Lebetswe's people") to send offerings to the Komana cult, so that the drought might end. By joining Komana, Madala—and especially the heirs of Lebetswe's old cultic practices—would be widening and unifying a particular form of community for the Tswapong Hills per se. Here were the beginnings of ethnogenesis under the rubric given to the Tswapong Hills by the BaNgwato: that of MaTswapong.[14] The community would embrace all Tswapong "BaPedi." GooMoremi presented such a possibility to Madala in 1983 as if it were a revival of old ways, made possible by the decline of Ngwato power. I have labeled it [C] on the map.

And yet, was Madala's 1983 affiliation with the cultic activity in GooMoremi a recent thing or not? During the same interview on 8 May, M. volunteered:

> Khama allowed this work of the ancestors; others after him, when he had died, they began to hinder it; not Khama. Then people came to prevent it. Like these villages, they were cut up, cut up like this, I mean they weren't divided by Khama. We were oppressed but we just refused to be cut apart. Tshekedi [Khama's son and the Ngwato regent king, 1925–1949] was a person who liked to come here very much. Tshekedi believed in a road, thinking, let a road come up from GooMoremi [village] and climb up, following the river down [along its flow] to Moeng. Uh-uh, no. When it came thus, the ancestors would not assent to it. Tshekedi said, let the road enter, but when it was almost finished, the ancestors stopped it, while Tshekedi was in the road. Ah! Then the winds came and ripped down the trees, overturning them, a great noise came, and Tshekedi left there fleeing in a motorcar.[15]

So, M. was saying, the BaNgwato tried to sever Tswapong cultic unity. But when? Perhaps it is best to step back for a moment. These exchanges with M. point

---

[13] Ibid., 11–13.

[14] Pnina Motzafi-Haller in "Historical Narratives as Political Discourses of Identity," *Journal of Southern African Studies*, 20, 3 (September 1994), 417–32, usefully discusses the birth of the ethnonym "Tswapong" but she vitiates her analysis by treating oral traditions exclusively as group charters and by not cross-checking their history. In my opinion "BaTswapong" is incorrect, since although it joins the toponym to the prefix for people, the actual ethnonym was and remains the derogatory "MaTswapong."

[15] Interview with M., 8 May 1990, 23–24.

up some important ways one can listen to oral "history." M. used "Khama" as a generic name for the Ngwato kingship (later he also said "MoNgwato" in the same way). Since Khama ruled for a long time, from 1875 to 1923, many people used his name in this generic sense. In a similar fashion, however, M. used the name "Mapulana" to connote the entire edifice of Tswapong cultic and ancestral practice, while at the same time implicating GooMoremi's ruling lineage, of which Mapulana is a founder. M. called unity-and-fertility practices Komana, and placed them all in GooMoremi's hands. When M. began thinking about the "road," he shifted to specifics. Leaving hold of the generic "Khama," M. retracted his implied criticism of the actual ruler, the man Khama.

Problems came after Khama, with Tshekedi, who sought to fragment the unity of Tswapong's ancestral villages (to "cut up" Tswapong). A contradiction arose, since neither M. nor anyone else would place "Mapulana" in Tshekedi's time, but no matter. The narrative had moved along to the specificity of how the ancestors intervened to prevent the building of the road from the line of rail, across the north of the Hills, down to Moeng College. Tshekedi built Moeng College in the 1940s as a modern secondary boarding school, his answer to the London Missionary Society's segregationist Tiger Kloof College in the Cape Province. The road physically inscribed a line from the BaNgwato into Tswapong, a connection that offended the ancestors: without distinction, the ancestors of all "BaPedi" (see [A] on the map) and those of Tswapong (see [C]). They sent Tshekedi and his ridiculous automobiles packing.

One might provisionally conclude from this exegesis that M. had reasons to link himself or his family to (1) GooMoremi (perhaps to legitimize his own authority) and (2) the Ngwato regime ("Khama"), in the abstract. I think both motives were present. What, however, should be made of the unfriendly reference to Tshekedi? Perhaps M. had disliked the Ngwato autocrat. Tshekedi made many enemies in M.'s generation by insisting on reviving the use of Khama's unpaid "age-regiments" for work on Ngwato state projects—notably, to build Moeng College. Moreover, M. has never been a Christian, and Tshekedi was markedly a Christian king. One might reason that M. had been a detractor of Tshekedi's during his actual rule.

Here one would be wrong. Other sources, written and oral, show that M. allied himself with the Christian presence in the village in the 1940s, and that M. was one of Tshekedi's regional partisans during the 1948–1949 conflict over the succession of the Ngwato monarchy. In that crisis, most villagers supported Seretse Khama's right to assume the kingship with his English wife, Ruth Williams; some "traditionalists," and evidently M., did not. In addition, like Tshekedi himself, M. represented a sort of aristocratic resistance to the South African-based cache of returning male migrants. M. had ruled the village during an interregnum in the 1950s caused by his senior agnates' labor migracy; those men came back and deposed him (see genealogy) above.

If M. had liked Tshekedi, possibly even owed his chiefship to him, why did he recite the Moeng road story to me? I think M. wanted to position himself as a pillar of tradition in his declining years, but the cultic legacy of Lebetswe's lineage, and his own personal history, hindered him. Because the Moeng story criticized Tshekedi, it was useful for criticizing M.'s own past. Its currency made it safe to tell, and its acceptance in the Hills weakened its expressive content. This shows how critical it is to pay attention to what Jan Vansina calls genres in oral traditions.[16] Some of the forces that originally produced the Moeng road story have dissipated, but a few old people in the Hills still resent the "occupation" of a village site by young Ngwato elites. More importantly, the story has explanatory power. A road project was begun to Moeng, and then abandoned with no explanation to the local people; and there is yet no good road to the Moeng campus after fifty years. Clearly the government would not put trucks on the absurdly treacherous path to Moeng unless it had to.

Perhaps it is relevant to note that I personally drove the existing route several times, picking up hitchhiking Moeng College students in the back of my pickup truck along the way. On one occasion, while I attempted to dictate a cassette-letter into my lapel microphone, I foolishly banked a steep turn far too quickly, nearly turning over. The accident would have killed me, and more certainly, the two natty young men wearing sunglasses in the truck bed (where they had preferred to ride). After roaring to a stop, I hopped out and apologized to them. In the middle of my apology I suddenly realized that, viewed from the truck bed through the cab window, I had presented an odd spectacle. I had been talking animatedly, apparently to my collar, and gesturing, while I rocketed along too fast for any sane driver. I must have looked like a lunatic. But the two students never lost their composure.

M. and I Make a Falsehood

As I have mentioned, after 1983 Madala village actively joined GooMoremi in the annual activities of the Komana rain and fertility cult there. According to M., when the chief Komana adept came to Madala in 1983 he said,

> You, our people: the MoNgwato [Ngwato king] has given us power so our work can continue, the work of you, BaPedi; you must not go on hiding yourselves, you can meet with [this work] and with the BaNgwato [both]. Now we can act with them, even they themselves participate; even [the current Ngwato "tribal authority" for the Tswapong Hills] has entered it. [The Komana leader] told us, Just go in openly like cattle, there should be no more hiding. Thus we began, [in 1983,] it was done, a festival there [in GooMoremi]. . . .[In GooMoremi today, during the cultic festivals attended by delegations from Madala and other villages:] Foods, each one is cooked, and when we come back later, we are given the seeds we took. Now, these seeds [they say,] Ye go and farm at your place, and do not add medicines. Just cast them, and sorghum will ripen, and rain will fall.[17]

---

[16] While Vansina's work has been criticized for overelaborating a typology of oral tradition, it suggests useful ways for each researcher to develop his or her own relevant schema. On a basic level, the Moeng tale is a rather set text, and partakes of a stereotype: local ancestors drive away a hostile force. See Jan Vansina's revised *Oral Tradition as History* (Madison, 1985), especially 90, 139. For other versions of the Moeng story, see J. Lesotlho, "The Badimo in the Tswapong Hills: A Botswana Traditional Institution in Action," *Botswana Notes and Records* 15 (1982), 7–8; also Interviews: Mr. Mathuba a Madikwe, b. 1901, Mmakgabo village, 24 May 1990, and 16 June 1990; and M., 24 June 1990.

[17] Interview with M., 8 May 1990, 23–24.

According to other people, the leader of the Komana cult wished the people of Lebetswe, the rain-fetcher of old, to lead Madala into the cult. But it was M. and other old men attached to the current chiefship of Madala who did so. They profess no conflict between their actions and their abiding respect for Ngwato prerogatives: the regional representative of Ngwato authority (now more or less a bureaucrat), "even he" goes to it! Lebetswe's descendants, who lost the chiefship long ago, do not paint such a happy picture. Lebetswe's grandson derided M.'s lineage's relationship to the Ngwato kingship as a calculated subservience. Before he became chief, M.'s father supposedly "worked digging wells for Khama, he was Khama's 'boy.'"[18] But for better or worse it is M. who helps manage Madala's participation in the Komana cult now.

I was interested in how seeds were "blessed" in the previous decades, and especially how things were done in the 1920s and 1930s. "Before 1983, what did you do?" I asked M.

> The difference was we acted without meeting them [other villages], and we acted in fear. Nowadays [we all] come, we meet with them, and they say, "let it be done, straightforwardly." Before we were afraid. Before it was such that, there is a certain river [M. says "the Photo-photo," later corrected to Mannonye at my prodding], there is a certain place, you cannot enter it, even if you are whistling, you find you cannot whistle . . . if you go in it you might just get lost in the veldt. Now it is there that we did the work, there amongst the ancestors. It was met with, together, we went in with "them" [ancestors], we went in and there were no people who were not BaPedi there.[19]

M. skipped forward again to GooMoremi in recent times, a topic I saw as a divagation. He wanted to stress the present: while the requirements of Pedi ethnicity had once restricted people's cultic activity, this was emphatically not so today. I persisted: let's talk about the old days, by that river.

> It was a river which is very deep. If an animal goes in there it cannot get out. . . Now that is where it was done, and a person truly fears it. Even now you might fear it. So, it was there that those seeds were placed, they went there, and the ancestors were also there.[20]

M. began to talk about the forest in general, about ecological prohibitions symbolized in the command, "do not drink of the first rains." When one goes to the ancestors in such natural places, one is likely to become confused and disoriented, and woe to he or she who doesn't heed them. But,

> if this has already been understood, these things will become diminished. And those whom we went with, we saw we would not be confused or upset.[21]

---

[18] Interview: B., Lebetswe's grandson, b. 1923, Madala, 15 May 1990. "Boy" is of course the ubiquitous colonial term for African men in positions of service.

[19] Interview with M., 8 May 1990, 27–28.

[20] Ibid., 31.

[21] Ibid., 34.

Did they just hear the voices, see "them" (ancestors), or what? I asked.

> We would hear the drums crying, trilling, trilling, to make us happy. And the drums cry, and we just feel, Here is people's work. Now the next day after we had scattered, we would go and pick up those seeds, and we know they've been worked.[22]

What did "they" sound like?

> We hear a noise of "them" like *"tchwe-jwe-tchwe-jwe."* Sometimes you might hear cats, a noise arises, now we know there perhaps is something. . . at the river, we not knowing where they may be, here, or there. . . .[23]

Some time after this conversation, one morning in June, Baruteng came over to me in my house and said, "L. is here and wants to see you." "Who is L.?" I asked. "L. is M.'s son. He is an old man also." I quickly got myself together and walked out to the split-wood fence to the side of my house. L. was a lanky, weather-beaten man, with a darker complexion than his father. His clothes were torn and he wore an old Stetson hat. We exchanged greetings and pleasantries, and I may have attempted to secure him for a taped interview, as I did whenever I had the chance. I did not, as surely would have been proper, invite L. in for tea. Off my guard, I just waited to hear what he had come to tell me. Our conversation then went something like this:

L.: You have been going around asking a lot of questions here about the ancestors.

Me: About your "parents," you mean? Yes, Sir. I am interested in your history.

L.: Well, if you are going to do this, they want to meet you.

Me: Meet with whom, Sir?

L.: With them. [Pause.] You must come to GooMoremi and meet the ancestors at Komana. They want to see you and bless your work here.

Me: [Pause.] Is this necessary?

L.: Well, if you do not do it, something may happen. You might be in your house, at night, and you might hear something, a noise like a mouse or something, and you might shine your flashlight into the corner of your house, and you might accidentally see one of the ancestors.

Me: Ah, what would this mean, Sir?

L. They would be very angry with you.

We went to GooMoremi with L. very soon afterwards. I confess that I was not unaffected by the prospect of seeing some preternaturally ancient crone in my

---

[22] Ibid., 34–35. It does not concern us here, but I want to draw attention to the interesting way in which M. uses the word "work" or "activity," corresponding to Jean Comaroff's arguments about *tiro* in *Body of Power, Spirit of Resistance* (Chicago, 1985).

[23] Interview with M., 8 May 1990, 27–28.

kitchen in the small hours. Often I had heard mice at night and pointed my flashlight about, which is likely how L. knew I had one.[24]

Reading Myself

Recall my question about how the BaNgwato repressed Tswapong cultic activity before World War II, "By force, or just by asking?"

> They didn't ask, if they were doing this they didn't make a request, they just put a stop to it. If they heard of it being done, those people would be arrested.[25]

What was M. thinking about? How could I know? Ngwato governors did, in the 1930s and 1940s, occasionally arrest MaTswapong for trafficking in home-brewed alcoholic beverages. At the time I was still getting used to local categories of experience. Beer, like cults, was something the Ngwato regime disapproved of. Several people had alluded to further "troubles" during M.'s time as chief in Madala. I knew that M. was one of Tshekedi's partisans at a time when Tshekedi's popularity was very low, and M. had been accused of stealing hut-tax receipts. All these things affected M.'s perception of what Ngwato force was.

My navigation through this thicket of meaning, my motives in pushing M. to recount Madala's ritual activity, are not hard to describe. At one point M. had said,

> If it is *ngwao* [our nature, custom], we do not ourselves imitate the BaNgwato, we just go—we, the masters here, we keep going with our prayers and we offer them, but we steal ourselves away, not openly doing these things.

Why? I asked M.

> Because it began that way. When we say it began, we mean in this *ngwao*. Nowadays we no longer act alone or in secret.[26]

In secret, he said! "In secret" in SeTswana is *ka sephiri*, a powerful term that literally means "in the manner of a wolf."[27] M. said, "We, the masters here," and there was dignity in *sephiri* if it covered an ancient regional cult, Komana. By the end of

---

[24] The coda to this vignette is as follows. When we got to GooMoremi, L. drank a lot of beer and "forgot" to introduce me to the cultists. I transported a trussed goat from a pasture to the village in the back of my truck, its head whacking the wheel-well until it fainted in its own urine. In the village I watched as it was sacrificially slaughtered. That night the chief led me to a house yard some distance from the village courtyard, and I was told to stay there. Someone gave me a cloth cot on which to sleep. The night was wintry, and the wind felt like icy water running under me. Cramped and drowsy from the cold, I heard drumming and voices faintly in the distance. The next day the *dikomana* cultists introduced themselves to me as I was leaving. Two of them fit the common description of diviners in southern Africa: thin, nervous. They had small smears of ash on their foreheads, exactly like Catholics on Ash Wednesday, that showed their direct contact with the ancestors. They told me that "they" had instructed them to say to me that I should go ahead with my work, unimpeded.

[25] Interview with M., 8 May 1990, 11–13.

[26] Ibid., 22.

[27] *Phiri* is translated locally as "wolf," an artifact of low Dutch suggesting a correspondence between Western and Tswana anthropomorphisms of sneakiness. A *phiri* is a hyena; there are no "wolves" (C. *lupus*) in Botswana.

our interviews M. was implying to me that some men attended Komana in secret long before open ties were established in the 1980s. My questions could not have led him to this position had not he also wanted to go there—on other issues M. and other senior men easily contradicted or disavowed the direction of my questions. But in the end it is I who pushed M. so far.

I wanted it to be true that after Lebetswe's Transvaal-centered rites were ended, a secret cultic tradition continued. The whole complex was, I hoped, centuries old. As other informants had stressed, a cult was a cult: they were all "the same thing." John Janzen's fine book, *Ngoma*, gives substance to this way of thinking. Though Janzen did not note it, what was elsewhere *ngoma* became *komana* among Northern Sotho and Tswana people; *-ana* is just a suffix, and the *ng-* to *k-* shift is very common. In the Venda Transvaal it was *gomana*.[28] Had senior men from Madala journeyed to a sacred grove to witness the ancestors' presence every year, hidden from the bookish vigilance of the Ngwato Christian kingdom? I liked this image.

But I grew to doubt it. And, at the end of the encounter described at the beginning of this essay, I rejected it. History is not just some strange sort of fiction. If it were, I would not have reluctantly seen that Madala's chiefly *kgotla* did little, apart from its Christian praying, to ensure the Tswapong Hills' fertility. I would have gone on hinting of an agricultural Eleusinian Mystery, which secretly persisted and then recrudesced in the 1980s. I cannot, because I doubt it did.

M. was a very complex man, and a cautious man. In his own way he had told me that we were headed down the wrong road. "Who was making noises at the river?" I asked.

> You may hear it said, they are the dead of ages past. . . ghosts only, which you can't identify. But they also are people; it is our history and nature [*ngwao*], they come from GooMoremi, they come from the land of the BaPedi, and also from Mapulana.[29]

For M. the ancestors were figures uniting people from all directions; he had had enough divisiveness in his life.

"What is Truth?" M.'s and Mine

In that same May of 1990 I wrote in my notebook,

> Was there a "mixing" somewhere in the past? Who was in the hills before the BaPedi came there? And then there is the figure of "Ngwali," a man "who eats like people," who came . . . blessing people's seeds on the spot

---

[28] John Janzen, *Ngoma: Discourses of Healing in Central and Southern Africa* (Berkeley, 1992). These cults are surely part of the phenomenon he describes; *ng-* to *k-* is the standard consonant shift from Nguni to Sotho–Tswana languages. Eileen J. Krige was apparently the first anthropologist to describe a drumming cult called Komana in "Agricultural Ceremonies and Practices of the Balobedu," *Bantu Studies* V, 3 (Sept. 1931), 207–40; in *The Realm of the Rain Queen* (Oxford, 1943) she and J. D. Krige call it Gomana and remark its final performance as having occurred in 1892. In a conversation with Molaodi Thakeng, an even older man than M., I had tried to distinguish GooMoremi's rain cult from the old circumcision ceremonies: which ones did Khama act to prevent, and when? Molaodi finally cut me off: "It's the same thing, that and Komana. *Go rupa* [initiation]."

[29] Interview with M., 8 May 1990, 35.

in Madala. Where were [such people] from? One dares to hope—from GooMoremi?[30]

Everyone who does field research to some degree reinvents the wheel. As I reviewed my empiricist notes I saw that some of my university-bought categories were wrong. It began to dawn on me that entities such as "the Mwali (or Ngwali) Cult," "the ancestors," and "Pedi ethnicity," were not so concrete, and could not disentangle people's experiences. I had to grasp that people's lives as lived gave other, unforeseen categories a much greater assumptive importance.

When I looked back on my material, one such categorical division in Madala struck me with force. I refer to the three conceptions of community I have already mentioned. Although they were manifested only in people's allegiances and behavior, I have rather concretely mapped them as [A], [B], and [C].

[A] was an old community, I think. It was regional, and straddled the northwest Transvaal, and part of Botswana (the Tswapong and Tshweneng Hills); it drew on an "old Pedi" ethnicity, made up from Tswapong "Pedi," Transvaal Nguni, Venda, and North Sotho ancestors. It embraced Madala. After a period of desuetude, it was half revived by the labor migration into South Africa of many young adults, especially after 1950. From its vantage point the BaNgwato like the Boers were distrusted overlords.

[B] was central to my research agenda in Tswapong. It was made from literacy, Christianity, Ngwato royal authority, and British colonial administration; it lay across the Ngwato (now "Central") District of the Bechuanaland Protectorate (i.e., Botswana). Elsewhere I call it the Realm of the Word.

[C] is the last community on the map. It is focused on GooMoremi and on GooMoremi's proto-ancestor "Mapulana." By the late twentieth century it meant the "new Pedi" ethnicity of the descendants of the Tswapong Hills' earliest settlers, as an identity somewhat different from related Transvaal people. Because it was bounded in this way, I feel sure it is newer than the others, but even more certainly, it did not include Madala until recently.

As I see it, M. lied in order to place this third ethnic construction of community, [C], back in time, all the way into the period of the making of the first and second communities, [A] and [B]. In addition, M. said that Madala had long belonged to [C]. Now, M. is a demoted chief of Madala. His own authority is now premised on [C], the Tswapong Pedi ethnicity, because he has been helping to lead Madala's delegations to GooMoremi's ancestor cult since Madala began its involvement in 1983. By reading Madala's participation in the [C] community back into the 1920s, M. made venerable Madala's cultic subordination to GooMoremi (to "Mapulana"), and so legitimated his own recent political rehabilitation.

What made M. hesitate about this transposition was that it placed the origins of Madala's fealty to GooMoremi and the "new Pedi" community in a period when the Ngwato kingdom clearly disapproved of any cultic activity. Thus the activity had to be "in secret," *ka sephiri*. Here I stepped in and persuaded him to embellish the story. As I was a white man, with a trace of SeNgwato accent (though perhaps I flatter myself here), studying Christianity and fresh from living in Gaborone and Serowe, M. at first assumed I resented the idea that Tswapong villages participated

---

[30] 2 May 1990.

in "heathen" ceremonies at all. Gradually he saw that I relished the idea of a subversive tradition.

M. had old links in Madala to Tshekedi Khama, and shared the patriarchal component of Tshekedi's antipathy toward South Africa.[31] M. felt he had to stress, as he repeatedly did, that "the BaNgwato" today embrace the GooMoremi Komana cult. Rather than attacking Khama III, the paragon of Ngwato-ness, M. implicated Tshekedi, his own somewhat discredited patron, for violating the "previous" regional community that M. claimed was [C], premised on GooMoremi. For this he quoted the well-known story about Tshekedi and the Moeng road. Khama III too much represented "the BaNgwato" and the "old days" in general, and so was above serious reproach.

M.'s falsehood, such as it was, could only take place in the interstices of traditions and tales. For instance, if M. had merely slanted or varied a genealogical tradition, like everyone else, it hardly would merit such a designation. Had M. shared rumors or gossip with me, as did Lebetswe's grandson, I would also be wrong to call them lies. But M.'s lie was a claim that something happened in his lifetime that, I strongly believe, did not happen. Madala did not send delegates to GooMoremi's fertility cult in the 1920s and 1930s. It would be grotesque to congratulate myself for contradicting this hospitable villager; but it would be irresponsible for me to pretend I was not, and obscure my interpretation with the claim that M. and I had different notions of what constituted "truth." In the end I felt that M. knew very well that he was not telling it.

This seems quite tidy, but in fact I was sometimes troubled by forebodings in Madala. Was it all a wild game, I wondered. Here I was trying to penetrate the weave of people's expressions of local and regional history, of cults and churches; just over the border lay the last white supremacist government in Africa. How impossible it was in my months in the village to know, in the decades past, what had transpired even between the old men who sat in the *kgotla*! Each one was unfailingly pleasant to the other, gamely seating himself on his tiny stool and uttering greetings. I too wished to be seen as a friendly neighbor, but once in a while an isolated elderly person mistook me for a tax collector or a district officer, even though Botswana had been independent since 1966. At such times I was just an inquisitive white man, and heard only, "Yes, sir; yes; greetings, our father," or uncomfortable denials of any knowledge whatsoever. At other times I seemed very much like a missionary; it was often difficult, in the living language of rural Botswana, to distinguish "I am here to learn about your history and religion" from "I am a bible student." Even had I more time in Madala, was there any way to be sure the entire edifice of my local history would not be made of the tissues of semi-truths, each one told to a different "me" for peculiar reasons, each one connected to my imagined status?

Perhaps it was great hubris to think I was reconstructing one true narrative from such testimony. Where was, after all, the aerie on which I could perch, so as to discern the merits of various disagreeing accounts? I held no text from which the tales and justifications of these men might fly away and return. At times I had imagined something like a play by Harold Pinter, in which different characters'

---

[31] Recall that M. served as chief while young men left in ever greater numbers for the mines, returning with greater ambitions, money, and attitudes.

reflections of an event might be pitched up against the ultimately knowing gaze of an abstract audience. M.'s discourse, which I could just barely manage to evaluate so directly as to call it false, was not even the most complex I encountered. And yet I was taking each individual story I heard as a weird synechdochical version of "the" whole story, unknown in its entirety. Even if I were a master logician, and could somehow deduce a meta-narrative from the sum of its deciphered, partial permutations, and see the whole structure emerge as one, what would I have in my notebook then? Something less, I think, than the details I would necessarily have amassed about people already, in the process of correlating and "correcting" their individual accounts.

Yet context is not (at any given moment) text. One cannot be in a language and outside it at the same time. I could evaluate everyone's words in the growing context established by other evaluations; I just could not look ahead to the whole text and work back to the parts. It is true that in Madala I had no fixed vantage point, but so what? At some period my work, my research and my thought both, would slow to a stop; I would come to some resting place (even if not a plateau) in my activities. There would then be one semi-coherent text, because my words would form one. That is what I had set out to do; and whether it is defensible seems to me to be more of a political issue than an epistemological one. By the time I completed my envisioned narrative, the annotations in my surveys did indeed overspill the pages of my little books and drown my particularizing queries. So I ended up with a different narrative, but a narrative still.

All in all, the mental gymnastics in my search for truth served me well. Like all stories, mine are representations about the real: as philosophers know, they can only be true or false, not the real itself. One has guidelines for establishing the truth-value of historical propositions: they include written or "independent" oral confirmation; and with attention to genre, agreement against the grain of apparent interest; common assumptions underlying disputes; and even, the apparent trustworthiness of informants. This is how I reasoned, aiming also to make my representations capable of "talking" with the Tswapong categories I found in use. One cannot get further than a representation anyway.

In life we go about and describe very many things, without bothering to pause and mull over how our criteria for doing so are ephemeral. We look for a moment at a room, and we can describe it to a certain extent; if we look longer and harder, sit on a chaise, pace about, and count cornices, we can describe more of it. Willfully placing a Tiffany lamp in the description is not allowed. In intending to say that chains of signification are endless, scholars sometimes warn that historians have no claim on the truth. Of course, but to me this is an odd remark; it sounds like saying: the observer has no claim on the Tiffany lamp, there or not.[32]

I have already admitted that each one of my "true" stories would remain part of the broader, ineffable picture any historian gets of the place he or she studies. Why then go about like Hercule Poirot in a doggedly positivist way, searching for true regnal lists and unearthing "the" history of power and politics among non-

---

[32] The assumption behind such equations is that to classify is to possess. This by now old chestnut has some charm, but strictly speaking, it is false; let's put it away. For others concerned about questions like "What is historical truth," in my opinion one might consult Ludwig Wittgenstein's later works (from the *Blue Book* on), but Thomas Kuhn, Paul Feyerabend, and other philosophers might do just as well.

literate folk? Consider this: despite all my caveats and confessions, I was not so awfully far from Madala's modes of historical thinking when I worked there. The old folks usually understood what I was getting at; they held that "Mpeo" did or did not really rule, in a particular real place; they critiqued one another's traditions as telescoped ("but he's forgotten Maifala"), or ignorant, or well-informed. Historians are understandably fascinated with such discussions. They should also be careful to credit their integrity. Not a man nor woman in Madala village would dissent from the idea that some historical narratives are true, and others false.

8

A Moment in the Middle: Fieldwork in the Nuba Hills

Janet J. Ewald

The general question I set for myself is this: how does fieldwork shape our historical knowledge? Before pursuing that question, we have to consider another: what exactly is "fieldwork," a term for a similar—but not identical—set of methods used by historians, anthropologists, geographers, and others? Fieldworkers have tended to conceive of fieldwork in terms of the "field" as a particular place and time in our own lives. We go into the field, stay there for a time, and then come out. During that special time and place of fieldwork, we seek to orient ourselves in unfamiliar surroundings and learn to manage in daily life; we find particular identities and have identities thrust upon us. Fieldworkers have reflected on their lives and identities in the field. Putting the worker at the center of fieldwork, these analyses offer valuable insights into how fieldwork leads to a particular kind of knowledge.[1]

Here I take a different approach, defining fieldwork primarily by the work, rather than the worker, in the field. And I will address in particular the work of historians: gaining knowledge about the past based on evidence, or traces of the past in the present.[2] Sometimes those traces of the past in the present are consciously preserved as artifacts, in their original form or in a form dating from some point in the past. This evidence exists in what I will call an archive.[3] Although

---

[1] Because of the particular centrality of fieldwork to anthropology, anthropologists have produced a huge corpus analyzing fieldwork. Only a few among the many works focusing on the experiences of the worker in the field are these collections of essays: Kirsten Hastrup and Peter Hervik, eds., *Social Experience and Anthropological Knowledge* (London and New York, 1994); George W. Stocking Jr., ed., *Observers Observed: Essays on Ethnographic Fieldwork*, History of Anthropology, I (Madison, 1983); and Tony Larry Whitehead and Mary Ellen Conaway, eds., *Self, Sex, and Gender in Cross-Cultural Fieldwork* (Urbana, IL, 1986).

[2] Adopting the term from François Simiand, Marc Bloch wrote of the "tracks" of the past in the present: "the mark[s], perceptible to the senses, which some phenomenon, in itself inaccessible, has left behind." *The Historian's Craft*, trans. Peter Putnam (New York, 1953), 54–55.

[3] Clearly, I am using "archive" in a much broader sense than usual. By my definition, "archives" include libraries and private collections of documents and other artifacts.

A Moment in the Middle: Fieldwork in the Nuba Hills 95

interpretations of it may change radically, the evidence itself no longer changes. Guarding against researchers bringing in pens or departing with the artifacts themselves, trustworthy archive keepers ensure the physical integrity of the evidence.

In the field, traces of the past exist in a very different relationship to the present. The evidence remains subject not simply to re-interpretation but also alteration and sometimes obliteration.[4] Evidence in the field thus exists in a field of forces. For historians and other scholars in the field, these forces are human forces. Generations of French proprietors altered the fields in whose dimensions Marc Bloch found traces of the past; they continued to alter them even as Bloch—or, as he put it, "the traveler in northern France"—walked those fields.[5] Serbian singers did not simply perform ancient songs for Albert Lord, but re-worked old formulae to create new songs in their performances.[6] The task of the historian working with evidence in and from the field is thus to understand how human forces, past and present, have put and continue to put their imprint on that evidence. The fieldworker listens to an oral narrative or gazes at ruins, and tries imaginatively to excavate the layers representing the present, the recent past, and the more distant past.

The specificities of time and place define the work of the field—the evidence—no less than defining the experience of the fieldworkers. Historians find the place of fieldwork where evidence remains subject to people who continue to change it. A particular time, too, defines the evidence in the field. The historian encounters traces of the past at a particular moment in their flux of change. Long before the worker arrives in the field, evidence has changed; evidence remaining in the field will continue to change long after the fieldworker leaves. The fieldworker, however, records evidence—writing notes, taping interviews, taking photographs—and removes it from the field of forces. No longer subject to change, this evidence now becomes an archive, or part of an archive.

Fieldwork thus represents a particular moment in a particular place: a moment in the middle, bracketed by what precedes it and what follows it. Historical knowledge based on evidence from the field emerges not only from the moment of fieldwork, but from those stages before and after it. We must appreciate how the evidence took shape in the years preceding and during fieldwork, and how evidence taken from the field in turn shapes the historian's knowledge after she or he leaves the field.

My historical knowledge about the Taqali kingdom emerged from the particular moment when I did fieldwork, and the times before and after that moment. For me, the moment in the middle lasted from January 1977 to March 1979, when I lived among people in the northeastern Nuba hills and its nearby plains in the Republic of the Sudan.[7] At the heart of the region rises a high massif: the core of the Taqali kingdom, which

---

[4] For an earlier formulation of this concept, see Janet Ewald, "Foxes in the Field: An Essay on Historical Methodology," *African Studies Review*, 30, 2 (1987), 9–15.

[5] Bloch, *The Historian's Craft*, 39, and *French Rural History: An Essay on Its Basic Characteristics*, trans. Janet Sondheimer (Berkeley, 1970), xxvii.

[6] Albert B. Lord, *The Singer of Tales* (New York, 1971), especially 13–14, 21–26. Lord indicates stages of learning the skills of epic song, from the first stages of repeating memorized formulae to the most advanced "freedom [to] move in tradition" (p. 26) to compose new songs.

[7] I was conducting Ph.D. research, which I had defined as an inquiry into how Muslim leaders arose in the Nuba hills, a socially diverse and politically fragmented frontier zone.

flourished between about 1750 and 1885. In the context of geography and politics, as well as of my fieldwork, the northeastern Nuba hills between 1977 and 1979 stood in the middle. The hills rose in the center of the Sudan, on the border between the Arab north and predominantly Nilotic south. And the years of my fieldwork fell during the all too brief period of peace between a 1972 truce that ended the Sudanese civil war and the resumption of open hostilities in 1983.

During the moment in the middle, evidence emerged as I encountered particular men and women who responded to my presence and my queries. I did not simply walk alone across the landscape; they led me to ruins and pointed out significant features. I did not listen to an already existing oral narrative; they composed one for me. But they did not create evidence out of nothing for my benefit. Their ancestors had built the houses, walls, and terraces that by 1977 lay in ruins in the mountains. They had heard stories about the past from their parents and grandparents. When I asked them questions, they remembered these tales as best they could and pieced them together into narratives which I recorded. Evidence in the field had taken shape for decades, even centuries, before the moment in the middle of my fieldwork. It took shape again during fieldwork, when local people answered the questions of an American researcher. My informants and I were the human forces shaping the evidence.

Acting as my guides to history and my teachers in everyday life, local men and women helped me, as a stranger, orient myself in new surroundings. But as I followed their guidance, I realized that the historical evidence to which they pointed also served to orient them in time and place. They firmly located the Taqali kingdom in the ranks of the earliest kingdoms of the upper Nile valley. They traced the origins of the royal dynasty to an Arab founder from the northern Sudan. During—and, even more importantly, after—fieldwork, I realized that local people's preoccupation with orienting themselves had emerged from their own past. Their ancestors had struggled to survive in the dangerous middle of various regional systems. The evidence presented during the moment in the middle indeed took shape during these past struggles.

Before the Moment in the Middle

Highland warriors and mediators rose to power in response to the dangers of living in the middle beginning in the last half of the eighteenth century. To the east of the Nuba hills, the sultans of Sinnar were losing power to alliances of merchants, Muslim clerics, and nobles. To the west, the sultans of Dar Fur ruled over an expanding and consolidating empire. Armies from both empires, their tributaries, and their dissident factions fought in and around the Nuba hills.[8] As well as raiders, traders came to the hills in search of gold and slaves. Confronting traders, raiders, and refugees from raids, Nuba highlanders turned to warriors who could

---

[8] For secondary sources about the histories of the sultanates of Sinnar and Dar Fur, and their involvement in the marches between them which included the Nuba hills, see R. S. O'Fahey and J. L. Spaulding, "Hashim and the Musaba'at," *Bulletin of the School of Oriental and African Studies* 35 (1974), 316–33; O'Fahey and Spaulding, *Kingdoms of the Sudan* (London, 1974); R. S. O'Fahey, *State and Society in Dar Fur* (London, 1980); and J. L. Spaulding, *The Heroic Age in Sinnar* (East Lansing, 1985).

defend them from dangers and mediate with outsiders.[9] Taqali's warrior-kings entrenched themselves after 1820, when a new wave of soldiers and merchants, based in the Turkish-ruled Sudan, threatened the Nuba hills.

Taqali's kings rooted themselves in a physical and social environment distinct to the Nuba hills. Throughout the hills, mediators and warriors dealt with raiders and traders. More than other parts of the hills, however, the Taqali massif lay near routes leading to the Nile valley and northern Sudan. Taqali's kings thus drew on a repertoire of regalia, symbols, and titles common to a Sudanic tradition of kingship. Most important, unlike most other Nuba hill leaders, the rulers of Taqali were Muslims.

Two events marked an increasing orientation of Taqali's elite away from the highlands and towards the Arab northern Sudan. Around 1860, a king came to power whose mother belonged to an Arab pastoralist community on the plains. King Adam al-Arabi cultivated allies from both plains Arabs and Muslim teachers. Abandoning the old royal compound in the heart of the massif, Adam built his most important residence perched at the edge of the escarpment and overlooking the plains to the east and west. The second, and more significant, event occurred after 1884 when King Adam died while in captivity of the Ansar, soldiers of the militant Islamic reform movement (or Mahdiyya) in the Sudan. A few months after Adam's death, the Ansar invaded the hills. For the first time in the kingdom's history, soldiers from beyond Taqali decisively defeated highlanders in the massif. Capturing large numbers of highlanders, the Ansar forced them to migrate to the Sudanese Nile valley. This mass migration brought highlanders, including many members of the royal family, into close contact with the Arab Sudan. During this crisis, Taqali's exiles learned about other Sudanese polities—especially the shaykhdoms of the Blue Nile highlands—which bore striking similarities to their own kingdom.

Returning to the highlands from their diaspora after the defeat of the Ansar in 1898, the descendants of the kings both reconstructed their own history and reconstituted their kingdom. After the disruption of the Mahdiyya, and perhaps stimulated by the questions of colonial officials, the elite speculated about their past. On the basis of what they remembered about the reign of Adam al-Arabi and what they had experienced during the Mahdiyya, they gradually composed a founding story. At the center of this story stood a figure stereotypical in Sudanese founding tales: the Wise Stranger.[10] The Taqali story depicted the Wise Stranger as an immigrant Arab from the northern river valley. At the same time as the rise of Sinnar's kings in the sixteenth century, this stranger supposedly arrived in the massif, converted the people to Islam, and established a line of kings. By 1930, local notables claimed to be descendants and heirs of the Arab Wise Stranger.

These local notables also held political office. Under the Anglo-Egyptian colonial regime, men from the royal family assumed positions in local administration. They looked increasingly to the northern Sudan. Upon the advice of colonial offi-

---

[9] For conditions in the Nuba hills during the last half of the eighteenth century, as well as a fuller account of the history of the Taqali kingdom as summarized in the text of this essay, see Janet J. Ewald, *Soldiers, Traders, and Slaves: State Formation and Economic Transformation in the Greater Nile Valley, 1700–1885* (Madison, 1990).

[10] For references to the Wise Stranger motif from other parts of the Sudan, see P. M. Holt, "Funj Origins: A Critique and New Evidence," *Journal of African History* 4, 1 (1963), 39–55; O'Fahey and Spaulding, *Kingdoms of the Sudan*, 110 and 114; and O'Fahey, *State and Society in Dar Fur*, 123.

cials and hoping to cultivate commercial ties with the north and east, in 1929 the royal family descended from their highland residence overlooking the plains to a site several miles from the foot of the hills. There they built the new town of al-Abbasiyya, with a mosque and market at its center. Based in al-Abbasiyya the descendants of Taqali's kings continued to hold local political offices even after independence in 1956.

By the 1970s, however, local government was no longer in the hands of the kings' descendants. An aged and blind man, the man who held the title of king exercised no official authority. People agreed that he would be the last king; after his death, Taqali people would not choose a new king. The current president of the Sudan, according to a local anecdote, had commented sarcastically on their claims to historical glory. When a local delegation told President Nimeiri that their kings had ruled ninety-nine hills, he made the snide aside, "Why don't we give them Jabal Awlia [a hill on the banks of the Nile] and they can make it one hundred." More significantly, when President Nimeiri came to power in 1969 he instituted administrative reforms. Officers sent from Khartoum replaced Taqali's old elite in the local bureaucracy. In the mid-1970s, provincial reorganization separated the Nuba hills from a predominantly Arab, northern Sudanese province. The new province of Southern Kordofan itself included people of many different ethnicities, religions, and languages. But the center of provincial political power did not rest with people who identified themselves—as did Taqali's notables—with the Arab, northern Sudan. Al-Abbasiyya itself lay on the opposite side of the province from the new provincial capital, Kadugli, a hard journey across the rugged hills to the west.

In late December 1976, a group consisting mainly of young female schoolteachers and middle-aged male notables made the overnight trip to Kadugli. There they joined the New Year's celebration commemorating Sudanese independence. As part of the events, various groups sponsored exhibits. The schoolteachers and notables from Taqali mounted an exhibit on the history of the Taqali kingdom, displaying items of royal regalia and an article from an Egyptian magazine relating the story of the Wise Stranger who founded the kingdom. Their exhibit won a prize.

On the last days of 1976, I too arrived from Khartoum in Kadugli. At the exhibits, I met the Taqali delegation and showed them the letters that their kin in Khartoum had written on my behalf. At this time, I knew very little of the narrative history of Taqali which I have sketched above. My knowledge about the Taqali kingdom began to take shape when I encountered evidence in the field. The field of forces preceding the moment in the middle had created that evidence; during the moment in the middle, a new field of human forces reshaped the evidence. How I came to Taqali and what I did there formed part of that field of forces.

During the Moment in the Middle

I arrived in the middle of the Sudan carried by the political and scholarly forces of a relatively peaceful moment.[11] Most broadly, I enjoyed an auspicious diplomatic

---

[11] In addition, I was carried by funds for travel supplied by the University of Wisconsin and sustained during my first year in the Sudan by a NDEA Title VI fellowship. By this time I was well aware of the importance of favorable circumstances in research; my earlier plans to conduct research in the desert edge of Mali had failed partly because of the drought which had afflicted that country in the middle 1970s.

moment for my journey. Hoping to cultivate an ally in northeastern Africa, my own government was providing aid and support to the Sudanese government. Sudanese students had begun to come to the United States in greater numbers in the early 1970s. One of these Sudanese graduate students taught my introductory class in Arabic at the University of Wisconsin in Madison. The University itself hosted a reception for a Sudanese government delegation in 1976. On that occasion, I made the initial contacts easing my travel clearance to the Sudan. Once in Khartoum, the family of my Arabic instructor hosted me in their household. I easily gained government permission to travel from Khartoum to the new province of Southern Kordofan; in the provincial capital, Kadugli, I stayed with the family of another University of Wisconsin graduate. With that household as my base, I attended the Independence Day celebrations and exhibitions.

Meeting me at a moment when they were presenting themselves to an audience of outsiders, descendants of Taqali's kings both claimed me as their particular responsibility and construed me in terms of other strangers who had come to their kingdom. I was not a Wise Stranger, as was the mythical founder of their kingdom; instead I was a stranger who was going to become wiser, enlightened by local notables about the history of the Taqali kingdom. The Taqali delegation to the Kadugli celebrations made room for me in the bus traveling back to al-Abbasiyya; on January 8, 1977, the historian from America arrived in al-Abbasiyya along with the prize that they had won for their exhibition. In al-Abbasiyya, Taqali's elite men and women eagerly assumed the role of field guides for me. And this is literal. Within a week of arriving from the provincial capital, they took me into the hills to visit the ruins of the kingdom's capital. They pointed out the artifacts to me, such as a four-hundred year old well where a maiden-eating snake had lived, and the graves of past kings. They also told me the founding story, and several other narratives about the reigns of Taqali kings.

The forces which had brought me to Taqali with such ease had given my presence something of an official stamp; I soon realized that I was receiving the official version of Taqali's history. Men and women from the local elite were actively interpreting for me, or drawing my attention to, the particular traces of the past that supported their sense of themselves as heirs to a long line of Muslim kings of Arab descent. All of Taqali's elite apparently agreed on the evidence and its interpretation. As an academic historian-in-training, I was suspicious of this degree of consensus. I also evaluated the elite's use of evidence as sometimes implausible and their focus on the kings alone as limited. I sought to reconstruct a different kind of history, using different rules of evidence. But how was I to find the traces of the past in the present which would allow me to go beyond the official version?

Most fundamentally, I discovered a wider range of evidence simply by extending the moment in the middle to a relatively long time—almost two years, separated by a break for archival work.[12] After all, I had heard the official version

---

[12] I was able to extend my stay because of generous support from the Social Science Research Council and Fulbright-Hays, which granted me fellowships after I had already spent almost one year in the Sudan. Before I arrived in al-Abbasiyya in 1977, I had conducted about two months of archival research in Khartoum. In October 1977, I left the Sudan for London where I worked in the Public Records Office and other archives; in February 1978, I returned to the Sudan. At the end of the moment in the middle, I returned to the Khartoum archives and also worked in the archives of the Missionari Comboniani in Rome.

of history during the first few intense weeks after my arrival in al-Abbasiyya. The longer I stayed, the less people saw me as part of the audience of outsiders to whom they proudly presented their official history. With time, the elite themselves spoke more freely, and in richer and more idiosyncratic detail about the past. In general, everyone became much more casual about my presence, freeing me to poke about by myself.

I used this freedom to move out from the geographic and social center of Taqali, away from al-Abbasiyya and its elite. I studied the enormously detailed Sudanesegovernment survey maps, which I had brought with me, to gain an idea of the location of physical features and villages. I visited as many of these villages as I could, learning the special characteristics of each. The people in this village possessed powerful magic; the wells in that village were reliable even in the dry season. In particular, I lived for several weeks in a village far up in the hills, where people spoke the local language as well as Arabic and had little contact with Taqali's notables.

I also extended my social map, asking as many different kinds of people as possible about the pasts of their families and the past of the Taqali kingdom. I interviewed people who lived in highland and outlying villages, as well as elite and non-elite men and women in al-Abbasiyya. People in outlying villages offered particularly valuable information about local religious practices which continued well into the twentieth century. I thus saw beyond the official version, depicting Islam as dominant from the distant origins of the kingdom. Perhaps the most helpful single informant, however, was an old man in al-Abbasiyya who belonged to the royal family. Ali lived on the fringes of the town and on the fringes of political power; he had lost out in a succession dispute in the 1920s. Since then, he had been brooding about the lost glories of the past. Although he never directly contradicted the notables, he did offer alternate or fuller accounts of events. In particular, Ali told me a variant version of the kingdom's origins, differing significantly from the story of the Arab Wise Stranger told by notables at the center of town.

At the same time that I tried to broaden my fieldwork beyond the world of elite men and women, I followed a second strategy which drew on the historical conceptualization of the same notables. Their organizing principle of history—i.e., the succession of kings—allowed me to reach most deeply into the past, giving me a central narrative structure for the history of the area. I used the reigns of Taqali's kings as a kind of stairway into the past. In interviews, I asked most informants to tell me what they knew about events or personalities during the times of various kings. Men and women, whether elite or not, revealed their special and distinctly non-stereotypical knowledge when I asked them to elaborate or explain points that came up during their accounts of the reigns of kings.

Even though I was collecting information about the past, that information formed a mosaic rather than a historical reconstruction. I was getting a little bit of information from here, and a little from there. I had not yet put them together into a coherent history of the Taqali kingdom, beyond the version told to me by elite men and women. Because I had not perceived the underlying dynamics behind the stories of events and personalities, this mosaic possessed a flat, unidimensional quality; it was a kind of historical map in the same way that the Sudanese government survey documents were topographical maps. It was only after my moment in the middle that I learned to read my historical map in the same way that a skilled geologist reads a topographical map, projecting a vision of the processes that created forms and features. This kind of historical map reading relied on analysis of evidence removed from its field of human forces. For me, this meant removing myself from the middle of the Sudan.

After the Moment in the Middle

The moment in the middle ended in March 1979. I finished my stay in Taqali as I had begun it, with a trip to the ruins in the highlands. Then I left al-Abbasiyya and returned to the United States. There, an academic setting allowed me to concentrate on analyzing evidence from the field and comparing it to evidence collected in archives and libraries.[13] Critically analyzing my evidence, I tried to understand the historical forces that had produced oral narratives themselves. I dealt with an apparent paradox. Only by removing evidence from the field of forces that had shaped it was I able to reconstruct that past field of forces. In this endeavor, I found written sources invaluable. With the notable exception of the founding story, written sources, where available, corroborated the larger corpus of oral evidence; this gave me confidence in the general validity of oral sources. Moreover, written sources allowed me to date events fairly precisely, including the rise of the warrior-kings.

However important the archival sources, fieldwork provided the center of the historical knowledge I gained about Taqali. Fieldwork first provided certain information unavailable in written sources. But more fundamentally, I approached the history of the Taqali kingdom in a certain way because of my experience in the field. The perspective of my informants to some extent became my perspective; their concerns informed my analysis; the very nature of oral evidence influenced how I came to regard the nature of political life in Taqali. Yet my specific interpretations of Taqali history diverged from those of the people whom I encountered during the moment in the middle.

I diverged most radically from my informants in my critique of the founding story, which I analyzed in light of both Ali's alternate story and written sources. The dominant founding story, I argued, represented only the most recent of a series of stories relating the origins of the Taqali kingdom. Two of these stories attributed the founding of a dynasty to the arrival of Wise Strangers from other parts of the Sudan. Stories about origins thus also put forth claims to identity and oriented Taqali within the wider region. I further argued that the elite composed a story presenting their founder as an Arab from the northern Nile valley only after the trauma and forced removals of the Mahdiyya. That founding story itself bore details suggesting that Taqali people composed it using knowledge gained during the Mahdiyya, when they encountered people of the Upper Blue Nile hills. As traces of the past in the present, the dominant founding story and its variants thus yielded a kind of archaeology of Taqali people's intellectual history: specifically, their changing speculations about their place in the world.[14]

---

[13] The first result of my work was a Ph.D. dissertation, "Leadership and Social Change on an Islamic Frontier: The Kingdom of Taqali, 1680–1898" (University of Wisconsin, 1982).

[14] Janet J. Ewald, "Experience and Speculation: History and Founding Stories in the Kingdom of Taqali, 1780–1935," *International Journal of African Historical Studies* 18, 2 (1985), 265–87.

Speculating about Taqali's place in the world informed my own historical reconstruction of the kingdom. I shared a general perspective with my Taqali informants: that Taqali stood at the center of a broader historical narrative and that at the core of Taqali history was the story of how warrior-kings arose and then maintained their power. The book that I wrote attempted to maintain this perspective, both examining the history of the greater Nile valley from the vantage point of Taqali and analyzing political dynamics within Taqali itself.

Fieldwork alone enabled me to make the Taqali highlands, a region which previously published works regarded as peripheral, into the center of a historical narrative. Until I left the field, very few records produced by people from Taqali existed outside the field of forces that created and acted on them; Taqali people had not created an archive. Indeed, some archives bore witness to events or personalities in Taqali, but their authors were outsiders who looked on Taqali as an almost legendary realm, tributary regime, or rebellious hinterland. Basing their work on such archival sources, historians of the Sudan had looked at Taqali out of the corners of their eyes; the kingdom was peripheral both to the men who, from the vantage point of riverain or savanna states, composed the documents which entered the archives and to the men who later worked in the archives.[15] Focusing on evidence from the field puts Taqali itself in the center of historical knowledge. Following the tracks that Taqali people themselves left depicts them as historical actors who struggled, with often unintended results, to find a safe place in the face of the dangers presented by life on the violent frontiers of the eighteenth and nineteenth centuries.

It is, of course, far too naive to speak of "Taqali people" as an undifferentiated group. Taqali was a kingdom, and all states rest on hierarchy and inequality between the rulers and the ruled. In the 1970s, men and women in al-Abbasiyya recognized this inequality by speaking of sultans and *ahl al-sudan,* or commoners. Putting the kings at the center of an historical narrative emerged unequivocally and with very little analysis from the narratives that the men and women of al-Abbasiyya—the descendants of the kings—related to me. I easily perceived, for example, how crises of succession within the royal house stimulated contenders for the kingship to behave in certain ways toward the traders and soldiers who represented the forces of the greater Nile valley.

The more difficult task was to detect and present highland subjects of the kings as historical actors. But a close reading and analysis of the oral narratives revealed that highlanders resisting royal power shaped politics in Taqali. Under the aegis of a variety of local leaders, the *ahl al-sudan* struggled to keep local land and labor out of the hands of the kings and their entourages. They succeeded in direct relation to the ability—largely based on location and topography—of their villages to defend themselves against the kings or raiders from the plains. Preventing the kings from gaining wide access to highland production, the *ahl al-sudan* forced the kings to

---

[15] For representative references to Taqali in some of the excellent monographs focusing on the riverain and savanna states, see P. M. Holt, *The Mahdist State in the Sudan, 1881–1898: A Study of Its Origins, Development, and Overthrow,* 2nd ed. (Oxford, 1970), 53–54; Richard Hill, *Egypt in the Sudan, 1820–1881* (London, 1959), 77; O'Fahey and Spaulding, *Kingdoms of the Sudan,* 64–65, 185; and Spaulding, *The Heroic Age in Sinnar,* 3. In a short article, Spaulding turns his attention to the Nuba hills which he nonetheless views in terms of their relationship to the kingdom of Sinnar. Jay Spaulding, "A Premise for Precolonial Nuba History," *History in Africa* 14 (1987), 369–74.

base a large part of their power on acting as warriors, hosts, or mediators in a regional setting. Highlanders who successfully insulated their villages from royal demands also unwittingly encouraged the kings to tighten their control over their own households and elaborate their domestic realm into the central institution of the state.

Finally, some of my knowledge about the Taqali kingdom emerged as I pondered the very nature of evidence from the field. That evidence included only a very few written documents. For the most part, Taqali's kings and their subjects chose to make and record their political relations in face-to-face confrontation, and by word of mouth. The preference for the spoken word itself provided evidence both for Taqali's internal political dynamics and its resistance to certain external forces. The characteristics of the spoken word reflected the realities of Taqali's political life. Like oral communication, political ties in Taqali were fluid, context-bound, and often ephemeral. Moreover, both kings and subjects generally valued ambiguity in political relations. And even if kings had wanted to issue documents, highlanders did not recognize their authority. The *ahl al-sudan* rejected writing, which presented itself in the form of Muslim clerics teaching Arabic literacy, as part of their rejection of the regional system which Arabic and Islam represented.[16]

The time after the moment in the middle closed as I eventually finished a monograph about the history of Taqali during the roughly two centuries preceding that moment. In the creation of historical knowledge, then, the moment in the middle came first. The engaged encounter of that moment afterwards sustained a more distanced analysis, which produced a history characterized by analyzing evidence itself as the result of historical forces; regarding the northeastern Nuba hills as a center rather than a periphery and highlanders as political actors; stressing process and ambiguity.

The book that I wrote now belongs to an archive. It is itself an historical artifact, the product of the field of human forces in the northeastern Nuba hills between 1977 and 1979. In its exact form, it could have resulted only from that time and place. My fieldwork produced historical knowledge deeply marked by the imprint of a particular moment in the middle when particular traces of the past emerged. At another moment, those traces would assume a different form; some might disappear while new traces might reveal themselves. A slightly or perhaps greatly different book would result.[17]

Knowledge resulting from fieldwork is thus contingent; it depends on a particular moment in the middle. But contingency does not invalidate it. Fieldworkers know—or ought to—that their particular historical knowledge represents not the only truth, but one of many possible truths. Nor does dependence on the moment in the middle separate fieldworkers from other historians. Fieldworkers indeed work as Marc Bloch enjoined all historians to work, moving from the present to the past carefully and self-consciously.[18] For fieldworkers, such care requires a constant awareness of the human forces that have shaped evidence before and during the moment in the middle.

---

[16] Janet Ewald, "Speaking, Writing, and Authority: Explorations in and from the Kingdom of Taqali," *Comparative Studies in Society and History*, 30, 2 (1988), 199–224.

[17] But such histories of the place where I worked are not immediately forthcoming. The peace and stability that helped bring me to the Sudan in 1976 ended in the 1980s. For the Sudanese, the moment in the middle between civil wars proved sadly short.

[18] Bloch, *The Historian's Craft*, 43–46, and *French Rural History*, xxvi–xxx.

9

A Double Exile: Extended African Residences and the Paradoxes of Homecoming

Richard M. Shain

Unspoken rules organize the fieldwork of North American Africanists. One of the most binding of these unarticulated regulations is an African residence limited to two years. While financial constraints partially determine the duration, North American cultural conceptions of fieldwork also play a major role. In the eyes of the profession, remaining in Africa more than two years to conduct research violates expected codes of behavior. When a researcher extends a stay overseas, many back "home" question whether the personal has not overtaken the professional.

Although this perception appears unduly judgmental, long research residences do present challenges for professional and personal growth. Many like myself who temporarily settled in Africa found that our academic and personal agendas overlapped. Although these multiple priorities meshed well while we were overseas, they made our "homecoming" problematic. Anyone who has lived and worked in another cultural environment expects to experience some disorientation upon return. However, I found that my professional dilemmas on coming back from eight years in Nigeria were far more complex than I had anticipated. They affected my emotional readjustment to North American life and threatened to curb my professional development.

The Long-Term Researcher as Exile

During my period of readjustment, I gained a clearer perspective on my long stay abroad. I initially remained in Africa because my position as a Nigerian university lecturer afforded me rare opportunities as an oral historian. My "insider" status enhanced my research program. However, I was not aware until my return of the full implications of my stay abroad. My long research residence constituted a self-imposed "exile."

The term *exile* is highly charged and it is crucial to enumerate the broad range of situations it identifies. A research "exile," for example, differs from the exile of political banishment or an artist's residence abroad. Political exiles, of course, leave impossible situations at home, usually involuntarily. A regime in power forces their uprooting. Once abroad, they contend with the complications of a precarious situation. Artists who relocate abroad manifest a highly ambiguous attitude towards their "home" cultures. They voluntarily leave their communities to escape a cultural climate they find confining and provincial.

Neither political positions nor artistic frustration, however, play a part in a research exile. While internal politics in the host country can abbreviate a research residence, politics at home do not get in the way of repatriation. Unlike an artist, a research exile does not go abroad initially for personal and aesthetic expansion; and, unlike many artists and political exiles, researchers rarely confront poverty. Their research grants and academic appointments ensure that they live comfortably and can effectively carry out their work.

Nevertheless, a long-term researcher still experiences the estrangements of exile. It is important to distinguish this estrangement from the culture shock of returning development workers or international volunteers. This group expects to be changed by their prolonged cross-cultural contact. However, academic researchers, particularly historians of Africa, are often caught unawares by the disorientation of homecoming. Some of this disorientation has its origins in graduate training which emphasizes intellectual and emotional detachment in the field. Historians are taught to avoid emotionally charged relationships with their subject in order to promote scholarly objectivity and ease the transition back into North American academic life. This avoidance of emotional involvement causes researchers to lose sight of how much their experiences abroad transform them intellectually.

I was primed for the emotional adjustments of homecoming. What took me by surprise, though, was a deepening intellectual anxiety. I came to recognize this uneasiness as part of the aftershocks of my self-imposed exile. My long research residence had changed me in more ways than I knew. My years in Nigeria, for example, expanded my awareness of the globalization of culture. While I was in Nigeria I wrote about this process with appropriate professional distance. When I returned to the United States, I realized I could not continue to write about this globalization from the sidelines. My long Nigerian stay had fundamentally altered my perceptions of the production of knowledge about Africa. This shift went beyond the theoretical plane. I became conscious that I was writing for a transnational audience. My scholarship began to address the predicaments of a readership divided between Africa and the rest of the world.

At Home Abroad: My Years in Nigeria

The challenges I faced on returning to America arose out of a fieldwork situation which encompassed the dual status of local professional and foreign student. Through a series of fortuitous accidents, I became part of Nigerian academia even before I began my historical research there. In 1978, I applied for a Fulbright dissertation research grant for Nigeria.[1] Because of an uncertain research climate, no one had been awarded a Fulbright to do work in Nigeria for several years. I needed a Nigerian university to support my research to have my application considered. In search of such a sponsor, I sent a packet about my research to a number of Nigerian history departments. I received a reply from the University of Jos offering me not only research backing but also a lectureship to replace a departing faculty member. I accepted the university's offer and soon was on my way to the Central Nigerian highlands.

Because of my lectureship at Jos, I was never a researcher on a full-time basis. However, straddling the Nigerian and North American academic worlds strengthened my research. In addition to formal research directed along standard North American lines, I also was carrying out a long-term informal research program. The longer I stayed in Nigeria, the more significant this informal research became. As I carried out my daily routine at the university, government offices, taxi parks, banks, drinking places, markets, food stalls, and dispensaries, Nigerians disclosed the idioms and languages they used to think and talk about the past.

Although this informal research resembled anthropological "participant observation," there were important differences. Anthropologists carefully choose fixed sites for their intercultural exchanges which limit the social roles they assume. My dual status as internal university lecturer and external researcher ensured that I had multiple points of contact with Nigerian society. I worked in numerous social arenas at once. The multidimensionality of my life made it impossible for me to limit myself to any one particular role.

Among these diverse roles, Nigerians most readily identified me with my academic position. The Etulo speakers, the subject of my historical research, saw me first and foremost as a lecturer from the University of Jos. My position enabled them to precisely situate me in Nigerian social and political terms.[2] My lectureship also reinforced my reputation as an "authority" on Central Nigerian history. The elders who tended to be nervous about unveiling Etulo's past, particularly to a young outsider, decided that my "expertise" compensated for my lack of maturity. Even more significantly, my teaching job meant I was far more accountable to the Etulo speakers than a visiting scholar would have been. I would not complete my work and vanish. When the community feared that my research was misleading or erroneous, they sought me out and voiced their concerns.

---

[1] My dissertation research dealt with the history of the Etulo of Central Nigeria. The Etulo are a small, riverain community whose language is related to Idoma and Egede. For two and a half centuries, they have had close ties with the peoples of the "Middle Belt" kingdom of Kwararrafa. My dissertation emphasized the construction of an Etulo identity, particularly how interregional relations and sacral kingship have provided a focal point for Etulo culture. See Richard M. Shain, *Water and Fire: A Cultural and Political History of the Etulo Speakers of Central Nigeria, c. 1630s–1890s* (Ph.D. dissertation, Johns Hopkins University, 1992). A Fulbright dissertation grant partially funded research in Nigeria between 1980 and 1982. Otherwise I was employed at the University of Jos as a lecturer in history and my salary covered my research expenses. Although archives were consulted at Kaduna and Ibadan, nine-tenths of my time was spent in the field in Etulo.

[2] In the 1980s, the University of Jos was recognized as the regional university of Nigeria's "Middle Belt," the region of many of Northern Nigeria's "minority" ethnic groups. Contemporary Etulo speakers identify themselves as belonging to the "Middle Belt." My affiliation added even more credibility to my research project.

My Nigerian university ties, first in Jos and then at the University of Cross River State, did more than enhance my research. They brought home to me the transnational implications of my work. While teaching or attending academic conferences, I was continually struck by the global reach of Nigerian history education. Nigerian historians resist the limitations of a singly Eurocentric or Afrocentric view of the world. When I served as chair of the history curriculum revision committee in my second post, I found myself supporting more local history courses while my Nigerian colleagues pushed for a greater emphasis on American and European topics. Similarly, my experiences as an external examiner[3] at three colleges of education showed that even at the community college level, Nigerian historians were oriented towards a global perspective.

This transnational orientation was particularly acute in the classroom. The irony of having an inexperienced North American teach Nigerian history to Nigerians was not lost on me or my students. For all of us, it was a source of much mirth, though little tension. In the United States, professors proclaim how much they learn from their students. In Nigeria, though, I did learn a tremendous amount from students. As I expected, they continually transmitted the details of their communities' past: genealogies, traditions of origin, and anecdotes about renowned leaders. Supervising senior research projects revealed the students' transnational language and method for representing their history. Their methodology, for example, incorporated elements of orality.[4] A particularly popular strategy used oral genres like foundation traditions as cues for formulaic reconstructions of the past.[5] Epistemologically, their projects reappropriated Western social science models not as tools to advance "theory" but as weapons in local and regional political contests. For example, Durkheim's distinction between mechanical and organic solidarity surfaced as a criteria for distinguishing between a "cultured" community and its uncouth neighbor. These projects represented serious historical investigations, yet they were different in form and function from anything I had seen produced at home.

My interactions with professional Nigerian historians further illustrated that academic history in Nigeria was developing along transnational lines. The length of my stay in Nigeria and the fact that I entered the system at a very low rank facilitated my integration into the Nigerian historical community. Nigerian academics were accustomed to senior North American scholars who secure a visiting appointment for a short time at a high rank. Younger expatriate historians like myself who entered Nigerian academia at the bottom and gradually worked their way up were a rarity. Indeed, my case was so novel many attributed my presence to the Central Intelligence Agency. Others, fortunately, were less suspicious. Slowly, I formed close friendships with the first postcolonial generation of Nigerian historians, scholars who had received most, if not all, of their training at home.

This postcolonial generation greatly influenced my historical writing. I was particularly impressed with their intellectual self-confidence and their ability to

---

[3] An external examiner is a one-person accreditation committee.

[4] For more on orality, see Walter Ong, *Orality and Literacy* (London, 1982) and Ruth Finnegan, *Oral Traditions and the Verbal Arts: A Guide to Research Practices* (London, 1992). Both Ong and Finnegan confine their analyses to oral literature rather than oral history.

[5] For an insightful treatment of formulaic constructions, see Elizabeth Tonkin, *Narrating Our Pasts: The Social Construction of Oral History* (Cambridge, 1991).

direct their work simultaneously to local and international concerns. An earlier generation of academic historians in the 1950s sought to prove to skeptical European readers that the Nigerian past was complex and multidimensional.[6] They wanted their Nigerian readers to appreciate the intellectual depth and aesthetic richness of African culture. After independence, a new cohort of Nigerian historians searched for a usable past that could contribute to the task of nation-building.[7] These historians had an ambiguous relationship with their non-African readers. While they wrote their monographs in impeccable academic prose and employed Western paradigms with consummate skill, an intellectual restlessness permeated their texts. As they strove to reconcile African "tradition" with European modernity, Western models of history writing became increasingly problematic for them. Yet for this generation of Nigerian historians to abandon these Western models would have been unthinkable. Their very ability to incorporate them attested to the decolonization of African intellectual life. Their work stood as a rebuke to a Western-exoticized Africa.

These transnational predicaments impinge far less on the current generation of Nigerian historians. Unlike their predecessors, they write primarily for an African readership. Shifts in international publishing and academic developments within Nigeria primarily account for this reorientation. Relatively plentiful opportunities once existed for postcolonial Nigerian historians to have their work appear abroad. Starting in the early 1980s, though, multinational academic publishers drastically cut back their African operations. With the scarcity of new publishing contracts abroad, local presses attempted to fill the void.[8] This increase in local book production has encouraged Nigerian historians to address more exclusively a local audience.

Developments within the academy further promote the localization of history writing. In the last twenty years, a number of new indigenous historiographic schools have emerged in Nigeria. The competition among them has meant that external approval has come to matter less. Moreover, with the expansion of higher education in the 1970s and 1980s, the historical community grew large enough to provide an audience for its own work. Nigerian authors no longer had to write for foreign readers.

Paradoxically, this localization of history writing coincided with the internationalization of Nigerian culture. The global market now encompasses Nigerian intellectual and cultural production. Books written by Chinua Achebe and Wole Soyinka are widely read and taught in the United States, and musicians Fela Anikulapo Kuti and King Sunny Ade are acclaimed in concerts around the world. Re-creations of Yoruba religion attract adherents in New York and Washington. Nigerian artists receive commissions to embellish North American university buildings. Most saliently, a recent diaspora of Nigerian academics to the Persian Gulf

---

[6] See, for example, K. Onwuka Dike, *Trade and Politics in the Niger Delta, 1830–1885* (Oxford, 1956) and S. O. Biobaku, *The Egba and Their Neighbors, 1842–1872* (Oxford, 1957).

[7] See, for example, E. J. Alagoa, *A Short History of the Niger Delta* (Ibadan, 1972) and J. F. A. Ajayi *Christian Missions in Nigeria, 1841–1891* (Evanston, 1965).

[8] I was production manager for one such venture in Jos—the Jos Oral History and Literature Texts. We published annotated collections of Nigerian oral traditions in editions of around one hundred copies. Our aim was to market these volumes internationally, but we found domestic demand was high.

region and North America has created transcontinental Nigerian cultural networks. This globalization of Nigerian culture has transformed the relationship between Nigerian history writing and the wider world. While Nigerians keep abreast of intellectual trends elsewhere and participate in transnational academic dialogues, many new developments abroad hold little interest for them. They have set their own impressive academic agendas independent of what transpires in North American and European seminar rooms.

Since I was living and working in Nigeria, it was inevitable that I would adopt some of these agendas. I was particularly excited by the younger historians' insertion of cultural politics into their work. I was attracted to their historical idioms and strove to incorporate them in my work. When I returned to North America I realized that these choices entangled me in my own transnational predicaments.

Abroad at Home: Infant, Victim, Tourist

Once back home, an Africanist researcher can find the familiar shockingly foreign. Commonplace activities like going to a laundromat or a post office become novelties. The array of consumer choices, for example, render every shopping trip an excursion into the exotic. An air of enchantment permeates the researcher's daily routines.

This thrill soon gives way to anxiety and alienation. Finding a comfortable professional niche proves elusive. Colleagues at home resent the "holier-than-thou" attitude of returnees or feel threatened by their unconventional career paths. Returning researchers also tend to make harsh judgments about colleagues' lack of commitment and expertise, adding to the tension.

The shock of reentry ultimately lessens. However, I would argue that the strains of reabsorption never entirely dissipate for the extended-residence-abroad researcher. Even after coming to terms with "home," the issues involved in reabsorption continue to influence professional development. Instead of being culturally rooted in both the United States and Africa, the returning researcher is no longer at ease in either place.

It is tempting to attribute this process of gradual estrangement to "reverse culture shock," to say that the returning long-term researcher passes through the four stages of culture shock identified by the anthropologist Kalervo Oberg.[9] On the surface, the exhilaration of reexperiencing one's society may resemble the excitement of beginning fieldwork when a researcher starts to "learn" another culture. The disillusionment with old friends and colleagues may be similar to Oberg's second stage of "irritation and hostility." Coming to grips with the demands of one's society may be roughly equivalent to Oberg's period of gradual adjustment when one learns how to function effectively in another culture. But this process of adjustment does not culminate in a fourth phase of biculturalism in which one moves with proficiency in two cultures.

Despite apparent analogies, my experience does not sustain Oberg's model. The chances of a research exile achieving bicultural fluency are small; no matter

---

[9] Kalervo Oberg, "Culture Shock: Adjustments to New Cultural Environments," *Practical Anthropology* (July–August 1960), 177–82.

how great the effort, this remains an elusive goal. Closer to the mark, Sidney Mintz has attempted to explain the bicultural predicament with a model of acclimation to the field which consists of three phases: "infant," "victim," and "tourist."[10] During the first months in the field, researchers have yet to learn the proper etiquette of their hosts. Their inexperience leads them to commit such gaffes as misunderstanding local social hierarchies, mispronouncing names and greetings, and miscuing dress codes. Often, the hosts overlook these transgressions in much the same way as they tolerate inappropriate behavior in children. They assume the researcher eventually will outgrow this awkwardness.

Most researchers move beyond this stage and function as partially integrated "strangers" in another culture. This marginal social position is fraught with difficulties. It underscores how inadequately any outsider can "know" another culture. Bombarded by complex and foreign signs, symbols, and gestures, researchers can become disoriented and, as a result, withdrawn and suspicious.

The partially assimilated researcher grapples with other challenges during this "victim" phase. Burgeoning friendships are particularly problematic. As Mintz observes, researchers love to be loved by those they encounter in the field. This need to be loved, particularly marked in North American researchers, can complicate fieldwork. Some researchers function under the illusion that being well-liked guarantees the collection of otherwise inaccessible data. The opposite can be the case. The harder some researchers try to be liked, the more amusing they often appear to their hosts; and laughable guests are not to be entrusted with privileged information.

According to Mintz's model, this "victim" awareness does not lead to bicultural fluency. Instead, researchers finally have to come to grips with the structural limitations of their position. No matter how deeply one enters another culture, the sense of belonging is compromised by the fact that the researcher can leave whenever it is convenient and return to his country of origin. With this option to pack up and go at will, the researcher resembles a tourist, albeit a well-informed, culturally sensitive one.

Research exiles must also renegotiate their relationships with their "home" cultures on their return. They have to relearn social behaviors, adjusting language and etiquette. I had to be very careful when I returned to my "home" university not to lapse into the harsh jocularity that characterizes social interactions in many parts of Nigeria. I also had to lower my voice and be less physically demonstrative. I found it particularly difficult to approach senior professors in an appropriate manner. In Nigeria, academic superiors are accorded "maximum" respect at all times. In the United States, such deference appears exaggerated or sarcastic.

Returning research exiles become vagabonds and lack a fixed address since it is extremely difficult while abroad to arrange for suitable housing at "home." As a result, most long-term researchers come home to no home and spend countless nights on the couches of family, friends, and colleagues. I was luckier than most. An old friend from Surinam ran something like a halfway house for disoriented Africanists in a run-down building near my old university. Despite this initial anchor, I grew increasingly skittish. I began to travel constantly, both locally and in-

---

[10] Sidney Mintz, "Infant, Victim, and Tourist: The Anthropologist in the Field," *Johns Hopkins Magazine* XXVIII, 5 (September 1977), 58.

ternationally. Some of this perpetual movement evoked the exhilarating restlessness of Nigeria. On another level, it reflected my anxiety that coming back was less a homecoming than a continuous visit.

This placelessness was heightened by an environment aesthetically foreign to me. In Nigeria, I had become accustomed to landscapes embodying historical and ritual meanings. By contrast, North American cities and suburbs resembled movie-set facades, a series of postcard images that seemed to elicit a touristic response. I felt more like a tourist in my own land the longer I stayed home. I realized I was in a state of always being abroad, whether in North America or Africa. Besides creating psychological impasses, this mind-set had implications for my historical writing. If I felt slightly out of place in both North America and Africa, for whom was my writing intended? Where was my implied reader?

Dilemmas of a Double Readership

Historians in North America tend to take their audience for granted. Most assume they are writing for other academic historians in the United States, particularly those with expertise in the same period and geographical area. Professional success depends on the esteem of this audience and the opinion of those outside the North American academy matters little. While they may cite the work of foreign researchers and be grateful for their interest and praise, most North American scholars never consider them potential readers of their work.

Even Africanists in recent years have been guilty of this neglect. The discipline has undergone a number of changes in the past three decades. African history writing in the United States has had to incorporate the methodologies of the wider history community. This synthesis has benefited the field by providing a common methodology that facilitates comparative analysis. In this process of establishing a common practice, African history has borrowed specialized languages. Many in the field have strongly criticized this discourse which appropriates terms and tropes from other disciplines.[11] As Roland Barthes observed, such languages are inherently "reductive and exclusionary" to such an intense degree they can be categorized as "terrorist."[12] Only a select band of initiates, trained in a few graduate programs, can use this language with any sophistication.

Returning long-term researchers are especially sensitive to the exclusionary nature of this discourse. Often well-versed in this language, they are ambivalent about using it. If their work is couched in North American terms, they risk alienating their African readership. Orienting their research towards predominantly African concerns means their work will confound their North American colleagues. Returning research exiles as a result are rarely prolific. They retreat to silence as they sort out these predicaments.

---

[11] This debate is not restricted to the history community. Similar controversies exist in literary studies. The journal, *Public Culture*, for example, devoted one of its issues to the debate surrounding Aijaz Ahmad's *In Theory* (December 1993). Ahmad argues that most poststructuralist thought is hegemonic in relation to non-European subjects. He especially faults the "post-structuralists" for theorizing about "Third World literature."

[12] Roland Barthes, "Taking Sides," in *Critical Essays*, trans. Richard Howard (Evanston, 1972), 163–70.

Identifying an implied reader represents a significant step in breaking this silence. However, given the transnational nature of a research exile's work, it is particularly difficult to specify an ideal reader. The three categories of readers described by Wolfgang Iser help to clarify this intractable problem: superreader, informed reader, and intended reader.[13] Superreader refers to a community of readers of varying ability whose common reactions are related to a text's meaning. The informed reader not only possesses sophisticated reading skills but also has the ability to monitor and control reactions during the processing of a text. The intended reader is implied by an author, a fictitious reader to whom the text is directed. Of the three, the intended reader most accurately describes the complex relationship between the writer, the audience, and the text for a returning long-term researcher. The intended reader concept accounts for mediating between one's own perspective, the implied reader's perspective, and the text itself.

When I first returned to North America, I assumed I belonged to a transnational intellectual community that would be receptive to my work. Despite my awareness of the differing orientations of North American and Nigerian researchers, I soon learned that more than separate research agendas divided the two groups. Of far greater significance were the differing relationships between author, reader, and text in the two historiographic traditions. In Nigeria, a community of superreaders, only some of whom are academic historians, have as active a role as a writer in creating a text's meaning. Many foreign scholars realize that their texts take on a life of their own in Africa and discover interpretations they never anticipated. In North America, highly-trained informed readers comprise the only audience for a historical monograph. As a result, they have more fixed meanings and a more restricted impact.

As my doctoral dissertation progressed, I recognized the elusive nature of this transnational readership. Identifying an implied reader seemed an insurmountable obstacle. Because my conception of my intended reader was so fragmented, my writing vacillated between different styles. Some of my early drafts were thick ethnographic descriptions so dense they were impenetrable. At another point, I saw my work as advocating the Nigerian cause in the United States. I dropped this advocacy when I remembered that Nigeria had no shortage of brilliant indigenous writers and academics to argue its case internationally. In other drafts, I employed an autobiographical voice to translate African historical experience into North American terms. However, the more I strove for authenticity, the more my writing sounded stilted. I then decided that theory would help extricate me from my stylistic dead ends. This option was intellectually stimulating for me but alienating for my readers.

Although this dilemma of a double readership did not keep me from completing my doctorate, it is implicit in my dissertation and continues to influence my work. Attempting to reconcile the differing priorities of reading communities in the United States and Nigeria has blurred for me the boundaries between "home" and "abroad." Like many former research exiles, I find myself writing outside my national academic tradition without having been fully integrated into another culture. In this in-between space, "home" becomes an elusive state of mind where the local and the foreign intersect. At this crossroads lies a double exile.

---

[13] Wolfgang Iser, *The Act of Reading: A Theory of Aesthetic Response* (Baltimore, 1978), 30–38.

10

Venture into Tio Country

Jan Vansina

"*Other Experience:* 1963–1964 Fieldwork: Tio (Congo Brazzaville)" is a laconic line in a curriculum vitae, a typical entry in such a document.[1] Behind such a terse and bland statement there always lurks a complicated story that is rarely told in academic print. After all, academics are only interested in the results of research, not in the story of how they were obtained. Moreover, to tell the hidden history of any fieldwork is difficult because the tale revolves around several plots which mix several established literary genres. It includes an episode in the ongoing film of history of the local people, a snippet of the researcher's own private life history, an often epic account of how the researcher triumphed over practical obstacles or failed to do so, a tale of how the researcher was eventually adopted by the local people, and a tale (perhaps along the lines of how the ugly duckling grew into a radiant swan) of how the researcher's first vague glimmer of the subject studied became the confident understanding presented in his or her authoritative account. Among these topics perhaps the dominant theme should be the last one, for it is an account that allows others to assess the quality of the academic results brought back from the field. Hence, this story tells of a short spell of fieldwork among the Tio and how its first vague goals ultimately turned into social history.[2]

Opening Gambit

My wife, Claudine, and I arrived in Brazzaville on Friday, October 11, 1963, three years after the independence of Congo and after the coup that had swept away the neocolonial government of Congo during the "glorious days" of August. Our goal was to do

---

[1] J. Vansina, *The Tio Kingdom of the Middle Congo, 1880–1892* (London, 1973) is the main publication that resulted from this research. This essay is mainly based on the original fieldnotes (notebooks, diagrams, and sketches). Fieldwork was financed by a small unsolicited grant from the Social Science Research Council (1963).

[2] The term "social history" was actually used (*Tio Kingdom,* xvi) even though it was then an anomaly. This instance shows how an ethnography rooted in a given time does almost automatically become social history.

fieldwork and our luggage consisted of eighty pounds of camping materials. We had a good idea of the practical side of fieldwork because Claudine had been born and reared in tropical Africa and I had years of earlier fieldwork experience elsewhere in the area. We had about six months and the goal was to gather the traditions relating to an old and hitherto unstudied major kingdom. There were two of these in Congo, both known to Europeans from the sixteenth century onwards: Loango on the coast, and the "kingdom of Makoko" (the Tio kingdom) north of Brazzaville. I had no doubts that rich oral materials going back to 1500 or earlier were to be collected, and expected these data to illuminate the available written reports. So, on the day of our arrival we conferred with the geographer attached to the local French research institute, and the next day decided to study the Tio kingdom. Its first advantage was that it seemed to be the oldest kingdom. Moreover, Tio ethnography and the Tio language had never been studied. It should be possible in the time available to complete an ethnographic survey and a sketch of the language in addition to a preliminary collection of very ancient traditions. We would gather as much as we could and return later for in-depth research. The Tio were also attractive from a practical standpoint. We could not afford a car and the Tio capital, Mbe, was only one hundred miles away from Brazzaville. A Land Rover from the research institute would drive us up there and then we would stay there for the whole period.

Everything went smoothly and very fas. By Tuesday we had visited Mbe for a few hours and found it to be a large village isolated on the empty and endless level of the high plateau of Mbe, a sea covered with short grasses. We met the ruling king and I hired a local French-speaking youth, Bernard, as an assistant. On Friday we were back, and work began on the 19th. We were lucky to find people finishing the walls of a small one-room shop on the main square and were able to rent it. For the first week or two we had a room in the dispensary, away from town, while they were finishing the building. Claudine immediately found a basketweaver from whom she ordered a huge basket for storage and mats for the floor and, inspired by the well-known practice in Rwanda, also commissioned him to build rounded partitions for rooms. That caused intense interest because the Tio only build on straight lines. Nearly all adult villagers came to visit this strange installation and were received with the customary wine and kolanuts.[3] In return we walked during the first evenings from one yard to the other as people were sitting for a chat around their fires. Soon everyone knew us by sight. Almost from the very first day Claudine began to sketch objects, something that greatly intrigued people. Onlookers would see how the pencil made a pattern that became the object sketched. They thought it was great and soon began to bring their favorite object to be portrayed.

Fitting In

We were certainly odd. At first no one believed my name, which was understood as *va nsina* (sit down), a phrase that happened to be the refrain in a then

---

[3] In those days, it was deemed important to reward persons interviewed not with pay, but with a gift standard for the culture. This happened to be two kolanuts and a glass of wine. But soon it became evident that almost everyone preferred the equivalent in money. Hence the kolanuts and wine became a sum in francs. With the exception of Lipie, whose august status allowed for more, all other persons were paid the same amount, however long or short, however interesting or dull their contribution was.

very popular song on the radio. Even women would interrupt their work on the fields to ask my name, laugh, and demand to see my passport to make sure their leg was not being pulled. Clearly we were not the usual Europeans. The Tio knew of itinerant traders, missionaries, and tourists from Brazzaville, coming of a Sunday to see them as "folklore" and to admire the butterflies for which the river a few miles away was famous. They also had seen at least two previous ethnographers who had stayed for a day and a night each time, and they remembered the roles of former administrators from the recent colonial past. Moreover, most of the adults had spent time in Brazzaville where they had met Europeans in a host of occupations. But we were different. We were not French; we stayed on and on; we were poor because we had no car and no machinery, not even a radio; we were soon eating whatever food was on sale locally; Claudine was not fussy and evidently quite used to a life "in the bush"; I was diligently learning the language, half a day every day and on the main square (people did check up on the progress—or lack of progress—I made); and we were walking around a lot. Indeed, a week or so after my arrival, the resident rural policeman came to complain to me that I was running around too much and too far away so that he could not follow me. He explained that he had been entrusted by the authorities to report regularly on my activities to the security services. From then on, I wrote his reports, so that he did not have to trail me everywhere. As our routine developed and it became clearer what exactly we were interested in, and capable of, our roles also became better defined. In some ways we were much like the local schoolteacher, a Congolese from another region, who also lived in Mbe day in and day out, with whom we got along very well.

On the other hand, we were normal people in many ways. We were a married couple, and it was soon known that our small son was with his grandparents in Europe. We lived in the village and shared the concerns of everyone about shortages of water and food. Mbe society was sharply divided by age, gender, and ward affiliation. Because we were married and because I dealt mostly with subjects of interest to the older people in town, we were grouped with them, rather than with the mostly unmarried and "irresponsible" youth. The separation and conflict between the sexes was particularly strong in Mbe. Women and men lived apart from each other the whole day; women worked much more than men and felt exploited as a result, especially in comparison with the younger unmarried men. They expressed their frustration in their own public rituals and in court cases as well as in gossip. The level of hostility and suspicion was such that it was improper for unrelated men and nubile married women to even chat with each other for more than two or three minutes. This applied to me as well, and I could only interview two very old women in Mbe. As Claudine did not understand much Tio and very few women had any French, they did not spend much time talking either, but Claudine did observe women's activities around their homes on our "street" much more than I could have done. Mbe was divided in four wards, each inhabited by a family group.[4] My assistant, Bernard, was the elder son of Ngateo who headed the by far most powerful and largest ward of Mbe. In a sense we were "owned" by this group, because I paid a salary to one of its men, a fact that gave rise to some jeal-

---

[4] For a sketch map, see *Tio Kingdom*, 506.

ousy.[5] But we lived in another ward and although I interviewed Ngateo often, I conversed just as much with the middle-aged and older men of the other wards, and they were just as helpful to me as Ngateo was. Evidently, the people of Mbe soon identified us as belonging to a one-house ward of our own.

Obviously, we never learned exactly what people thought of us at each stage of our stay, nor which roles they had assigned to us, but by December we were accepted as innocuous and perhaps useful, especially by the older people whom I was constantly interviewing about old times and court cases. The sign of our acceptance was that we were now keyed into the local gossip and a month or so later even warned about the importunities of the European Sunday tourists. It helped that the latter on more than one occasion included us and our house in their folkloric sights and that we had to ward them off just as much as the Tio did. I was also admonished by the tale about researchers in Brazzaville. They were "Frenchmen" who busily wrote on paper, then took the plane back to Paris and threw their notes out the window, for no one had ever seen, let alone read, what the results of all that writing had been! They wanted me to make the Tio known, preserve their memories on paper, and send the printed results to Mbe for them to read.[6]

Life in Mbe

Most of our time at Mbe was spent in routine. Early every weekday Bernard would appear and we would be off to interview one or another older person for an hour or two, while Claudine did the housework[7] and then took her special basket-stool to go and sketch. Meanwhile, the women were in the fields and most of the men were busy with their work in or out of the village. The front yard of our house gave us a splendid view of the main square and all the people who were coming or going between the parts of the village and on the way to or from the fields. In the early afternoon the women returned and everybody turned in for a siesta. Claudine and I, however, went out to the river more than a mile away and twelve hundred feet lower than the plateau to swim before the women came down in chattering swarms to bathe and fetch their water supply. After our return we pottered around the village or did small chores. Later in the afternoon, I either went with Bernard to another interview or sometimes went around by myself to watch any goings-on. When the weather was fine, we stayed most evenings to chat under the starry skies in our front yard, just as other people did. When it rained, we went to sleep, just like everyone else. On Sundays, no formal work was done. Everyone stayed around in the village and relaxed. The older people slept late and visited each other, the children played in the streets, and the young men, dressed in their best finery, strutted about on the square to be ogled by the young women. Usually I spent part of the day checking notes or tabulating statistics, while Claudine sketched.

---

[5] A letter from the *chef de canton* Olala Ngandzion dated January 27 defending *"mon fils"* Bernard asserted this.

[6] Although *The Tio Kingdom* was published in English, a copy was sent to Mbe. Ten years later, a group of young Tio academics began to translate it into French for publication in Brazzaville itself.

[7] Although we had hired a servant, Claudine cooked and did the housework.

The urban reader may well think that such a life must have been very boring. After all, what else but placid routine happens in a remote village? What unusual events can ever happen there? In fact, a lot transpired. There was the odd truck that arrived in the middle of the night to halt on the square, where the driver was soon met by the sleepy congregation of the whole village to tell them the gossip from Brazzaville. I will always remember the announcement that the Americans were about to hide the moon with a Coca Cola sign, a garbled version of the moon-landing program. This greatly upset everyone because the waxing and the waning of the moon regulates all fertility. But, apart from such trucker gossip, there were special events of great local importance. We witnessed and played a modest role as part of the public in many of these. The following summary lists the major events that occurred during our stay; most special events were related to illness and death, and to a lesser extent with birth and marriage. During these rituals or court cases, the whole settlement acted very much as if it were a single family. But the summary also reveals that Mbe was not wholly immune from national politics, and in particular not from the turmoil then caused in Brazzaville by the struggle between revolutionary youth and state administrators.[8]

CHRONOLOGY OF SPECIAL EVENTS: OCTOBER 18, 1963–APRIL 1, 1964[A]

October 20	Woman died at Ngabe and is praised in song at Mbe
November 18	Lightning strikes school, special exorcism
24	Learn about assassination of John F. Kennedy and Lee Harvey Oswald from people in Mbe
26	Public announcement by Mbiinu Mbiinu about lightning and need to clean royal tombs
December 5	Public announcement by Ookondzaadza against witchcraft related to the lightning
8	Elections, voting at school
12	Death of a child
13	Burial of the child
28	Birth
29	Public meeting on the return of bridewealth and accusations of witchcraft
30	Women ordered by the revolutionary youth to clean the village square as part of a national campaign inspired at Brazzaville[b]
30–31	First case in outbreak of epidemic of measles
30	Decision to have *itsuuwa*, a spectacular, complex healing ritual for Catherine, a wife of the king, herself of royal extraction, who suffers from tuberculosis. Nine-day public ritual begins.
31	Public ball for the elders on New Year's Eve
January 18	Catherine leaves *itsuuwa* house; the cure was a failure
18	Court: divorce case
22–24	Court: Kyeliko's divorce
26–27	Court: divorce of the king
29	Letter from Brazzaville about Julienne, a child treated there for complications of measles

---

[8] Cf. P. Bonnafé, "Une Classe d'âge politique: La J.M.N.R. de la République du Congo-Brazzaville, *Cahiers d'Études Africaines* 8, 31 (1968), 327–68.

February	1	Court: Kyeliko's divorce
	3	Public announcement by Mbiinu Mbiinu of a political denunciation of the *chef de canton* of Ngabe by John Doe from Mbe
	3	Court: Kyeliko's divorce
	4	Julienne returns from Brazzaville's hospital
	4	Court: Oyo's adultery case
	6	Exorcism ritual for Julienne
	8	Another exorcism ritual for Julienne
	8	Court: mediation in a marriage dispute
	10	Ookondzaadza's public speech against witches concerning Julienne
	13	Court: Oyo's adultery case
	14	Death and burial of Julienne
	14	Death of Catherine and public grief
	15	Birth
	15	Public wake and construction of a regal catafalque for Catherine
	16	Spectacular burial of Catherine, filed by Brazzaville television as "folklore"
	19	Death and immediate burial of a boy who showed the signs of a contagious disease
	21	Illness of an insane wife of the king living near Brazzaville announced
	22	Announcement of another serious measles case
	23	Exorcism for the measles case
	24	Exorcism for the insane wife
	25	Public announcement about witchcraft in yet another serious measles case
	26	Public announcement about witchcraft in yet another serious measles case
	27	Court: a marriage settlement at Imbããw [c]
	28	Two exorcism cases for ill people at Imbããw
February 29– March	1	Court: bridewealth return at Imbããw [d]
	1	Healing ritual by major medicine man at Imbããw
	1	Court: marriage settlement at Imbããw
	4	Spectacular healing rituals at Imbããw
	5	Spectacular healing rituals at Imbããw
	22	Revolutionary youth or "gorillas" from Brazzaville invade Mbe to demonstrate against the king. This would lead to a political coup from Brazzaville on April 20 and the installation of a new king.
	24	Consecration of a family shrine
	24	*Itsuuwa* for an angina case
	25	Public denunciation by Mbiinu Mbiinu of witches

Notes to Chronology:

[a] Visits to Mbe by Tio from elsewhere (quite often), Sunday tourist daytrippers from Brazzaville (several in January), and trips by three researchers (not connected with us) in January, February, and March are excluded.

[b] Later, almost every Saturday saw some action inspired by them, but directed by the oldest leaders of the village.

[c] We were then staying in the tiny village of Imbããw, twenty miles from Mbe.

[d] Proceedings in *Tio Kingdom*, 527–39. On request, I acted as court recorder on this occasion.

The Shaping of the Research Program

On arrival in Mbe, I did not know what I would find there. After all, we had chosen to live there precisely because so little was known about the Tio. So I started out in a stereotyped way: to obtain a first overall sketch of Tio society and its language. In the morning, Bernard and I sat down to study the language, progressing from the most elementary features of phonemes to the structure of nouns and sentences. This would be the pattern for most days until I had a whole sketch of Tio grammar and a substantial vocabulary two months later. The first afternoons we discussed kinship terminology. As soon as it could be arranged, an afternoon was spent at town meetings. At the first of these I explained again (this had already been discussed on the preliminary visit of October 15) what research I planned to do and then asked standard ethnographic questions about social structure. Nearly all the ward leaders and other elders assisted at first, but they left most of the speaking to Ngateo with only occasional comment by others. The next four sessions took place at Ngateo's and dealt with generalities of economics, political structure, religion, and the life cycle. Time was also spent walking around in the village and in the fields and I began to draw up a provisional plan of the village and its surroundings. We also borrowed a moped to visit a famous abandoned site miles away and a small village beyond it. I took a roll or two of pictures, but then the camera jammed, and henceforth we were to rely on Claudine's drawings. Those really attracted people and almost from the beginning they began to bring out unusual objects to be drawn.

By the last days of October these preliminaries were finished. I had a bird's eye view now of the Tio way. Now my task was to turn the generalized normative statements I had been given into something more concrete. So I set out to make a census and record genealogies, and to use these to make sense of the social patterns of settlement in the wards. I could now begin to interview other leading people besides Ngateo about points that had come up earlier. Finally, the time was also ripe to inquire into the traditions of the kingdom. So far, all I had been told was that the children and grandchildren of kings were keepers of these traditions. Now, however, it became soon apparent that no one seemed to know anything about kings before Iloo, the one who had signed the treaty with Pierre de Brazza in 1880, although I was told a good deal about Iloo's successors. There were also some stories about a culture hero who lived in a misty, distant past. Perhaps, I thought, this was so because no one wanted to broach the topic before the king had set the tone. Hence, I secured an appointment with him for November 11 and was promised that he would then tell me the story of all the kings. Almost from the outset of this interview, however, it became only all too evident that the king knew no more than anyone else. Late-sixteenth- and seventeenth-century written sources mentioned that a people called Jaga or Yaka had then provoked major political upheavals in and around the kingdom. In order to shake off the king's reticence, I mentioned them and stated that they had played a major part in the past history of the Tio. What did he know about them? He hesitated and replied, "The Yāā have been here; they drove a part of the population away towards the Kasai."[9] Even as he spoke, it was obvious to me that he was making it up; he really knew nothing.

---

[9] Notebook I, 171.

There was no royal historical tradition here, and hence the rationale for my research project was no more. It was suddenly clear that a coherent Tio historical consciousness only began with Iloo. A little later, I even found out how and why this was so. Indeed, on November 29, the king would confess that he did not know the Yāā. "It was the Mpfuninga who had moved away towards the Kasai."[10] With that realization on November 11, the first phase of my research in Tio history screeched to a halt.

What now? Just gather material for an ethnographic survey? The first glimmer of another project came to me later that same day. It was then common practice in social anthropology to distrust general normative statements. Hence, one looked for concrete information. Ask not how much bridewealth is to be paid, ask how much was paid for the marriage of a sister, a mother, or a grandmother. Having already gathered the normative earlier, I was now beginning to hunt for just that concrete data. At the same time the great weakness of ethnographic surveys was that they were atemporal. Whatever the point in time referred to by each concrete bit of information had been, it was rubbed out from the overall description which was cast in an ethnographic present as permanent as God in heaven. Was it not possible to pinpoint the date of each concrete occurrence and eventually to reconstruct a panorama of the Tio way of life that would be valid for the same dated period in the past, say for the same generation? The stumbling block here was, however, that anthropologists were adamant about their belief that only direct participant observation allowed one to construct a valid ethnography. Hence, an ethnography for any earlier period was impossible for lack of direct observation by a trained anthropologist. Was this not just professional prejudice? Surely, this axiom could be challenged. Was not social history an ethnography in the past tense? So I dreamed of painstakingly reconstructing a social panorama valid for the earliest possible generation, perhaps the time of King Iloo, two generations before the current one to which fifty- or sixty-year-old people belonged.

A few days later (November 14) my formal census of Mbe was finished.[11] The town counted 328 inhabitants, 168 of them adults. Each inhabitant was now firmly placed socially (in a genealogy), in space (in a particular ward and spot in the ward), and by rough relative age (genealogy). It now became possible to systematically interview at least every middle-aged or old man. Given the latent war between the sexes in Mbe, only two of the older women, however, agreed to be interviewed, although we found more volunteers in Ngabe.

As I began to inquire even more pointedly for concrete "cases," we slid inevitably into personal reminiscences, then into bits of life histories to date these, and then into the wider historical context to find an absolute date. In doing this, the history of the kings gradually turned into a history of the families in Mbe. Research that had hitherto focused on an alien historical framework, the history of kings, now tapped the genuine historical consciousness of the Tio. Our interest in material culture fitted in well. The Tio saw objects as monuments from the past in the present, and they delighted in Claudine's sketches. Such objects sometimes provoked spontaneous reminiscences. In addition, they provided us with a solid

---

[10] Notebook II, 98.
[11] *Tio Kingdom*, 503.

scene in which to imagine those bits of life history which appeared during interviews. Yet weeks later I still felt uneasy about the possibilities of this "ethnography of the past." It seemed as if the research was drifting, as if I were collecting antiquarian curiosities here and there without any further rationale. The turning point came on December 11 during an interview with one of the oldest women of Mbe, Abili Ndyōō. For the first time I asked her directly about concrete childhood memories about work and crops, the layout of their village, marriage proposals, inheritance, and bridewealth. She lit up. Her spirited answers and vivid vignettes from a fairly well-dated past utterly convinced me that I was on the right track. From that day onwards, most interviews turned into rich reminiscences. I had finally learned how to prompt people to tell us about significant memories in their past. At the same time, Claudine and I became enough a part of village life to take part in its social dramas. The health crises and the rituals accompanying them taught us how the Tio perceived and struggled to ensure their physical survival, while the court cases revealed the sometimes sordid and bitter tensions as groups fought for relative advantage within the community. In each instance, the unique concrete detail of such events greatly widened my horizon and enriched later interview conversations. For me, the high-water mark came when I spent a long evening and two full days (January 21–23) conversing with Lipie, a gaunt, gnarled giant of a man, the high priest of the kingdom, who was visiting a friend of his in Mbe. He was a person so old that he remembered the daily life when de Brazza arrived in 1880. Each of my tentative queries unleashed a flood of reminiscences, a flood which I no longer had to interrupt for clarification. I had learned enough to follow him in his wandering through his memories.

Throughout this phase, however, I also kept the issue of representativity firmly in mind. It was not enough to converse even with all mature men in Mbe and occasional passersby. We had to go further. So we also talked to people in the hamlets around the town and managed to spend ten days in Ngabe, twenty-five miles away. Ngabe was Mbe's rival on the Congo River. Its colonial history had been very much intertwined with that of Mbe and it was from Ngabe that the most notorious Tio politician of the colonial age, Queen Ngalifourou, had lorded it over the country.

By the last days of January, the second phase of research was ending. The linguistic sketch and the gathering of a whole series of social statistics were coming to a close. A cornucopia of data about Tio life around 1900 was available. It was time for a third phase. I foresaw that this would consist in systematically cross-checking all the information I had gathered from one person with the reminiscences of all other known persons of the same age, and would begin around February 20.[12] But first we should live a week or two in an isolated, tiny village lost on the plateau, twenty miles away from Mbe and even further from other settlements, to counterbalance the "view from the center" which Mbe provided. There was also an opportunity to accompany the geographer of the French research institute in Brazzaville on a visit more than a hundred miles away to the place which was believed to have been the cradle of the kingdom and interview people there. Then we planned to visit another famous site which, according to the Tio in Mbe, had

---

[12] Letter to my parents, January 30, 1964.

been the hub of the kingdom before it moved to Mbe, perhaps in the eighteenth century. After that, we could start the cross-checking phase which was to last a month or so. Then we could leave Mbe and spend two to three weeks at Brazzaville to read colonial archives to establish a context for the colonial period before catching the plane on May 1. All went as planned except for the visit to the second historical site. We did not go there because the geographer with whom we were traveling cut his trip short and returned to Brazzaville.

On April 2, we distributed all our household goods, said our good-byes, and left for Brazzaville. Bernard continued to record local news and plots of Tio tales during the next three months. The colonial archives which I wanted to consult were then housed at the French embassy at Brazzaville. but after the first morning there, a suspicious diplomat denied us further access because we were of foreign nationality. As it was impossible to return to Mbe without equipment, we spent the last three weeks of our stay in the country working in a library. I also wrote a systematic provisional sketch of our findings. The results were reassuring. Although we had only spent five and a half months on the plateau, they showed that we had gathered a reasonably full record of social life in Mbe before and around the turn of the century. But would these data by themselves suffice to write more than a sketchy social history of the Tio? I certainly could not use observations about rituals and procedures common in 1963–1964 directly to reconstruct life around 1900. I had hopes that some of the earliest archival materials would throw light on this question, but I had no access to them, and that was that.[13]

A year later, a most improbable event occurred. I received a letter from Professor Brunschwig in Paris telling me that a huge quantity of de Brazza's papers had been donated to the French archives by one of his descendants. These included diaries of his travels, the existence of which had hitherto remained totally unknown. As he was about to edit these for publication, he wanted me to go through them to provide "ethnographic notes."[14] The conjunction of the fieldwork and the diaries proved to be a goldmine. The data from the fieldwork not only provided a context for the diaries, but specific remembrances about internal Tio politics of that time were recorded in the diaries. The reminiscences and even observations of rituals and courts made in 1963–1964 illuminated the written record from the 1880s and were in turn illuminated by it. Even de Brazza's seemingly innocuous sentences describing the landscape or the layout of a village were pregnant with information about crops and patterns of family residence for one who had gathered reminiscences about these features. If anyone doubts how useful historical fieldwork can be for the interpretation of a written record, they should study these editions. The diaries of de Brazza are not unique. For instance, a diligent library search eventually turned up records of many other visitors among the Tio between 1880 and 1892 besides de Brazza, and these texts too acquire a whole new dimension in the con-

---

[13] Later, the archaeologist J. P. Emphoux was able to send us photographs of a few relevant colonial documents from this archive.

[14] H. Brunschwig, "La négociation du traité Makoko," *Cahiers d'Études Africaine* 5/1, 17 (1965), 5–56; "Les Cahiers de Brazza (1880–1882)," *Cahiers d'Études Africaines* 6/2, 22 (1966), 157–227; and *Brazza l'explorateur. L'Ogooué, 1875–1879* (Paris, 1966). See also C. Coquery-Vidrovitch, *Brazza et la prise de possession du Congo (1883–1885)* (Paris, 1969).

text of the fieldwork data. Eventually the social history of the Tio I had envisaged would be written after all and dated 1880–1892, the generation of Iloo.[15]

Epilogue

The publication of *The Tio Kingdom* gave rise to a polemic in *Cahiers d'Études Africaines* that began when C. Vidal dismissed it as an "ethnography in the imperfect tense." It was flawed because it pretended to reconstruct a social history for a past period. Answering several rebuttals to her critique, she summed up her main objection as follows:

> Precisely: J. Vansina does too much, says too much about the Tio kingdom, he says all that can be imagined about such a society, he knows all . . . after having spent only seven months in the field. That is why the bride is too beautiful.

and

> If I am to believe the experience of J. Vansina a few months in the field have been enough to dissipate the obscurities left in (or perhaps constructed in) the written record.[16]

How does one answer this charge? In general, one could say that the success of fieldwork cannot be reduced to the length of time spent in the field. A long time spent in the field is not a guarantee of success. Previous experience of fieldwork matters. It matters how one lives and what one does there. If one stays in comfortable lodgings and tours around to collect more or less formalized traditions, it may take a very long time. It matters how much effort one puts into learning the local language. Last but not least, the specific context in which the host society finds itself during the stay of the fieldworker matters. But nevertheless, five and a half months is a very short time indeed. After all is said and done, how is it possible that so much was learned in so short a time?

First, the place was favorable. Very few people live on the huge plateau of Mbe. Only 66 men and 102 women lived in Mbe, while all the villages for fifty miles around Mbe including Ngabe (28 men and 38 women) together contained only another 82 men and 120 women. This small population explains why it was possible to obtain a whole series of quantitative materials about everyone, especially in Mbe, and also why an unusually high percentage of the population could be interviewed (e.g., over 40 percent of all men in Mbe). More importantly, the small population made it possible to have face-to-face contact with everyone and

---

[15] But even as late as 1968 I remained worried about possible anachronisms: "Yet it is clear that I cannot take facts from 1963, project them back to 1880, and then rediscover them again with great glee, as has frequently been done. Obviously, this magician's trick of extrapolation will not do, nor can a coherent account of Tio society and culture for 1880 be given by the oral or written data from [sic!] that period." "How the Kingdom of the Great Makoko and Certain Clapperless Bells Became Topics of Research," in L. P. Curtis, Jr., ed., *The Historian's Workshop: Original Essays by Sixteen Historians* (New York, 1970), 233. Yet the manuscript of *The Tio Kingdom* was completed by Spring 1970. In it I asserted, "Still fieldwork was more of a necessary precondition than a direct source about the way of life seventy years before" (p. 23)

[16] C. Vidal, "Quand la mariée est trop belle . . . ou plaidoyer pour la tradition orale," *Cahiers d'Études Africaines* 17/2–3, 66–67 (1977), 378.

to easily identify all those who could contribute to the study. This is a far cry from the situation to which Vidal refers, namely Rwanda where Vidal and I had both worked.[17] Rwanda is a country which counted nearly three million inhabitants around 1960. A second favorable feature in this case was the frequency with which the Tio traveled. This explains how we could interview so many people from faraway places in Mbe, despite the fact that we had no car: the people came to us. And so despite our relative immobility, in the end only 29 of 67 people interviewed lived in Mbe and nearly all those who lived in Mbe had lived elsewhere as well. Hence, the data gathered were valid not just for the plateau of Mbe but also for the bigger neighboring plateau of Ngo.

The timing of the research was also favorable. Congo had just undergone its post-independence revolution. The population was freer than it had been earlier and less harassed by the authorities. The latter were only beginning to build constraints of their own on the population. There was an air of freedom about. Moreover, we could not be confused with colonial agents anymore, yet the people still felt that to have "white people" was potentially useful. They hoped that we could do something for the recognition of Tio culture. They suffered from being viewed by the Brazzavillois as an odd folkloric remnant in the new republic. For their part, the administrative authorities were not worried about this possible result of our research because Tio ethnicity was not then the highly charged political question it was to become a decade later.

Previous experience certainly helped us considerably. We came with the essentials we needed, we could be whisked out of Brazzaville in record time, and we followed the right protocol in announcing our stay and explaining what we were about. Experience counted in the choice of a place to stay smack in the middle of the village for all to see and for us to see all. We also knew in general what village life in Central Africa was like. I had had much experience in conducting interviews, and knew not to pursue an unwanted topic or one that seemed strange or silly to my interlocutor, to wait patiently for unsolicited and unexpected information, and to recognize expressions of enthusiastic recollection when they came. Moreover, there were two of us, and four eyes and ears are better than two. True, we also were somewhat handicapped: we had no tape recorder, camera, or car, hence we could not record complete conversations, photograph or film special events, nor drive to all the places of interest we learned about. Then also there had been no time to do the necessary library research first, nor to prepare for learning the Tio language. But even handicaps have their advantages: the local people liked that we were just as dependent on occasional transport as they were, they relished the feeling that they heard the news over the radio and we did not, and the sketches were a big success. But the lack of bibliographical information had no advantages. I don't believe those who hold that this keeps one's mind unsullied and fresh for the wonders of discovery. All I know is that it certainly prevented me from asking a series of pertinent and probing questions.

Even all those favorable circumstances do not really explain why almost everyone was so helpful to us and why everything went so well. I don't know why

---

[17] Vidal, "Quand la mariée," 378n.1. Her comment, "where J. Vansina spent some time [*fit un séjour*], a few years ago," betrays either her lack of information or deliberate ill will. The phrase implies a short stay rather than the three years I spent there.

but the fact was that people were quite forthcoming and delighted to teach us about their way of life. Of course, they also expected us to learn, and that kept us on our toes as they were in the habit of more or less discreetly checking our progress, and not just in my understanding of the language. I will never forget my embarrassment when, early during our stay, a middle-aged man was walking with me to the fields perhaps two miles away and kept pointing to various plants, mostly grasses, saying their names and having me memorize those. Halfway through, he began to give me names for clusters of different plants in the same fashion. All went well until we returned. We were barely on the way back when he stopped, pointed to a plant, and asked me for its name. He kept doing that all the long way home. To me, one blade of grass looked like any other, one shrub like another, and I miserably failed my test. At least, I was much better with the stuff anthropologists learn about, such as bridewealth, preferential marriages, death payments, or witches. But we were not always the pupils. The Tio were just as curious about the ways of the Europeans as we were about theirs, and they often asked questions like: How did people pick marriage partners? What was dowry? Could one marry first cousins? What sort of clans were there? To some extent then conversations became a genuine exchange of information and not just one-way debriefings. Perhaps it was this more than any other feature which explains why we felt quite comfortable in Mbe and people felt comfortable with us.

No doubt Fortune smiled on us in Mbe. We did accumulate a large amount of information. Yet when we left Congo, I was still uncertain as to how useful the field data would be. The quality of the information was good. Most of it was based on reminiscences and most of these tallied with other reminiscences from other people. But would the data suffice by themselves to paint a reliable and reasonably full picture of Tio life, say before 1910? Eventually, the discovery of many written records and the fact that the written and oral data slotted into each other like pieces of a jigsaw puzzle showed that fieldwork in Mbe had been a necessary precondition for a proper understanding of the documents, just as the writings were a necessary precondition for making full use of the reminiscences collected. Vidal's charge that I had used ethnological data from contemporary fieldwork to fill the lacunae between the written documents of the 1880s in order to form a seamless but spurious historical account is patently false, even in the rare instance where I compared the description of the *itsuuwa* ritual I saw in 1963 to the written account of a similar ritual in 1883. The comparison merely showed that the overall plot of the ritual and some of its sequences and actions had remained the same. This was not a heinous anachronism, a projection of the present into the past. The document of 1883 exists on its own. All I did was merely to recognize the past in the present. That, of course, is the goal of all field experience by researchers, even if they merely go to see the landscape on which the history they study from written documents was played out.

The Vidal polemic raises another troubling issue. How could she as a reader evaluate the quality of fieldwork when she had only the book that resulted from it? She had no access to my records, and even if she had, that would not have been enough. She also would need information about the research design and its goals as they changed over time, since that determines what is recorded and when. In general, open access to the data can be achieved by depositing the records in a public repository, but that is not enough in this case and probably in many others.[18] My notebooks and other records about this piece of fieldwork merely include substantive information, nothing else. There is no account there about decisions made concerning details of the research design (e.g., sampling) or the future conduct of research, no mention of satisfaction or disappointment with the state of play at a given moment, no evaluation at all of the people I worked with, and nothing about work routines or practical arrangements. Hence this essay. Most of its substance stems from recollection not from the written record, which acted mostly as a cue to the recollection. For instance, the crucial portion of the momentous interview with the king on November 11 is listed as "So the Yāā have been here; they put a part of the population to flight towards the Kasai." There is no mention at all of the fact that I did not believe him, because he seemed to draw inspiration from watching his large dog for a long while after having heard the question and because he then hesitatingly replied in the one short sentence that was written down. Nor does the notebook make any mention that later in the day as I was crossing over an open space to visit a Mr. Ba it struck me that a social history built up from reminiscences might be possible. All the record does about this turning point in the research is to preserve the exact date at which it happened. Hence, Vidal would need to have this article as well as the fieldnotes in order to be reasonably well-informed about this piece of fieldwork.

---

[18] I suspect that no fieldworker will ever agree to do this before their research is published and even then they may not do so for good reasons (for example, to preserve promised anonymity). Sooner or later, however, the data must be put on record.

EPILOGUE: FIELDWORK IN HISTORY

Jan Vansina

As the contributions in this book show, fieldwork is a treasured highlight in the lives of every historian of Africa who has experienced it. Many among them believe that fieldwork experience is a *sine qua non* for anyone who aspires to be an historian of Africa. Prospective academic employers, in North America at least, agree. The importance of fieldwork has seemed self-evident. Is it not an esoteric training procedure, similar to an initiation, which endows fledgling historians with the unchallenged authority of personal experience? Yet many respected historians, both foreign and African, have never conducted fieldwork, although most among them have visited or resided, or currently reside in Africa. It is therefore not self-evident that fieldwork experience is essential to the history of Africa. Moreover, the term "fieldwork by historians" is assumed to be a standard process that always produces the same effects. Yet a comparison of the activities of various scholars in the field soon shows that it is not a standard process, does not lead to a standardized experience, and consequently does not necessarily yield an equal level of expertise at the end. Before one can address the question of the contribution of fieldwork to the discipline, however, one must first look into the variety of practices covered by that word. Only then can one better understand why and how the practice is indeed essential to the discipline.

Avatars of Fieldwork

When Kenneth Dike set out in 1948 on a tour to collect oral traditions in the Niger Delta, he was probably the first academic historian to do so in Africa.[1] We do not know how he went about it, or whether he saw any analogy between his endeavors and fieldwork carried out by anthropologists. Two years later, the anthropolo-

---

[1] On K. O. Dike, see R. July, *An African Voice* (Durham, NC, 1987), 141–45. Fieldwork by scholars has a long pedigree however. Perhaps the first historian to do so was Pausanias (second century A.D.), doing research for his *Description of Greece*. See P. Veyne, *Did the Greeks Believe in Their Myths? An Essay on the Constitutive Imagination*, tran. Paula Wissig (Chicago, 1988).

gist Ian Cunnison was gathering oral traditions in the Luapula valley to study the link between "the Historical Notions of a Central African Tribe" and the sociopolitical order.[2] I may have been the first non-African historian to practice historical fieldwork proper, when in 1953 I began to gather oral traditions in addition to standard research in anthropology. Even though the requirements, practice, and field design for historical research are quite different from anthropological pursuits, nevertheless fieldwork in history was a take-off from the practice in anthropology. By the later 1950s, however, there still existed a consensus that historians should leave fieldwork to the specialists, anthropologists, who should collect the oral traditions needed by historians.[3] Soon thereafter this position was abandoned, and historians began to do fieldwork as a matter of routine from the 1960s onwards. Yet even though they did not work at all like anthropologists, they still believed that anthropological fieldwork remained the model to be followed.

Fieldwork has a long pedigree in social and cultural anthropology. The first professional academics began to practice it just before the turn of the century.[4] Still, it was not until Malinowski returned from his enforced residence on the Trobriand Islands that a full-fledged theory of fieldwork emerged. The anthropologist was supposed to be a "participant observer": that is, an *observer* rather than someone who disturbed the objects of study by asking questions of them; and a *participant* whose participation not only added direct experience of various activities to the observation proper, but supposedly led to a total blending of the observer into the background so that the ordinary behavior of the subjects was no longer disrupted by an alien presence.[5] The objective observation of behavior was the goal of all fieldwork, not the array of subjective explanations by which the objects of research, the people studied, explained their behavior. Between the 1930s and the 1960s, most anthropologists in Africa used functional and structural analyses to provide an overarching explanation for the behavior of their objects of study. It was this practice that early historians sought to emulate, even though they were rather more interested in what people had to say about the past than in their behavior. Yet that change in attitude altered the very nature of fieldwork.

Indeed, fieldwork carried out by historians differs from fieldwork carried out by anthropologists. Historians study a local society and its culture for its own sake

---

[2] I. Cunnison, *History on the Luapula*, Rhodes Livingstone Institute Papers No. 21 (London, 1951).

[3] This was evident during the debate about this question at a conference in 1957. Nevertheless, the last of its list of resolutions said, "The Conference would like to stress the urgent need for training historians for fieldwork in Africa *in concert with archaeologists and anthropologists*" (my emphasis). D. H. Jones, ed., *History and Archaeology in Africa: Second Conference Held in July 1957 at the School of Oriental and African Studies* (London, 1959), 52.

[4] For many anthropologists, Franz Boas was the first to practice fieldwork when he went to Baffin Island in 1883–1884. Some earlier professional anthropologists such as A. Bastian took notes "in the field" but did not stay very long in one spot. See A. Bastian, *Ein Besuch in San Salvador, der Hauptstadt des Königreichs Congo* (Bremen, 1859). E. Pechuël Loesche, however, stayed for two years (1874–1876) to carry out research on the coast of Loango and it is hard to deny that he did fieldwork or took refuge in his official label as "geographer" when in fact he was an anthropologist. See his *Volkskunde von Loango* (Stuttgart, 1907).

[5] See G. W. Stocking Jr., *The Ethnographer's Magic and Other Essays in the History of Anthropology* (Madison, 1992), especially "The Ethnographer's Magic: Fieldwork in British Anthropology from Tylor to Malinowski," 12–59; and A. Kuper, *Anthropologists and Anthropology: The British School, 1922–1972* (London, 1973), 13, 20 (Rivers), and index, "field methods."

in order to obtain data about its past, while anthropologists study a society as a case in order to obtain data pertinent to general theories. Hence, historical fieldwork tends to be more open-ended and anthropological fieldwork more restricted to *a priori* sets of issues. Historical fieldwork focuses on the recording of messages and their context: what people say is crucial. A generation ago anthropologists focused on observation of behavior often explicated for them by key informants who might or might not be representative. Now anthropologists are interested in messages, but study them as expressions of a "mode of thought," assumed to be different from our own. Thus, when anthropologists follow Cunnison in paying attention to local history-telling, they use these data as expressions of historical consciousness and often tie their particularities to particular social characteristics without regard to the validity of each message as a source, a crucial question for historians.

As a result, historians tend to expend more time and effort to learn the local language well than anthropologists do, if only because a study of messages as opposed to observation requires more advanced knowledge of language. Many anthropologists still cling to the fiction of participant observation, whereas most historians seem to adopt the role of pupils in need of guidance by their hosts. Anthropologists treat the situation at the time when they arrived on the scene (the point of "zero time") as unchanging and proceed to uncover the essence of a timeless society and culture unsullied by the mundane influences of modernity. This "ethnographic present" is anathema to historians. Although their concern with the gap between norms and practice often leads them to carry out statistical surveys within the community where they live, many anthropologists settle in a single small community and in practice often rely on a few key informants. They assume that a single community is representative of a whole homogeneous ethnic group. In comparison, most historians as they gather evidence must necessarily focus on individual or group differences between messages and cannot avoid confronting issues of sampling and representativity. As a result, many do not ensconce themselves in a single community. Finally, it should be remembered that fieldwork is the *sine qua non* of anthropology: until recently fieldwork was the badge that distinguished aspirants from genuine anthropologists. But among historians in general, fieldwork is unusual and confers an ambiguous cachet of exoticism and eccentricity to those who indulge in it. This strongly colors the self-image and the expectations of researchers.

So when historians turned to fieldwork, their practice became quite different from the usual anthropological routine from the outset. In the parlance of historians, the word "fieldwork" now covers a multitude of practices. It is used for any research activity in Africa, from a short visit to an archive to years of research in a community. Indeed it sometimes is even used to refer merely to residence in Africa, for instance, when teaching at a local university. It is therefore important to give some sense of the variety of practices involved.

For a start, one should distinguish between residence, fieldtrip, and fieldwork; and the term "fieldwork" should be reserved for the activity of collecting data during a lengthy stay by a researcher living within the community studied. When I went to Libya in 1978 to set up a center for research in oral tradition and organized the collection of oral evidence by Libyans about the colonial wars from 1911 to 1932, I was in residence there, not doing fieldwork. I did not myself gather data in the field, even though I did "participate" in Libyan administration and observe it. That was not fieldwork because I was not studying administration. For similar reasons, teaching spells at African universities or simply living in Africa should not be labeled fieldwork. When I went to Gabon for a month in 1980 to gather data in Libreville for a study in historical linguistics, I was not doing fieldwork either: I was on a fieldtrip. The stay was too short and I was not really living in a community that I was studying. Thus, historians consulting archival depots in Africa are not doing fieldwork: they too are on fieldtrips. According to this rule, nearly all stays by archaeologists in Africa are also fieldtrips.

But when I stayed over a period of several years (1953–1956) studying Kuba ways of life and history in a Kuba town and in Kuba villages in Zaire, I was doing fieldwork. And even though I only spent some seven months (1963–1964) studying Tio history at Mbe, a Tio village, this was clearly fieldwork as well. The case of my research in Rwanda and Burundi (1957–1960) is less evident. As was the case later in Libya, I was there to gather oral traditions and I did use assistants. But unlike the Libyan case, I gathered much of this data myself and had learned the local languages sufficiently well to interview the performers of oral tradition, although I still could not wholly dispense with an interpreter. This was then fieldwork of a different sort.

Yet the difference between the work done in Rwanda and Burundi and fieldwork among the Kuba and Tio was so great that an anthropologist might not look upon the former as fieldwork because I resided at home in Butare (Rwanda) and only very rarely stayed for a week or so in local communities, whereas in the two other cases I lived in local communities. This case not only shows how crucial living in the community is to the notion of fieldwork for anthropologists who view this as the essence of participant observation, but it also illustrates how very different activities can all be labeled fieldwork.

It is worth fussing about this definition of fieldwork because it underlines its unique contribution, which is the interaction between the unique experience undergone by researchers and the gathering of sources for history. All fieldwork then has two components: the gathering of data (an intellectual activity), and the gaining of experience (a personal emotional and cognitive happening). Even though both are closely interwoven in practice, it is still worth considering them separately. Let us begin with the gathering of data, the "research design."

Some readers may be surprised to note that the descriptive definition of fieldwork proposed does not specify any particular set of protocols to be followed or any specific technique to be used for gathering evidence. That is because research designs and practical information-gathering activities differ widely among fieldworkers. Yet, to put it in the jargon of historians, the heuristics of the sources are crucial because they condition their availability. In fact, the do-and-don't methodologies to obtain particular items of information are well-developed. For instance, the superior value of "information in spite of itself" is as well-known as the lack of value of anything obtained through "leading questions"; and one knows when to use samples and when not, when the sample must be random and when stratified. But there are no mandatory research designs covering the whole fieldwork operation.

In practice, most scholars use a design between two extremes. One extreme is to recover as much data as one can from within a single small community without worrying much about the representativity of the data gained with regard to the larger society to which the community belongs. Thus, the information is valid for the place where it was recorded and may or may not be applicable or typical for other places. Having chosen this research strategy and settled in their village or town, many researchers then follow no particular plan to recover information and are content to let things happen and to gather their data as they come. Thus, among scholars who choose this design, many rely for the most part on informal interaction rather than on formal interviews. This choice of research design maximizes the interaction between researcher and local people and thus maximizes fieldwork experience gained, even though it also leaves researchers especially vulnerable to manipulation by local social entrepreneurs.

On the opposite extreme, some researchers stress representativity to the extent that they do not settle in any particular locale but move from place to place according to a sample conducted *a priori* or derived from the experience of a first experiment, the "pilot experiment." Indeed, some eschew any sample and visit all the settlements within the geographic area they study. Such researchers develop standard protocols for interviews, often use questionnaires, and follow rigid, predetermined rules as to how many and what sort of people they formally interview in each of the places visited. In such a design, the representativity of any bit of information with regard to the whole will be evident, but at the cost of leaving a considerable distance between researcher and "interviewee." Such data gathering lacks the personal experience gained by the scholar and is much less intensive and intimate than the opposite method.

All the contributors to this volume have chosen research designs that are closer to the first extreme, although many others have come close to the other, and I have alternated between both according to the type of information sought, the size of the society studied, and the amount of financing and time available. In most cases, research designs elaborated before one goes to the field are altered as practical circumstance, practical experience, and sometimes sheer serendipity dictate. Each fieldwork project, therefore, has a story of how its research design evolved and was carried out. To assess the reliability and exact meaning of the information gathered therefore, one must not only have access to the specific circumstances (such as interview, observation, or questionnaire) during which the information was gathered, but one must also know how the whole research design evolved during fieldwork. To illustrate both differences between research designs and hence the need for others to have access to them, a thumbnail sketch of my own field research follows.

My research among the Kuba began as a straightforward ethnographic survey. After a few months it split into historical and anthropological fieldwork. The historical fieldwork aimed at gathering all formal traditions known to every single family in the country. That goal was achieved, but at the cost of hiring several assistants to collect these data.

In Rwanda and Burundi, different pilot schemes were set up. In the case of Rwanda, this led to an effort to find every community historian who knew historical narratives of a certain well-defined type in a population of several million people. The design was adjusted at least once during the period of fieldwork. This design was formally drawn up after the results of a house-by-house quest in a pilot settlement were known. A major alteration occurred as the result of both the publication of narratives about local histories gathered by the administration and by claims made by the emerging Hutu parties. In the case of Burundi, the pilot scheme led to the design of a sample that involved specific assumptions about social roles and spatial location. That research design did not need later adjustment and had been almost totally implemented by the time I left.

In Rwanda a number of assistants were involved, while in Burundi I relied on occasional assistance only in the last six months or so of research. Changes in research design during fieldwork among the Tio are the topic of Chapter 10.

In Libya the first phase of the research consisted of alerting all potential informants through the media and then working settlement by settlement until the whole country had been covered, a technique somewhat similar to the one used in Rwanda but significantly different in detail. Most of this procedure can easily be gathered from my notebooks, which are available for the research among the Kuba, Rwanda, and Rundi, but not yet for Tio country.[6] It is interesting that while some historians have rightly insisted that the concrete data gathered (usually oral traditions) should be made accessible to the public, even they have not realized the importance of obtaining access to information relating to the history of the research itself.[7]

The acquisition of knowledge from internalized personal experience is the second facet of fieldwork, a facet that is ultimately even more essential than the acquisition of new data, for the data cannot be understood without the experience. Yet that experience is never the same for different researchers and can never be replicated even by the same researcher, because it is shaped by a "once-only situation": the encounter between the here-and-now conditions at the time and place where research is conducted and the contemporary personal makeup of the researcher. The group of contributors to this volume may seem quite homogeneous. They have all lived in the communities they studied for at least one year, they were all much the same age at the time, they all settled primarily in one place rather than roaming around, their essay in this collection discusses their first stay in the field (except in my own case and McCurdy's), and the experience of fieldwork has clearly altered their personal outlook on life. They have very much in common and yet this collection of essays also shows how vastly different their experiences have been. A quick look at their personal situations shows how different they were. Some were women and others were men; some were bachelors and others were not; some lived alone and others lived with spouses or companions; some had brought their children and others did not; some lived in cities and others in villages; some ran their own households and others hired domestic help; and some used interpreters or assistants while others did not.

Just as important as their personal situation is the concrete context of the "here and now" in which fieldworkers find the communities in which they are to work. This includes the political climate, as illustrated in the contrast between Michele Wagner's research in Burundi and in Tanzania, but much besides this as well. When Claudine and I arrived in Mbe we found severe food shortages and a high incidence of tuberculosis there, and soon after we arrived a deadly outbreak of measles

---

[6] On microfilm at the Center for Research Libraries, Chicago.

[7] See the eloquent pleas by B. Heintze, "Primary Sources Only for the Collector?" *History in Africa*, 3 (1976), 47–56, and D. Henige, "In the Possession of the Author: The Problem of Source Monopoly in Oral Historiography," *International Journal of Oral History*, 1 (1980), 181–94.

occurred. In Rwanda we encountered civil war. But in Burundi (1957–1960) and among the Kuba (1953–1956), all was still quiet, even though the political climate kept changing during the research and tensions were building towards a climax. Every contributor to this book can easily point to the impact of changing political, social, economic, or religious circumstances that obtained during their stay and which have since continued to change to the point that their exact research experience could not be replicated today by anyone who would want "to check their data," including the original fieldworkers themselves. Yet almost no researcher kept careful track of these circumstances day by day for later reference, perhaps because they accepted the circumstances they found on arrival as "normal."

The time of arrival is the beginning of an era for every researcher. The newcomer tends to perceive the condition he or she finds on arrival as normal. Every later change is gauged against that benchmark that becomes a "zero time," the beginning of a mental era. The researcher has no direct experience of what happened before his or her arrival and must rely on the accounts of others to document past change. These are never so immediate or so concrete as personal experience, however, nor are they complete, so that sometimes massive change goes unreported. Thus, an opposition between Tutsi and Hutu was of no importance in Burundi society when I arrived there in 1957.[8] But a mere five years later, it had become the major social cleavage in the country, and it has since led to enduring civil war. By the time Michele Wagner arrived in the 1980s it seemed inconceivable that this cleavage had not "always" been there. Yet no documents at all describe the massive shift that occurred in the minds of all Barundi with regard to this question between late 1959 and 1972. Another consequence of the zero-time phenomenon is that it becomes very difficult to grasp the continuity of change before and after arrival because the contrast between immediate knowledge from personal experience and mediated information stemming from earlier sources creates an almost insurmountable hiatus.[9]

Just as it is a profound error to envisage fieldwork as an invariant technique and to study its results without reference to the conditions under which it was conducted, so it must be realized that the general context for all fieldwork in tropical Africa has changed with the times since the earliest days of the practice. One could write a short history of fieldwork practices from the days when Pechuël Loesche lived on the Loango coast in 1874–1876 as part of an expedition to set up a German base there in the style of the commercial factories of the day.[10] In early colonial days fieldwork was carried out by expeditions. After about 1930 extended stays became common while the logistics for foreign non-African researchers became easy, but researchers had to fend off colonial attitudes of all sorts and often had to struggle to free themselves from control by the local district commissioners. Before 1945 Africans could hardly carry out any fieldwork at all. In the early days of independence state control was happenstance so that both African and other

---

[8] The correct transcriptions are Tuutsi and Hútu, but in Western languages Tutsi and Hutu are now standard usage.

[9] This issue has apparently been completely overlooked in the literature, yet it is crucial for most aspects of recent history.

[10] For this background, see P. Güssfeldt, J. Falkenstein, and E. Pechuël Loesche, *Die Loango Expedition 1873–1876. Ein Reisewerk in Drei Abtheilungen* (Leipzig, 1888).

researchers went about more freely than either before or since. Logistics were becoming a bit more difficult but were not yet a major headache. Later the new governments began to control access to the field by issuing permits, at first in order to cope with an increasing number of researchers, later by restricting acceptable topics of investigation, and later still by instituting a more-or-less discrete surveillance of researchers (both foreign and African, but especially the latter). In some cases only official informants could be consulted. In the end, meaningful fieldwork became nearly impossible in some countries. At the same time general insecurity, especially but not exclusively in the larger cities, has increased and health services have deteriorated while logistics, especially with regard to transportation, have often become an expensive nightmare. In some cases dramatic internal problems, such as outbreaks of civil war or drought and famine conditions, have rendered fieldwork totally out of the question.

The Contribution of Fieldwork to African History

One may well ask whether the contribution of fieldwork to the history of Africa warrants the substantial efforts and hardships that are involved, for the efforts required are substantial indeed. They usually encompass about five years of the life of every non-African scholar who indulges in fieldwork. Languages must be learned well; the available documentary data must be consulted; and one or two years are spent in the field, usually under unfamiliar, uncomfortable, even risky circumstances and at significant expense. Then follow one or two more years of writing up and of readjustment to the society from which one hails. No wonder fieldwork marks for life the person who undertakes it.

African fieldworkers escape from some of these burdens but the difficulties they encounter are not less than those of other researchers. They run the same general risks of health and security as expatriates do. Their social position at home forces them to respond to many demands on their services which interrupt the time they can devote to fieldwork. Usually they also lack the financial support needed for uninterrupted research. As a result they rarely can engage in long continuous spells of fieldwork. In most cases they find only a few months at a time to be in the field. They return, however, year after year and often stay in contact with the communities in their field for much longer periods than expatriates before they can write up and publish their results.

Do the results of fieldwork justify these special efforts and could they not be obtained otherwise? Our view is that they do and they cannot be otherwise achieved. Fieldwork is absolutely essential if African history is to be more than a shallow and half-spurious tale. All too often the contribution of fieldwork is still thought to consist merely of the gathering of oral data. Certainly that is often one of the results, but not the major one. If it were, why then not rely on the oral traditions that have been recorded in written form already by others such as community historians, administrators, or missionaries, and avoid fieldwork altogether? Long before I arrived among the Kuba in 1953, E. Torday had gathered a number of Kuba traditions in 1908 and 1909 and published them, and local colonial administrators had vastly enlarged this corpus ever since 1919. Yet I felt compelled to start gathering traditions all over again.[11] I had to do so not just in order to gather traditions about social groups, events, situations, or institutions that had been overlooked in the record, but also primarily to obtain a systematic overview of existing variants (and thus of the nature and dynamics of historical consciousness at work) in order to develop an informed opinion about the historical validity of the contents of those traditions. Only then could I use them for historical reconstruction. There is far more involved here than just plucking traditions like buttercups in a meadow.[12] It is a matter of understanding first what is actually said in the original language; then what is implied, which context is implicitly referred to; and last but not least how local historians interpret such data and use them as strands to weave their own multiple understandings of their past.

The view that the usefulness of fieldwork is limited to the gathering of oral data has also led to the nefarious idea that while it may be a worthwhile activity in situations that deal with the precolonial history of the last centuries, it can be dispensed with for more recent periods because there are plenty of written data available, and also for older periods because these lie beyond the limits of what people recollect. That is nefarious for several reasons. First, the reams of colonial paper express the point of view of outsiders. They do not tell us how events and situations were perceived by colonial or postcolonial subjects and they do not allow us to transcend the interpretations of the official outlook embedded in them.[13] Moreover, the paper record also remains silent on many developments.

For instance, it is out of the question to write a well-grounded social history from those records alone. Momentous events, which are documented, are rare in the social history of communities, while changing trends often go unnoticed. Moreover, much of what was going on was simply not visible to outsiders. The change in mentality among Barundi between 1959 and 1972 is a perfect if poignant example. The records mention Hutu and Tutsi but not how these criteria of identity, which were at first rather minor ones compared to others, became the foremost criterion of ethnicity in everyone's mind. Thus, oral data, including biographies of people in various walks of life, are essential for any sound understanding of colonial or recent situations.[14] Indeed some of the richest results from fieldwork stem from the integration of oral, written, and iconographic materials and the testimony from places and objects into a single rich, multifaceted reconstruction that cannot

---

[11] E. Torday and T. Joyce, *Notes ethnographiques sur les peuples comunément appelés Bakuba ainsi que sur les peuplades apparentées. Les Bushongo* (Brussels, 1910); E. Torday, *On the Trail of the Bushongo* (Philadelphia, 1925); and L. Achten (district commissioner), "Dossiers ethnographiques," 394, 394 bis of the archive of the ethnographic section of the Royal Museum for Central Africa at Tervuren (Belgium). See also the dossiers 427, 640, 651, and 984.

[12] To approach fieldwork from this perspective is to completely misunderstand what it is all about and is a waste of one's effort.

[13] The fundamental problem with T. Ranger's *Revolt in Southern Rhodesia: 1896–1897* (Evanston, 1967) is precisely that the work relied on the interpretation of the official outlook and missed the oral sources that refute it.

[14] For an example of what is available, see B. Jewsiewicki, *Naitre et mourir au Zaire: Récits de vie* (Paris, 1993), a collection of biographies spanning most of the colonial period and later until c. 1990. Most of these accounts broach topics that are not represented in the written record at all or show how the reality of daily life differed from the regulations affecting it and the written descriptions of it

be achieved by using any of these sources on its own. Moreover, most fieldworkers, like many contributors to this volume, do carry out research on the twentieth century and routinely gather and evaluate oral, archival, and other sources during their fieldwork.

Fieldwork is also relevant to early periods. Marc Bloch used to observe and talk to French peasants in order to better understand the history of medieval farming and land tenure. He learned much about the factors that condition a farming life, from the quality of soils and the requirements of crops and tools, to issues relating to the management of labor, the risks and uncertainties involved, and the nature and substance of decision making. Without knowing this, the abundant written record concerning fief, corvée, land tenure, registers, yields, taxes, and records about peasant grievances and their insurrections remained a mere babble. And of course the climate, landscapes, monuments, and historical sites of France formed as much a part of Bloch's upbringing as the French language and overall culture.

Foreign-born historians of Africa especially need to learn such fundamentals and acquire them best through fieldwork. For instance, an historian of Angola or the Gold Coast in the seventeenth century has access to many written records but still learns from field experience about the impact of the climate on people's activities and expectations, the physical layout of landscapes, the presence of historical ruins, the gamut of old technologies ranging from farming to industrial production and from medicine to transport (including the tools used), as well as social mores; knowledge of which is essential to understand older records. Many threads link present or recent practices to past situations, whether social, political, religious, or economic. While change has indeed affected all of these practices (otherwise there would be no history), experiencing the present and doing research on daily life in the recent past illuminates seventeenth-century texts in the history of Angola just as much as Bloch's experiences did for his documents.

Fieldwork opens the eyes. Even though specialists may well call the sketches Antonio Cavazzi drew on the spot in the mid-seventeenth century "quaint," they are quaint only until the researchers carry out fieldwork and learn to recognize landscapes, objects, and their uses, and various social activities from music making to palavers. After fieldwork the sketches become a rich repository of data.[15] Similarly, records reread after fieldwork become more familiar as the researcher becomes better aware of the unspoken constraints the business of living imposed on the actors. She or he is now sensitized to the absence of many data about the social details, unmentioned because they are supposed to be well known, and hence the absence of much information about the social reality of the time. Moreover, the more thorough their knowledge of the language once spoken by these actors, the better researchers are able to understand the traces it leaves in the approximate translations preserved in texts written in European languages. Fieldwork then yields a nearly indispensable context.

As the last point discussed shows, fieldwork is not only, or even mainly, about the collection of oral data. It is about the experience of being steeped in a different culture and milieu in order to learn the context of past history and perceive the

---

[15] The drawings are printed and discussed in E. Bassani, "Un Cappucino nell'Africa nera del seicento," *Quaderni Poro*, 4 (1987).

traces it has left in the landscape, language, historical imagination, and habits of people. Often one of the most beneficial but unexpected results of this experience is a thorough reorientation of the framework in which one had conceived the topic to be studied, for fieldwork rarely develops exactly as foreseen in research proposals. X goes to study slavery and returns with a dissertation on the evolution of political ideology; Y plans a study of trade unions and comes up with one of religious consciousness. In thirty years of association with doctoral dissertations involving fieldwork, I remember only two that turned out to be just what the proposal foresaw, and I have my doubts about the thoroughness of the research involved. In my own case, historical fieldwork among the Kuba was not even on the agenda to begin with. The projects in Rwanda and Burundi were not formulated ahead of time. And in the Tio case, I went out to study the formal traditions of an ancient kingdom but returned with a "daily life" social history of the generation just before the turn of the century. Such examples show that fieldwork does more than provide a new slant on the topic of research; it often leads to the discovery of unsuspected new topics.

Still, it would be disingenuous to state that such topics arise solely from the concerns of the society studied. Fieldworkers also "recognize" them as potential topics for study because of the similarity to topics studied by historians elsewhere. The history of ideology or the study of religious consciousness and "daily life" topics have all been practiced long before the researchers discovered them on the ground. The novelty consists in the relevance of a topic to the society and culture studied and the recognition, despite dissimilar appearances, of the similarity between a set of concerns in the community studied and a topic that had been developed elsewhere in a different guise. The impulse then stems both from the fieldworkers and their hosts. As a result of such dynamics, fieldwork contributes to the continual expansion of the horizons of academic historiography.

Beyond this, fieldwork makes even more fundamental contributions. It leads to better-informed interpretations and a better understanding of the historical dynamics involved. Academic historiography is molded by Western conventions about the genre called history and by the expectation that understanding results from the perception of ultimately rational "explanations" for the motivations of the actors. But African history was played out by actors within different cultural contexts. Through personal experience the fieldworker learns how to translate these into a narrative that makes sense to academics and presents an interpretation without doing violence to the sources.[16]

Stated in the most general terms, the following occurs. All historical interpretation flows from the dialogue between the subjectivity of the authors of the sources and that of the interpreter. Variability in interpretation stems from the subjective situation of the participants in the fieldwork encounter. Without fieldwork the subjectivity of the outsider historian is rooted in a foreign cultural universe and will lead to basic distortions. The process of "experience" acquired in fieldwork amounts to an education of that subjectivity, including an *éducation sentimentale*, attuned to a cultural milieu that is the outcome of the historical period studied. Certainly

---

[16] See J. Vansina, *Living with Africa* (Madison, 1994), 238–43.

fieldworkers are not less subjective than other historians but their subjectivity is better informed.

But often there is more. When historians study written documents the voice of their authors is heard once and for all, i.e., the subjective interpretation they bring to the writing of a document is given once and for all. It can only be partially circumvented by comparing documents. But that does not hold in the case of oral information. Because one deals with living people, it is possible to find a larger number of points of view to compare and to acquire a better sense of what exactly informs the subjectivity of different sources. It follows that there is less room for the historical imagination of the historian than in the case of written sources that "cannot talk back."

It also follows that in the end the resulting interpretation of the historical work flows from a collaboration between the authors of the sources and the fieldworker historian. When in addition fieldworkers write for the benefit of the communities studied (which they rarely do), then the reception of their work heightens this effect and extends it to the full range of sources, not just oral material. In practice this means that fieldworkers are less free to attribute implicit or explicit motivations stemming from their own imagination to historical actors. They tend to break away more from an appeal to stock explanations for such motivations in Western historiography. Thus, class hatred, the search for profit, or the thirst for power may give way, for instance, to the fear of witchcraft, a desire to accumulate bridewealth, the need to placate ancestors after a disaster, or the desire to emulate local role models.

In addition, fieldwork experience allows historians to see the historiography on situations and topics similar to their own research with new eyes and to reinterpret this historiography fruitfully to yield more plausible reconstructions. Their better-educated sensibilities allow them to recast the documentation in the light of what they know from experience about the contexts involved, from the relevance of rainfall to government or to the local importance of oratory performance in healing. It allows them sometimes to bring together what looked hitherto like a set of disparate data into a meaningful, new, and unexpected synthesis.

But the technique of fieldwork is not without its drawbacks. It is not a magic wand that transforms every pumpkin it touches. There are four main generic drawbacks. First, the phenomenon of zero time tends to introduce a retrojection of later conditions into earlier situations if the fieldworker is not explicitly aware of its dangers. Reconstructing a history on this basis leads to fatal distortions. Second, fieldworkers with long experience are inclined to believe that no one has withheld any information from them concerning the topic of their research. That is not true. For instance, I knew Jules Lyeen, the Kuba royal sculptor, well and often talked to him. Yet he never told me that he was also a tax collector for the king. The Kuba, even those who criticized the king, never talked to me about the ruler's income from collecting state taxes, nor of the revenues that accrued to him from pressuring people to work for the local concessionary company in palm products, despite the fact that he himself had called his capital Pish a Mbééng, "the search for money"![17] Fieldworkers often forget that the community or society in which they work con-

---

[17] See J. Jacobs and J. Vansina, "Nshoong atoot, Het koninklijk epos der Bushong (Mushenge Belgisch-Kongo)," *Kongo Overzee*, 22, 1 (1956), 32–35.

sider them an asset in their search to maintain or achieve concrete common goals. To the Kuba my role was in part to strengthen their prestige in the context of the country and even beyond: I was good for indirect rule and for the tourist trade in Kuba objects. I was aware that the local Kuba used my presence in this way because I knew that the same strategy had met with resounding success in the case of my predecessor E. Torday forty-five years earlier. Yet I did not realize that this situation would not just lead people to help me, but also to conceal from me.

Third, a more insidious effect of fieldwork is the acquisition of a secondary ethnocentricity, a phenomenon not unknown among other historians who often tend to side with their historical actors against their historical adversaries. In this case, the phenomenon is even more insidious. As they shed some of their original ethnic preconceptions fieldworkers adopt local ones and tend to overevaluate the contributions and the virtues of their adopted ethnic group compared to its neighbors. For instance, Torday underlined how civilized the Kuba were, "as Romans were under Augustus,"[18] and I had to beware consciously of avoiding such judgments. Yet my first book on Kuba history was profoundly ethnocentric. It stuck so closely to the narrative traditions collected that it reflected the point of view of the political elites and the inhabitants of the capital to the extent that it reads as if one of them had composed it.[19] In a more benign form there is an unavoidable inclination to evaluate situations elsewhere unconsciously through the eyes of one's own acquired experience. Because such a stance is unconscious it is all the more insidious. Hence one must be very much on the lookout for evidence of secondary ethnicity in order to be able to counter or at least soften its effects. This is good reason for historians to attempt to widen their direct experience and thus lessen the potential impact of this factor.

Finally, the very intensity of personal experience leads to hubris and to an adoption of the argument of authority. It tends to make one overrate its value to the point of believing that one's interpretation has become the only plausible one. But this is no less true for historians studying their own culture than it is for fieldworkers.

These drawbacks merely underline that fieldworkers are just as fallible as other historians and should neither benefit from credence based on the argument of authority, nor be immune from scrutiny. Just as other historians are expected to justify their interpretation by referral to the written sources used, which can then be consulted by others, so should fieldworkers. Just as written records are available to other historians, the records pertaining to fieldwork, including diaries if any, should also be made available. Unfortunately, the crucial importance of this point often still eludes historians of Africa. The stringency of this requirement equals the crucial place of fieldwork in the discipline.

This is not an easy requirement to meet, however. First, some information cannot be checked because fieldwork itself cannot be replicated. Second, much of the

---

[18] E. Torday and T. Joyce, *Notes ethnographiques*, 13 and 60.

[19] J. Vansina. *Geschiedenis van de Kuba van ongeveer 1500 tot 1904* (Tervuren, 1963). Contrast this with the less ethnocentric *The Children of Woot: A History of the Kuba Peoples* (Madison, 1978). This did not please Bushong intellectuals such as Bope Nyim a Kwem, "La perception Kuba de leur histoire à travers l'oeuve de Vansina," *Annales Aequatoria* 14 (1993), 409–26, who concludes his article as follows (423): "We have ascertained that the publications of Vansina that provoke the most controversy are those from the period 1972–1978. Perhaps because the Belgian historian no longer asked questions of his informants."

information gathered is confidential. Third, many researchers feel that some of their records are too personal for public display. Fourth, there is the fear that others will exploit the hard-won data before the researcher can do so. Finally, organized repositories do not exist as yet to accept such materials. Such objections are weighty but they can be overcome, either by initially making the data available on demand only and later depositing them, or by depositing the records quickly with the requirement that they should remain closed for a specified number of years. But in the end, all records should be deposited. Moreover, an account of the vagaries that the research design has undergone from the inception to the conclusion of the research also needs to be deposited.

This requirement is all the more necessary because fieldwork practices are so variable. Each research has its own strengths and weaknesses and these should be assessed just as the credibility of each piece of information is assessed. Moreover, truly "bad fieldwork" is not unknown. In some cases, for instance, speculation has simply been presented as information gathered. Indeed, in one well-known case this has bedeviled the historiography of precolonial Zimbabwe for a full generation.[20] If African historiography is to flourish, such cases should be denounced with the indignation and condemnation hitherto reserved for the denunciation of fake or non-existing documents.

Studies based on fieldwork have left their imprint on the historiography of Africa not only by adding new sources, but also, even more importantly, by proposing new interpretations that bear an imprint of the historical memory and imagination of the people involved as much as that of the researcher. In the end, the dynamics of reinterpretation may lead to the total renovation of the historiography of Africa, but only if responsible fieldwork continues to be practiced and if academic historians learn to write more for concerned audiences in Africa itself. After all, the greatest contribution of fieldwork lies in its ability to produce a rich translation of culture in which the voices of the Africans concerned blend with the voice of the outside researcher. In this way fieldwork leads historiography to more authentic perspectives.

---

[20] See the condemnation by D. N. Beach, "The Contribution of Donald Abraham, 1958–1963," in his *A Zimbabwean Past* (Gweru, 1994), 227–37.

BIBLIOGRAPHY

Abemba, J. "Pouvoir politique traditionnel et Islam au Congo Oriental." *Cahiers du Centre d'Etude et de Documentation Africaines* (Serie 1: Sociologie). Brussels: CEDAF, Cahier 2, 1971.
Adenaike, Carolyn Keyes."Putting the Color Back in the History." In Robert W. Harms and others, eds., *Paths toward the Past: African Historical Essays in Honor of Jan Vansina*, 415–25. Atlanta: ASA Press, 1994.
Adenaike, Carolyn Keyes. See also Keyes, Carolyn.
Adorno, Theodor. "Keeping One's Distance." *Minima Moralia*. London: Verso, 1974.
Ajayi, J. F. A. *Christian Missions in Nigeria, 1841–1891*. Evanston, Ill.: Northwestern University Press, 1965.
Akinjogbin, I. A. *Dahomey and Its Neighbours 1708–1818*. Cambridge: Cambridge University Press, 1967.
Alagoa, E. J. *A Short History of the Niger Delta*. Ibadan: Ibadan University Press, 1972.
Angrosino, Michael V. "Son and Lover: The Anthropologist as Nonthreatening Male." In Whitehead and Conaway, eds., *Self, Sex, and Gender in Cross-Cultural Fieldwork*, 64–83. Urbana, Ill: University of Illinois Press, 1986.
Ardener, Shirley. "Gender Orientations in Fieldwork." In R. F. Ellen, ed., *Ethnographic Research: A Guide to General Conduct*, 118–29. London: Academic Press, 1984.
Ashton, E. H. *Medicine, Magic and Sorcery among the Southern Sotho*. University of Cape Town, School of African Studies, N.S. 10 (December 1943), 28–32.
Atkins, Keletso. *The Moon is Dead! Give Us Our Money: The Cultural Origins of an African Work Ethic, Natal, 1843–1900*. Portsmouth, NH: Heinemann, 1993.
Barthes, Roland. "Taking Sides." In *Critical Essays*, translated by Richard Howard. Evanston: Northwestern University Press, 1972.
Bassani, E. "Un Cappucino nell'Africa nera del seicento." *Quaderni Poro*, 4, 1987.
Bastian, A. *Ein Besuch in San Salvador, der Hauptstadt des Königreichs Congo*. Bremen: Heinrich Strack, 1859.
Beach, D. N. *A Zimbabwean Past*. Gweru: Mambo Press, 1994.
Bhebe, Ngwabe. *B. Burombo: African Politics in Zimbabwe, 1947-1958*. Harare: College Press, 1989.
Bimanyu, Deogratius. "The Waungwana of Eastern Zaïre, 1880–1900." Ph.D. dissertation, SOAS, University of London, 1976.
Biobaku, S. O. *The Egba and Their Neighbors, 1842–1872*. Oxford: Oxford University Press, 1957.
Bloch, Marc. *French Rural History: An Essay on Its Basic Characteristics*. Translated by Janet Sondheimer. Berkeley: University of California Press, 1970.
———.*The Historian's Craft*. Translated by Peter Putnam. New York: Knopf, 1953.
Bohannan, Laura [writing as Elenore Smith Bowen]. *Return to Laughter* [1954]. New York: Anchor Press, 1964.
Bonnafé, P. "Une Classe d'âge politique: La J.M.N.R. de la République du Congo-Brazzaville, *Cahiers d'Études Africaines*, 8, 31 (1968).

Bope Nyim a Kwem. "La Perception Kuba de leur histoire à travers l'oeuvre de Vansina." *Annales Aequatoria*, 14 (1993).
Boyd, Jean, and Beverly Mack. *The Collected Works of Nana Asma'u 1793–1864*. East Lansing: Michigan State University Press, forthcoming.
Briggs, Jean. "Kapluna Daughter." In Golde, ed., *Women in the Field: Anthropological Experiences*, 19–46. Chicago: Aldine, 1970.
British War Office, Transvaal Dept. of Native Affairs. *The Native Tribes of the Transvaal*. Pretoria: Government Printer, 1905.
Brown, Beverly. "Ujiji: The History of a Lakeside Town, c. 1800–1914." Ph.D. dissertation, Boston University, 1973.
Brunschwig, H. "La négociation du traité Makoko." *Cahiers d'Études Africaines*, 5/1, 17 (1965), 5–56.
———. "Les cahiers de Brazza (1880-1882)." *Cahiers d'Études Africaines*, 6/2, 22 (1966), 157–227.
———. *Brazza l'explorateur. L'Ogooué, 1875–1879*. Paris: Mouton, 1966.
Clammer, John. "Approaches to Ethnographic Research." In Ellen, ed., *Ethnographic Research: A Guide to General Conduct*, 63–85. London: Academic Press, 1984.
Codere, Helen. "Field Work in Rwanda, 1959–1960." In Golde, ed., *Women in the Field: Anthropological Experiences*, 143–64. Chicago: Aldine, 1970.
Cohen, Anthony P. "Informants." In Ellen, ed., *Ethnographic Research: A Guide to General Conduct*, 223–29. London: Academic Press, 1984.
———. "Post-Fieldwork Fieldwork." *Journal of Anthropological Research*, 48 (1992), 339–54.
Coles, Catherine, and Beverly Mack, eds. *Hausa Women in the Twentieth Century*. Madison: University of Wisconsin Press, 1991.
Comaroff, Jean. *Body of Power, Spirit of Resistance*. Chicago: University of Chicago Press, 1985.
Conaway, Mary Ellen. "The Pretense of the Neutral Researcher." In Whitehead and Conaway, eds., *Self, Sex, and Gender in Cross-Cultural Fieldwork*, 52–63. Urbana, Ill: University of Illinois Press, 1986.
Cooper, Frederick. *Plantation Slavery on the East Coast of Africa*. New Haven: Yale University Press, 1977.
Coquery-Vidrovitch, Catherine. *Brazza et la prise de possession du Congo (1883–1885)*. Paris: Mouton, 1969.
Cunnison, Ian. *History on the Luapula*. Rhodes Livingstone Institute Papers, 21. London, 1951.
Dike, Kenneth Onwuka. *Trade and Politics in the Niger Delta, 1830–1885*. Oxford: Oxford University Press, 1956.
Dimpe, Motswaedi. "Batswapong–Bangwato Relations: The Politics of Subordination and Exploitation, 1895–1949." Student research essay, University of Botswana, 1986.
Diop, Cheikh Anta. *Nations nègres et culture*. Paris: Présence Africaine, 1954.
Du Bois, Cora. "Studies in an Indian Town." In Peggy Golde, ed., *Women in the Field: Anthropological Experiences*, 221–36. Chicago: Aldine, 1970.
Ellen, R. F., ed. *Ethnographic Research: A Guide to General Conduct*. London: Academic Press, 1984.
Ewald, Janet J. "Experience and Speculation: History and Founding Stories in the Kingdom of Taqali, 1780–1935." *International Journal of African Historical Studies*, 18, 2 (1985), 265–87.
———. "Foxes in the Field: An Essay on Historical Methodology." *African Studies Review*, 30, 2 (1987), 9–15.
———. "Leadership and Social Change on an Islamic Frontier: The Kingdom of Taqali, 1680–1898." Ph.D. dissertation, University of Wisconsin–Madison, 1982.
———. *Soldiers, Traders, and Slaves: State Formation and Economic Transformation in the Greater Nile Valley, 1700–1885*. Madison: University of Wisconsin Press, 1990.
———. "Speaking, Writing, and Authority: Explorations in and from the Kingdom of Taqali." *Comparative Studies in Society and History*, 30, 2 (1988), 199–224.

Bibliography

Fair, Laura. "Women's Popular Culture and the Creation of a National Identity in Zanzibar, 1890 to 1930." Paper presented at the meeting of the Arts Council of the African Studies Association, New York, April, 1995.
Faithorn, Elizabeth. "Gender Bias and Sex Bias: Removing our Cultural Blinders in the Field." In Whitehead and Conaway, eds., *Self, Sex, and Gender in Cross-Cultural Fieldwork*, 275–88. Urbana, Ill: University of Illinois Press, 1986.
Finnegan, Ruth. *Oral Traditions and the Verbal Arts: A Guide to Research Practices*. London: Routledge, 1992.
Fluehr-Lobban, Carolyn, and Richard A. Lobban. "Families, Gender, and Methodology in the Sudan." In Whitehead and Conaway, eds., *Self, Sex, and Gender in Cross-Cultural Fieldwork*, 182–95. Urbana, Ill: University of Illinois Press, 1986.
Forkl, Hermann. "Publish or Perish, Or How to Write a Social History of the Wandala (Northern Cameroon)." *History in Africa*, 17 (1990), 77–94.
Freilich, Morris. "Field Work: An Introduction." In Freilich, ed., *Marginal Natives: Anthropologists at Work*, 1–37. New York: Harper and Row, 1970.
Freilich, Morris. "Mohawk Heroes and Trinidadian Peasants." In Freilich, ed., *Marginal Natives: Anthropologists at Work*, 185–250. New York: Harper and Row, 1970.
———. "Toward a Formalization of Field Work." In Freilich, ed., *Marginal Natives: Anthropologists at Work*, 489–585. New York: Harper and Row, 1970.
Friedl, Ernestine. "Field Work in a Greek Village." In Golde, ed., *Women in the Field: Anthropological Experiences*, 195–217. Chicago: Aldine, 1970.
Geertz, Clifford. *Local Knowledge*. New York: Basic Books, 1983.
Golde, Peggy. "Odyssey of Encounter." In Golde, ed., *Women in the Field: Anthropological Experiences*, 67–93. Chicago: Aldine, 1970.
Golde, Peggy, ed. *Women in the Field: Anthropological Experiences*. Chicago: Aldine, 1970.
Goward, Nicola. "Personal Interaction and Adjustment." In Ellen, ed., *Ethnographic Research: A Guide to General Conduct*, 100–118. London: Academic Press, 1984.
———. "Publications on Fieldwork Experience." In Ellen, ed., *Ethnographic Research: A Guide to General Conduct*, 88–100. London: Academic Press, 1984.
Gulick, John. "Village and City Field Work in Lebanon." In Freilich, ed., *Marginal Natives: Anthropologists at Work*, 123–52. New York: Harper and Row, 1970.
Güssfeldt, P., J. Falkenstein, and E. Pechuël Loesche. *Die Loango-Expedition, 1873–1876: Ein Reisewerk in Drei Abtheilungen*. 3 vols. Leipzig: Edward Baldamus, 1888.
Harrell-Bond, Barbara. "Studying Elites: Some Special Problems." In Rynkiewich and Spradley, eds., *Ethics and Anthropology: Dilemmas in Fieldwork*, 110–22. New York: John Wiley and Sons, 1976.
Hastrup, Kirsten, and Peter Hervik, eds. *Social Experience and Anthropological Knowledge*. London and New York: Routledge, 1994.
Heintze, Beatrix. "Primary Sources Only for the Collector?" *History in Africa*, 3 (1976), 47–56.
Henige, David. "In the Possession of the Author: The Problem of Source Monopoly in Oral Historiography." *International Journal of Oral History*, 1 (1980), 181–94.
———., ed. "Fieldwork in Zambia." *History in Africa*, 5 (1978), 273–326.
———., ed. "Silences in Fieldwork." *History in Africa*, 17 (1990), 319–58.
Higginson, John. *A Working Class in the Making: Belgian Colonial Labor Policy, Private Enterprise, and the African Mineworker, 1907–1951*. Madison: University of Wisconsin Press, 1989.
Hill, Richard. *Egypt in the Sudan, 1820–1881*. London: Royal Institute of International Affairs, 1959.
Hirschkind, Lynn. "Redefining the 'Field' in Fieldwork." *Ethnology*, 30, 3 (1991), 237–49.
Holt, P. M. "Funj Origins: A Critique and New Evidence." *Journal of African History*, 4, 1 (1963), 39–55.
———. *The Mahdist State in the Sudan, 1881–1898: A Study of Its Origins, Development, and Overthrow*. 2nd ed. Oxford: Clarendon Press, 1970.

Honigmann, John J. "Field Work in Two Northern Canadian Communities." In Freilich, ed., *Marginal Natives: Anthropologists at Work*, 39–72. New York: Harper and Row, 1970.

Howell, Nancy. *Surviving Fieldwork: A Report of the Advisory Panel on Health and Safety in Fieldwork, American Anthropological Association*. American Anthropological Association Special Publication, 26 (1990).

Iser, Wolfgang. *The Act of Reading: A Theory of Aesthetic Response*. Baltimore: The Johns Hopkins University Press, 1978.

Jackson, Jean. "On Trying To Be an Amazon." In Whitehead and Conaway, eds., *Self, Sex, and Gender in Cross-Cultural Fieldwork*, 263–74. Urbana, Ill: University of Illinois Press, 1986.

Jacobs, J., and J. Vansina. "Nshoong atoot, Het koninklijk epos der Bushong (Mushenge Belgisch-Kongo)." *Kongo Overzee*, 22, 1 (1956), 1–37.

Janzen, John. *Ngoma: Discourses of Healing in Central and Southern Africa*. Berkeley: University of California Press, 1992.

Jarvie, I. C. "The Problem of Ethical Integrity in Participant Observation." *Current Anthropology*, 10, 5 (1969), 505–508.

Jewsiewicki, B. *Naitre et mourir au Zaire: Récits de vie*. Paris: Harmattan, 1993.

Johnson, Samuel. *The History of the Yorubas*. Lagos: CSS Bookshops, 1921.

Jones, D. H., ed. *History and Archaeology in Africa. Second Conference Held in July 1957 at the School of Oriental and African Studies*. London: Universitiy of London, 1959.

Jorgenson, Joseph G. "On Ethics and Anthropology." *Current Anthropology*, 12, 2 (1971), 319–34.

July, Robert. *An African Voice*. Durham, N.C.: University of North Carolina, 1987.

———. *The Origins of Modern African Thought*. London: Faber, 1968.

Keyes, Carolyn. "*Adire*: Cloth, Gender, and Social Change in Southwestern Nigeria, 1841–1991." Ph.D. dissertation, Universityi of Wisconsin–Madison, 1993.

Kilbourne, Benjamin. "Fields of Shame: Anthropologists Abroad." *Ethos*, 20, 2 (1992), 230–63.

Krieger, Laurie. "Negotiating Gender Role Expectations in Cairo." In Whitehead and Conaway, eds., *Self, Sex, and Gender in Cross-Cultural Fieldwork*, 117–28. Urbana, Ill: University of Illinois Press, 1986.

Krige, Eileen J. "Agricultural Ceremonies and Practices of the Balobedu." *Bantu Studies*, V, 3 (Sept. 1931), 207–40.

Krige, Eileen J. and J. D. Krige. *The Realm of the Rain Queen*. Oxford: Oxford University Press, 1943.

Kuper, A. *Anthropologists and Anthropology: The British School, 1922–1972*. London: Allen Lane, 1973.

Lance, James. "What the Stranger Brings: The Social Dynamics of Fieldwork." *History in Africa*, 17 (1990), 335–39.

Landau, Paul Stuart. *The Realm of the Word: Language, Gender, and Christianity in a Southern African Kingdom*. Portsmouth, NH: Heinemann, 1995.

———. "When Rain Falls: Rainmaking and Community in a Tswana Village, c. 1870 to Recent Times." *International Journal of African Historical Studies*, 26, 1 (1993), 1–30.

Landes, Ruth. "A Woman Anthropologist in Brazil." In Golde, ed., *Women in the Field: Anthropological Experiences*, 119–39. Chicago: Aldine, 1970.

Lawless, Robert, Vinson H. Sutlive Jr., and Mario D. Zamora. "Introduction." In their *Fieldwork: The Human Experience*, xi–xxi. New York: Gordon and Breach, 1983.

Leakey, Mary. *Disclosing the Past: An Autobiography*. Garden City, NY: Doubleday, 1984.

Lesotlho, J. "The Badimo in the Tswapong Hills: A Botswana Traditional Institution in Action." *Botswana Notes and Records*, 15 (1982), 7–8.

Lord, Alfred B. *The Singer of Tales*. New York: Atheneum, 1971.

Mack, Beverly. "Hajiya Ma'daki: A Royal Hausa/Fulani Woman." In Patricia Romero, ed., *Life Histories of African Women*, 47–77. Trenton, NJ: Ashfield Press, 1987.

———. "Songs from Silence: Hausa Women's Poetry." In Carole Boyce Davies and Anne Adams Graves, eds., *Ngambika: Women in African Literature*, 181–90. Trenton, NJ: Africa World Press, 1985.

———, and Catherine Coles. *Hausa Women in the Twentieth Century*. Madison: University of Wisconsin Press, 1991.

Mack, Beverly. See also Boyd, Jean.

Mackenzie, John. *Ten Years North of the Orange River: A Story of Everyday Life and Work Among the South African Tribes*. Edinburgh: Edmonston and Douglas, 1871.

Malinowski, Bronislaw. *A Diary in the Strict Sense of the Term*. Translated by N. Guterman. New York: Harcourt, Brace and World, 1967.

Marshall, Gloria. "In a World of Women: Field Work in a Yoruba Community." In Golde, ed., *Women in the Field: Anthropological Experiences*, 167–91. Chicago: Aldine, 1970.

Maxwell, Robert J. "A Comparison of Field Research in Canada and Polynesia." In Morris Freilich, ed., *Marginal Natives: Anthropologists at Work*, 441–84. New York: Harper and Row, 1970.

McCurdy, Sheryl. "The 1932 'War' Between Rival Ujiji Associations: Understanding Women's Motivations for Inciting Political Unrest." *Canadian Journal of African Studies*, 30, 1 (1996).

———. "The Position of Women in Tanzania and Their Ability to Make Reproductive Choices." M.A. thesis in Development Studies, University of Dar es Salaam, 1987.

———. "Fertility and Healing Cults: Colonial Health Policies and the Rise of Female Associations in Ujiji and Mwanga/Kigoma, 1929–1993." Ph.D. dissertation, Columbia University, in progress.

Mintz, Sidney. "Infant, Victim, and Tourist: The Anthropologist in the Field." *Johns Hopkins Magazine*, XXVIII, 5 (September 1977), 54–60.

Mirza, Sarah, and Margaret Strobel. *Three Swahili Women: Life Histories from Mombasa, Kenya*. Bloomington: Indiana University Press, 1989.

Moore, Donald, and Richard Roberts. "Listening for Silences." *History in Africa*, 17/19 (1990/91).

Mothibe, Tefetso Henry. "Organized African Labor and Nationalism in Colonial Zimbabwe 1945–1971." Ph.D. dissertation, University of Wisconsin–Madison, 1993.

Motzafi-Haller, Pnina. "Historical Narratives as Political Discourses of Identity." *Journal of Southern African Studies*, 20, 3 (1994), 417–32.

Nader, Laura. "From Anguish to Exultation." In Golde, ed., *Women in the Field: Anthropological Experiences*, 104–105. Chicago: Aldine, 1970.

———. "Professional Standards and What We Study." In Rynkiewich and Spradley, eds., *Ethics and Anthropology: Dilemmas in Fieldwork*, 167–82. New York: John Wiley and Sons, 1976.

Newbury, David. *Kings and Clans: Ijwi Island and the Lake Kivu Rift, 1780–1840*. Madison: University of Wisconsin Press, 1991.

O'Fahey, R. S. *State and Society in Dar Fur*. London: Hurst, 1980.

O'Fahey, R. S., and J. L. Spaulding. "Hashim and the Musaba'at." *Bulletin of the School of Oriental and African Studies*, 35 (1974), 316–33.

———. *Kingdoms of the Sudan*. London: Methuen, 1974.

Oberg, Kalervo. "Culture Shock: Adjustments to New Cultural Environments." *Practical Anthropology* (July–August 1960), 177–82.

Oboler, Regina Smith. "For Better or Worse: Anthropologists and Husbands in the Field." In Whitehead and Conaway, eds., *Self, Sex, and Gender in Cross-Cultural Fieldwork*, 28–51. Urbana, Ill: University of Illinois Press, 1986.

Ong, Walter. *Orality and Literacy*. London: Methuen, 1982.

Parsons, Neil. "Settlement in East-central Botswana circa 1800–1920." *Symposium on Settlement in Botswana*. Gaborone: The Botswana Society, 1980.

Pechuël Loesche, E. *Volkskunde von Loango*. Stuttgart: Strecker and Schröder, 1907.

Pelto, Pertti J. *Anthropological Research: The Structure of Inquiry.* New York: Harper and Row, 1970.
———. "Research in Individualistic Societies." In Freilich, ed., *Marginal Natives: Anthropologists at Work,* 251–92. New York: Harper and Row, 1970.
Penvenne, Jeanne M. *African Workers and Colonial Racism: Mozambican Strategies and Struggles in Lourenço Marques, 1877–1962.* Portsmouth, NH: Heinemann, 1995.
Perrings, Charles. *Black Mineworkers in Central Africa.* New York: Africana Publishing Company, 1979.
Phimister, Ian. R. *An Economic and Social History of Zimbabwe, 1890–1948: Capital Accumulation and Class Struggle.* London: Longman, 1988.
Public Culture. "Controversies: Debating *In Theory.*" 6, 1 (Fall 1993).
Rabinow, Paul. *Reflections on Fieldwork in Morocco.* Berkeley: University of California Press, 1977.
Rae, Colin. *Maláboch or Notes from my Diary on the Boer Campaign of 1894.* Cape Town, 1898.
Ranger, Terence. *Revolt in Southern Rhodesia: 1896–1897.* Evanston: Northwestern University, 1967.
Roberts, Richard. "Reversible Social Processes, Historical Memory, and the Production of History." *History in Africa,* 17 (1990), 341–49.
Rynkiewich, Michael A. "The Underdevelopment of Anthropological Ethics." In Rynkiewich and Spradley, eds., *Ethics and Anthropology: Dilemmas in Fieldwork,* 47–60. New York: John Wiley and Sons, 1976.
Schapera, Isaac. *The Ethnic Origins of Tswana Tribes.* Monographs on Social Anthropology, 11. London: The London School of Economics and Political Science, 1952.
Schwab, William B. "Comparative Field Techniques in Urban Research in Africa." In Freilich, ed., *Marginal Natives: Anthropologists at Work,* 73–121. New York: Harper and Row, 1970.
Shain, Richard M. *Water and Fire: A Cultural and Political History of the Etulo Speakers of Central Nigeria, c. 1630s–1890s.* Ph.D. dissertation, Department of History, The Johns Hopkins University, 1992.
Spaulding, J. L. *The Heroic Age of Sinnar.* East Lansing: University of Michigan Press, 1985.
———. "A Premise for Precolonial Nuba History." *History in Africa,* 14 (1987), 369–74.
Stocking, George W., Jr. "The Ethnographer's Magic: Fieldwork in British Anthropology from Tylor to Malinowski." In his *Observers Observed: Essays on Ethnographic Fieldwork,* 70–120. Madison: University of Wisconsin Press, 1983.
———. *The Ethnographer's Magic and Other Essays in the History of Anthropology.* Madison: University of Wisconsin Press, 1992.
———. "History of Anthropology: Whence/Whither." In his *Observers Observed: Essays on Ethnographic Fieldwork,* 3–12. Madison: University of Wisconsin Press, 1983.
———, ed. *Observers Observed: Essays on Ethnographic Fieldwork.* History of Anthropology, 1. Madison: University of Wisconsin Press, 1983.
Strobel, Margaret. *Muslim Women in Mombasa: 1890–1975.* New Haven: Yale University Press, 1979.
Strother, Z. S. "Inventing Masks: Structures of Artistic Innovation Among the Central Pende of Zaïre." Ph.D. dissertation, Yale University, 1992.
———. *Masked Evidence.* Chicago: University of Chicago Press, forthcoming.
———. "Pende Constructions of Secrecy." In Mary H. Nooter, ed., *Secrecy: African Art that Conceals and Reveals,* 156–78. New York: Center for African Art, 1993.
Swantz, Marja Liisa. *Blood, Milk, and Death: Body Symbols and the Power of Regeneration Among the Zaramo of Tanzania.* Westport: Bergin and Garvey, 1995.
Thompson, Paul. *The Voice of the Past.* Oxford: Oxford University Press, 1988.
Tonkin, Elizabeth. *Narrating Our Pasts: The Social Construction of Oral History.* Cambridge: Cambridge University Press, 1991.
———. "Participant Observation." In Ellen, ed., *Ethnographic Research: A Guide to General Conduct,* 216–23. London: Academic Press, 1984.

Torday, E. *On the Trail of the Bushongo*. Philadelphia: Lippincott, 1925.

———, and T. Joyce. *Notes ethnographiques sur les peuples communément appelés Bakuba ainsi que sur les peuplades apparentées. Les Bushongo.* Brussels, 1910.

Townsend, Leslie H. "Out of Silence: Writing Interactive Women's Life Histories in Africa." *History in Africa*, 17 (1990), 351–58.

Urry, J. "A History of Field Methods." In Ellen, ed., *Ethnographic Research: A Guide to General Conduct*, 35–61. London: Academic Press, 1984.

Van Maanen, John, Peter K. Manning, and Marc L. Miller. "Editors' Introduction." In Warren, ed., *Gender Issues in Field Research*, 5–6. Newbury Park, CA: Sage, 1988.

Van Onselen, Charles. *Chibaro: African Labour in Southern Rhodesia, 1900–1933*. London: Pluto, 1976.

Vansina, Jan. *The Children of Woot: A History of the Kuba Peoples*. Madison: University of Wisconsin Press, 1978.

———.*Geschiedenis van de Kuba van ongeveer 1500 tot 1904.* Tervuren: Koninklijk Museum voor Midden Afrika, 1963.

———. "How the Kingdom of the Great Makoko and Certain Clapperless Bells Became Topics of Research." In Curtis Jr., ed. *The Historian's Workshop: Original Essays by Sixteen Historians*. New York: Alfred Knopf, 1970.

———. *Living with Africa*. Madison: University of Wisconsin Press, 1994.

———. *Oral Tradition as History*. Madison: University of Wisconsin Press, 1985.

———. *Paths in the Rainforests: Toward a History of Political Tradition in Equatorial Africa*. Madison: University of Wisconsin Press, 1990.

———. *The Tio Kingdom of the Middle Congo, 1880–1892*. London: Oxford University Press for International African Institute, 1973.

Veyne, P. *Did the Greeks Believe in Their Myths? An Essay on the Constitutive Imagination.* Translated by Paula Wissig. Chicago: University of Chicago Press, 1988.

Vidal, C. "Quand la mariée est trop belle . . . ou plaidoyer pour la tradition orale." *Cahiers d'Études Africaines*, 17/2–3, 66–67 (1977), 377–78.

Wagner, Michele. "Environment, Community, and History: Nature in the Mind in 19th and Early 20th Century Buha." In Gregory Maddox and others, eds., *Custodians of the Land*. London: James Currey, 1996.

———. "Whose History Is History? A History of the Baragane People of Buragane, Southern Burundi, 1850–1932." Ph.D. dissertation, University of Wisconsin–Madison, 1991.

Warren, Carol A. B., ed. *Gender Issues in Field Research*. Newbury Park, CA: Sage, 1988.

Weidman, Hazel Hitson. "On Ambivalence and the Field." In Golde, ed., *Women in the Field: Anthropological Experiences*, 239–63. Chicago: Aldine, 1970.

Wengle, John L. *Ethnographers in the Field: The Psychology of Research*. Tuscaloosa: University of Alabama Press, 1988.

Werbner, Richard P. "Continuity and Policy in Southern African High God Cults." In his *Regional Cults*. New York: Academic Press, 1977.

———. "Small Man Politics and the Rule of Law." *Journal of African Law* 21, 1 (1977), 24–39.

Whitehead, Tony Larry, and Mary Ellen Conaway, eds. *Self, Sex, and Gender in Cross-Cultural Fieldwork*. Urbana, Ill: University of Illinois Press, 1986.

Whittaker, Elvi. "The Birth of the Anthropological Self and Its Career." *Ethos*, 20, 2 (1992), 191–219.

Whitten, Norman E., Jr. "Network Analysis and Processes of Adaptation among Ecuadorian and Nova Scotian Negroes." In Morris Freilich, ed., *Marginal Natives: Anthropologists at Work*, 339–402. New: Harper and Row, 1970.

Wissmann, Hermann von, and others. *Im Innern Afrikas: Die Erforschung der Kassai während der Jahre 1883, 1884, und 1885*. [1888]. Nendeln: Kraus Reprint, 1974.

Yengoyan, Aram A. "Open Networks and Native Formalism: The Mandaya and Pitjandjara Cases." In Freilich, ed., *Marginal Natives: Anthropologists at Work*, 403–39. New York: Harper and Row, 1970.

INDEX

Abba Bayero, Hajiya, 30, 32, 33, 36–39
Accident, xx, 24, 39
Acculturation, 61
Actor (as in play), xiv, xxiii, 8, 74
Adaptation, xxii, xxv, 109
Adire (textiles), 1, 4, 7n14, 8
Afolayan Michael Oladejo, 1
African researcher, xiii, xxii, xxvii–xxviii, 11–17, 133–34
Africans and African history, xxiv
African Americans, xiii
Africanist, xix–xx, xxii, 110, 111
Afrocentric, 107
Age ascribed, xxxi, 4n8, 62
Agenda: academic xl, 104, 109, 112; personal, 104
al Abbasiya, 98–102
Americans: in Africa, 31, 34, 96, 97; perceptions of, xxvi, 61, 117
Amulet, 67, 69
Anachronism, 122–23, 125
Angola, 136
Anthropology and fieldwork, xi, xiv, xvii–xxii, xxiv–xli, 94n1, 127–30. See also Ethnographic present; Participant observation
Arab, 96–99, 101; initiated; 37, 49, 55
Arab slave trade, xxxi
Arabic: language, xii, 99, 100; literature; 30, 33, 36; literacy; 35, 103
Archaeologist, 110
Archaeology, xvii, 58, 59, 61, 101
Archive, xiv, xvii, xxxvi, xl, 11n1; as surviving record; 94–95, 103; understanding by fieldwork, xli, 7n5, 74, 101, 102, 129–30. See also Written record

Archives: consulted; xi, 8, 99; Brazzaville, 122; Belgium, 57n2; Burundi, 23, 26; Dar es Salaam, 46, 50, 52; France, 122; Khartoum, 99n12; London, 99n12; Nigeria, 30, 106; Rome, 99n12; Sudan, 99n12; Zimbabwe, 11n1, 13, 15, 16
Argument of authority, 139
Art, 61, 62, 68, 73
Art history, xiii, xxix, xliii, 57
Artifact, 94, 99, 103. See also Object
Artist, 60, 105, 108
Assault, xx, 32
Atkins, Keletso, xii
Attachment to place and people, xxi
Audience, 33, 99–100. See also Readership
Author, 112, 137–38

Bangwato. See Ngwato
Bapedi. See Pedi
Barthes, Roland, 111
Bayero University, 29, 31, 33, 35, 36
Bechuanaland Protectorate, 81, 90
Behavior: and identity, xxvi, xxviii, xxx, xxxi; learned, 110; observed, 37–38, 90, 128–29; proper, 32–33
Belgian Congo, 20, 58, 59
Belgians, 71, 139
Bi Amina, Hassan, 41, 44–55
Bias, xxxix, 2n3, 77
Biculturalism, 109–111
Bi Fatuma, 46–51, 55
Bloch, Marc, 94n2, 95, 103, 136
Boers, 79, 82, 90
Bohannan, Laura, xxvii, xxxvi
Bope Nyim a Kwem, 139n19
Boone, Sylvia, 61

148

Index

Botswana, xxiii, 75–93; University of Botswana, Lesotho, and Swaziland, 15
Brazzaville, 113–88, 121, 122, 124
Brunschwig, Henri, 122
British, 20, 34, 43, 90
Buha, 18–20
Bujumbura, 21–23, 26
Bulawayo, 13, 14, 15
Buragane, 18–20, 21, 25
Burundi, xxii, 18–18, 41n4, 43, 130–37; national archives, 23; University of, 27, 33

Case study, 129
Cavazzi, Antonio de Montecuccolo, 136
Cell leaders, 25, 27, 52
Charm, xxxvi, 46n13, 48; *wanga*, 60–61, 66–68, 73
Child: researcher as, xxxiv, 5–6, 14, 40, 61, 110. *See also* Pupil
Chokwe, 58, 73
Christianity, 21–22, 61, 69, 81, 90
Civil war, xii–xiii, 26, 96, 133–34
Cognition, xix, 130
Community college, 107
Colonial archives, 122
Colonial community, xxxii
Colonial concept, xxxix, 21
Colonial context, xxxii
Colonial domination, xxiv
Colonial experience, 20
Colonial history, 21, 26, 121, 134–35
Colonial period, xxvi, xxxii, 21, 37, 121, 123
Colonial regime: Anglo–Egyptian, 97; Belgian, 20, 58; British, 20, 43, 90; German, 43
Community: concept of, 18; duration of contact with, 134; events, xxxiii, 117–18; and fieldwork, 129–31, 132; history, xxv, 26; perceptions of, xxvi, xxxi–xxxii, 59–60, 63, 65–68; regional, 91; relationship with researchers, xxxvii, 14, 32, 62, 73, 138–139; secrets, 56; tensions, 121, topic of study, xii, xliii, 21, 24–26, 137. *See also* Town meeting

Columbia University, xiii
Conflict, xiii, xviii, xx, 43, 51, 117
Congo–Brazzaville, xxiii, 113–26
Context of fieldwork, 132–34
Cooking, xxx, 5–6, 38, 40, 114–15, 116
Cooper, Fred, xii
Cooperation, xxv, xxxvi–xxxvii, 2, 6, 25, 55
Cross River State, University of, 107
Cultural absolutes, xxii
Cultural adjustment, xxv
Cultural climate, 104–105
Cultural distance, 137
Cultural fluency, xiv, xl
Cultural milieu, 136–37
Cultural network, 1, 89
Cultural recognition, 124
Cultural relativity, 69
Cultural training, xxxiv
Culture: clash, xix, 74; coherence of, 37; communicability of, 26, 74, 110; globalized, 105; home, 110; internalized, xiii; and labor; and self, xix; traits, 14; translation of, 140; understanding, xiv
Culture area, xii, 109
Culture hero, 119
Culture shock, xv, xx, 2, 74, 105; reverse, 109–110
Cunnison, Ian, 128, 129

Dar es Salaam, 20, 27, 46, 50, 52, 54; University of, 41n3
de Brazza, Pierre Savorgnan, 119, 121, 122
Deceit by researcher, xix, xxvi, xxxv, 55
Deposit of fieldnotes, 125–26, 139–40
Dike, Kenneth, 127
Disease, xx, 6, 35, 41–42, 132–33
Disorientation, 10, 110
Drawings, 114, 116, 119, 120–21, 124, 137
Dress: researcher's, xxviii, 4, 8, 27, 32–33, 46n13, 67; codes, 110; footwear, xvii, 3–4; glasses, 65, 67–70, 73, 85
Durkheim, Emile, 107

Elder, xxv, xlii, 14, 20, 25–28, 47–48, 106; women, 62, 63
Elite, xiv, 20, 25, 85; accounts by, 97, 99–101, 139

Emotions, xix, xxxv, 24
Emotional detachment, xviii, xxiv–xxv, xxxix, 52, 105
Emotional distance, xiv, xxii, 131
Emotional involvment, xii–xiii, xix, xxxv, 105, 130
Emotional sensitivity, xii–xiii, xlii, 26
Empiricism, 77, 90
English, 14, 20, 29n2
Epistemology, xxv, 92, 107
Ethics, xxv, 44, 60, 74; about divulging information, xxii, 45, 56
Ethnic group, 73, 81, 82, 129
Ethnic strife, xviii
Ethnicity, xxxi, 28, 98, 124, 135
Ethnocentricity, 107, 139
Ethnogenesis, 83
Ethnographer, xvii, 71, 77, 112, 115
Ethnographic present, 120, 129
Ethnography, xx, 114, 119–23, 130
Etulo, speakers of, xii, l, 106
Europeans, xxvi, 11, 114, 115, 125; westerners; 7, 43–49, 53, 108
Evaluation: of testimony, xll, 71, 125–26
Exegesis, xliii, 63, 65
Exile: researcher as, xxiii, xl, 13, 104–112
Expatriate community, xxxii, 31, 34, 35, 36
Expatriates, xxvi, 31, 107, 134
Expert, 51, 62, 73
Expertise, xv, 106, 109, 111

Factions, 43–44, 51
Falsehood, xxiii, 75–77, 90–93, 119–20, 126
Fashion, xiv. *See also* Dress
Fear: of political regime, xxxiv–xxxv, 23–28; internalized, xxxix, 87–88
Fetish, 48. *See also* Amulet; Charm
Field research, xi, xix, 29, 130
Field trip, 64, 129–30
Fieldwork; access to information about, xix, 125–26, 131, 140, defined; xvii, xxv, xxxiii, 95–96, 127, 129–30; duration and contributors, xxiv–xxv, 132; duration and funding, xviii, 134; goals, xxiv–xxxvi, xl, 128–30; history of, xi–xiii, xxiv,127–29; implications of long duration, xxiii, 104–112; importance of, 134–40; intensive, xii–xiv; need for long duration, xii, xxi, 129; replicability of, 127, 139, 140; specific cases of duration, 1, 27, 36, 37, 41n3, 123, 124n12, and written evidence, 101–102, 122–23
Folklore, 115, 116, 118, 124
Formula: literary. 95, 107
French language, 20, 21, 114, 115, 138
French people, 115, 116, 122, 136
French research institute, 114, 121
Foreigner, xxxi, 23, 38, 53, 55, 73; by nationality, xlii, 122; researcher as, xxvi, 133–34, 136; scholar, 108, 112; student, xv, xxviii, 105. *See also* Expatriate; Outsider
Friends: of researchers; xliii, 2n5, 4, 61, 107; as facilitators, xxvii, xxxviii, 13, 45, 55; at home; xxxvii, 40, 62, 109–110; as protectors, 34–35, 64, 72
Fulani, 29n1, 32, 39
Fulbright grants, xiii n3, 1, 18n, 22, 29, 35, 57n2, 75n2, 99n12, 105–106
Funding: and African researchers, xv, 16, 17, 134; constraints, 20, 46, 131; and duration of fieldwork, xii, xviii, xxi, 104; sources of contributor's, 1, 11n1, 18,1, 41n3, 57n2, 75n2, 99n12, 105–106, 113n1. *See also* Grants

Gabon, 130
Gaborone, 77, 90
Gender, xiii, xxii, xxv, xxviii–xxxi, xxxvi, 38; and Hausa, 29n1, 38; and Tio, 115
Genealogy, 26, 79–91, 107, 119, 120
Genres: 137; oral, 85, 107, 113
German, 43, 133
"Going native," xxxix
Gold Coast, 136
GooMoremi village, 75–91
Gossip: 69, 115, 116, 117; and identity xxvi–xxvii. *See also* Rumor
Grant. *See* Fulbright grant, funding
Guest, 24–25, 37–38, 64, 110

Ha: people, 20, 41n3
Hajiya: as term of address, xxviii, 40

Index

Harare, 13, 15
Hausa, xii, 29–40
Health: researcher's, xix–xx, xxxii–xxxiii, 6, 35, 134
Health service, xv, 12, 42n5, 52, 134
Heuristics, 130. *See also* Research design
Higginson, John, xii
Historian; academic, xv, 104, 113, 127, 105–112; local, 135; oral, 104
Historical account, 171
Historical actor, 102, 136–39
Historical conceptualization, 100
Historical consciousness, xii, xiii, xiv, xv, xxiii
Historical imagination, 137, 138, 140
Historical information; access to, 132, 139–40; concealed, xviii, 138–39; confidential 45, 140; context, 54, 77; crosschecked, xli, 26, 121, 122; in pieces, xliii, 100; privileged, 51, 110; reliability of, xxiii, 24–25, 71, 31; spontaneity of, xviii, 124, 130
Historical interpretation, 135–40; local xxxiii, 63, 99, 135, 140; and fieldwork, xiii, xv, xxv, 122–23; by researcher, 91, 101, 139n19
Historical reconstruction, 97, 99, 100–102
Historical society of Kasulu, 28
Historical understanding, xiv, xvii, xxi, xli, 137; of evidence, xiii, xv, 136
History; academic, xxiii, xxiv; colonial, 26; conception of, xxiii, xlii; construction of, 71; family, xxiii, xliii, 100, 120–21, 131; intellectual, 101; interest in, 27; local, xxiii, xli, 28, 44, 56, 91, 100, 135; meaning of, xxiii; Muslim, xviii, 97, 99, 100; practice of, xviii, xlii. *See also* Fieldwork
Historiography, xi, xviii, xxiii, 107–112, 137–38, 140
"Home" and "field," xxii, xxiii, 55, 107; coming home, 54, 104–105, 109–111; field becomes home, xxxv, xxxvi n5, 9, 10
Host, xiv, 73, 110,129; community, 74, 123; family, 44, 49, 53, 67, 70
Hostility, 14, 49, 51, 74; gender, 115
House keeping, *See* Life style

Howell, Nancy, xix, xxi
Human rights, 21
Hutu, 20n2, 26, 28, 132, 133, 135

Ibadan, 1–2, 6–7, 9, 10; archives, 106n1; University of, 3, 6, 7
Iconographic data, 135. *See also* Drawing; Photograph
Identity; assigned to researcher, xxv–xxxii, 43, 91, 94, 106, 115–116; ethnic, 26, 49, 81, 101, 135
Identity papers, 23, 45, 115
Imbāāw, 118
Informant, 132, 134, 139n19; notion of, xii, xviii, xxxvii, xxxviii; Botswana, 77, 92; Tanzania, xli, 42–56; Taqali, 96, 100–102; Zimbabwe, 13–17. *See also* Interviewee; Key informant
Initiation: fieldwork as, 127; boys, xxix, 57, 63–67; women; xxx, xxxiii, 41–56, 62
Initiate, 83
Insider, xxiii, xxvii–xxviii, xxxi, 105
Intellectual decolonization, 108
Internalization, xiii, xxv, xxxix, 132; of fear, xxxv, 23, 26
International Monetary Fund, 12
Interpreter, 31, 130, 132
Interview; Abili Ndyōō, 121; Ali, 100, 101, cited, 15; formal, xlii, 8, 50n18,13; group, xlii, 25, 27–28, 62, 63, 119; King's, 119–20, 126; Lipie, 114n3, 121; M., 75–77; 81–93; Ngoma Kandaku Mbuya, 71; on record, 95, remuneration of, 55, 114n1; schedule, xviii; technique, xii, xviii, 120, 123
Interviewee, xxviii, xlii, 13–14, 55, 131. *See also* informant
Introductions, xxxvii, 13, 15, 30, 36, 98
Iser, Wolfgang, 112
Islam, 29n1, 30, 31, 35, 97
Islamic reform movement, 97, 100, 103
Isolation, xxxiv–xxxv, 6n12, 7, 49, 51

Johns Hopkins University, xiii
Jos, University of, 105, 107

Kano, xxvii, 29–40
Kasulu, 27–28

Kenya, 27
Key informants, xxxviii, xxxix, 129
Khadija, 44, 56
Khama III, 79n5, 81–84, 86, 91
Kigoma; urban area, 41–43, 46, 49–52, 55; town, 50, 52–54
Khartoum, 98, 99
Komana cult, 76, 83, 85–91
Kombo Kabenga, 58n3, 59–61, 70–72
Kombo Kakese, 58n3, 63, 65–66, 69–70, 72
Kombo Kiboto, 58–59, 62–65, 67, 70
Kombo, a.k.a. Munzenze Kavuka, 69, 70
Kordofan: southern, 98,99
Kuba, 130, 132–35, 138–39

Labor; consciousness, xii; history, xii, xiv, 11–17; migration, 84, 90
Lagos, xvii, 2, 3, 9; university, 33
Language, command 8, 14, 29, 66; difficulties, xv; instruction, xii, xxiv, 23, 40, 130; local 100; peculiarities, 90, 110, 111; self-taught, 65–115, 119, 124; skills needed, xii, 40, 123, 129, 134, 135
Leading questions, xlii, 130
Learning process, xviii, xxi–xxii, 4–6, 125; by doing, xxxiii, xli, 2, 8; control over, xxxvii, 45. *See also* Child; Pupil
Legitimacy: academic, xliii, 111–12
Libya, 129–130, 132
Life histories, 121; in colonial times, 16, 135; of women, xxii, xxxvi, 34, 37, 44
Life style: researcher's, xxxi–xxxiii, 3–8, 31–33, 39–40, 114–16. *See also* Cooking; Dress
Linguistics, xxxvii, 36, 119, 121, 130
Logistics, xii, 25, 46, 133–34
Lord, Albert, 95
Lyeen, Jules, 138

Madala, 76–81, 83–86, 88–93
Madison. *See* Wisconsin–Madison, University of
Magic, xi, 4, 100
Mahdiyya, 97, 101
Makamba, 19, 22–27
Malaria, xx, xxxiii, 6, 35, 44, 60
Malinowski, Bronislaw, 128

Manda, 57–59, 61, 65, 68, 72
Manuals, xiv, xviii, xxi
Manyema, 43, 49
Marital status, xxviii–xxx, xxxii, 34–39, 54, 115, 132
Mason, Hercule, 72, 76
Matebele. *See* Ndebele
Matswapong. *See* Tswapong
Mbe, 114, 125, 130, 132
Memoirs, xvii, xviii, xx–xxi, xxvi n31, xxviii, 64
Memories; of past by Africans, 79, 81, 116, 140; of childhood, 121; of colonial past, xxxi; about researchers, xvii,xxvi. *See also* Reminiscences.
Mentality, xii, xxiv; Ujamaa, 27–28; of ethnicity, 133, 135
Methods: anthropological, xxxiii, xxxix; field, 63, 65, 94, 130; historical, xl–xliv, 13, 99, 107, 111; manuals of, xiii, xiv, xviii. *See also* Participant observation; Sampling
Message as object of study, 129
Minnesota, University of, 41n3
Mintz, Sidney, 110
Mode of thought, 93, 129
Moeng; college 84–85; road, 83, 84, 91
Monuments, 120, 136.*See also* Object, Ruin
Motivation, attributed to actors, 137–38
Mueller, Hans, 58n4
Muslim; history xliii, society, xxii, 31, 32, 34; teachers, 32, 96, 99, 103; women, xxii, 30, 40
Mwanga, 41–43, 47–53, 54–55

Name standing for an era, 84
Ndebele, 14, 79, 81–82
Ndjindji, 59–73
Negotiation; about identity, xxvi, xxviii; about research, 17, 41, 45, 46, 47, 55
Neighbors; becoming, 8, 31–33; enmity of, 74; protected by, xxviii, 6–7, 9, 32; trusted by, 25
Neocolonial; attitude, 21; context, xxxii
Ngabe, 118, 120, 121
Ngateo, 115, 116, 119
Ngwato kingdom and people, 77–91

Index

Nigeria, xvii, xxii, xxiii, 1–10, 29–40, 104–112
Nile valley, 96–102
Norm, xxv, xxviii, 7n15, 55, 73, 119, 120, 129
North America, xi, xii, xxxi, 127. *See also* United States
Nuba Hills, 94–10
Nzambi, 58–60, 69, 72

Oberg, Kalervo, 109–110
Objects, 114, 119; art, xiii, xxix, 62; historical significance of, 120–21, 136. *See also* Amulet; Artifact; Charm
Objectivity, abandoned, xxv, xxxix, 105; as excuse, xxxviii–xxxix, 28, 74; required, xiv, xviii, xxxviii, 105, 128
Observation,115, 128–29, 131
Observers and observed, xviii, xxxiv–xxxv, 37–38, 48, 67, 68
Oral evidence, 16, 114, 129–30; and fieldwork, xv, xxiv, 13, 14, 136; and subjectivity, 138; and written sources, 84, 101, 114, 122, 125, 135–36; in writing, 134
Oral history, 18, 28, 50, 57, 71, 76, 84
Oral literature, xxii, 29, 30, 33, 36
Oral narrative, 95, 96, 101, 139
Oral tradition, 13, 93, 50, 54, 134–35; and fieldwork, xi–xii, xiv, 127–28; formal, 121, 131, 137; genealogy, 82, 91; genres, 85, 107, official, 99–100; subversive, 82, 91; Tio, 114, 119–20
Orality, 103, 107
Outsider, xxxi, 55, 56, 73; audience, 99, 100, 102; researcher ambiguous, xxiii, xxvii; researcher as, xv, xxv, 34, 51, 74, 140

Participant observation, xviii, xxxiii, xxix, 106, 120, 128–30
Past and present; impact of present, xxiii; traces of past in present, 94–95, 99, 101, 136; use of present to understand past, 125
Peace Corps, xxxiii
Pechüel Loesche, E.,133
Pedi, 77–79, 81–86, 88, 90

Pende, xii, 57–74
Penvenne, Jeanne, xii
Performance, 43, 46n12, 63n10, 138
Performer, 29, 30, 33, 36, 60, 130
Perrings, Charles, xii
Person-centered fieldwork, xxxv–xxxvi
Personal experience, 8, 132, 133, 139
Personality: impact of fieldworker's, xii, xiii, xiv, 5, 132
Photograph, xxxvi, 95,119, 124
Pilot experiment, 131–32
Police, 21–23, 27, 35, 115
Politics: national and local, xxii, xliii; Burundi, 22–26; Congo, 118; Nigeria, 9; Tanzania, 27–28, 41, 44; Sudan, 98, 102–103
Political situation, and research, xxii, xxxiv, xxxvii, xliii, 11, 18–28, 132–33
Positivism, 75, 92–93
Postcolonial experience, 20, 107, 108, 135
Postmodernism, 28
Precolonial hisory, 20, 135
Privacy, 7, 34, 38, 44, 52
Professor; in field, xxv, xxvii, 4, 22, 33, 54; at home, 107, 110
Prostitution: as a topic for research, 34
Protocols, 130, 131
Pseudonym, 50n2, 75n2
Psychology, xix, xx, xxix, 111
Pupil: researcher as, 41–56 (*somo*), 125-29

Questionnaire, 131
Qu'ran, 32, 35, 37

Race, xxvi, xxxi; black, 14–15, relations, 12; white, 39, 61, 81, 90, 91, 124
Ramadan, xxxiii, 39–40, 51–52
Rapport, xxxvii–xxxviii, xxxix, 16
Readership, xxiii, xxiv, 92, 105, 111–12; African, 116, 140; non–African, 108
Recital: history, 63n10, 69
Relationships:close personal; development of, xxii, xxxiii–xxiv, xxxv–xxxix, xliii; deterioration of, 69; duration of, 9–10; importance of, 71; and objectivity, xxv. *See also* Friends
Reminiscences, 121, 122, 125, 126

Research; academic results, xvi, 113; informal, 106; languages, xii; peripatetic, xi, xii, 131, 132; proposal, xli; standard, 106; urban, 1–17, 29–56, 132, 134
Research assistants, xii, 28, 65–66, 76, 115, 130–32; Baruteng, 76, 81, 87; Bernard, 115, 116, 119, 122; security agent as, xlii, 25–26; Shabani, 53
Research clearance, xliii, 21–23, 33, 34, 134
Research design, xli, 20, 125–26, 130–32, 140
Research project, xi, xvii, xliii, 50; altered in field, xiv, xli, 45, 120
Research team, xiii, 28, 63
Research topic, xii–xiv, xliii, 14, 44, 134, 137
Researcher: perception of, 49–50, 53, 55–56
Residence in Africa *vs.* fieldwork, 129–30
Residence permit, 35
Respect; dress and, 4, 33; toward elders, 27–28, 48n17, 56, 110; toward researcher, 14, 15; involving researcher, xxxiv, xxxvi, 23, 26, 69
Risks, xix–xxi, 25, 134
Rivalry, xxxvii, 43–44, 51, 55
Riots, 9, 39
Role: assigned, xxv, xvii, 115–16, 139; assumed, xxxviii, 106; gender, xxix, 6, 30–32; social, 14, 34, 132
Ruins, xxxiii, 136; specific, 58–59, 95, 96, 99, 101, 119
Rumor: and identity, xxvii–xxiii, xxvii; specific, 20, 55–59, 66–68, 91. *See also* Gossip
Rundi, xii. *See also* Burundi
Rwanda, 114, 124, 130, 132, 133, 137

Sampling, xiii, 126, 129–32
Sanji, 63n10, 65, 70
Seclusion; of women, xlii, 32, 34, 38, 39; of chief, 69,70
Secret, xxii, xlii, 15, 44–56, 70, 82–90
Security agent, xxxiii, xxxiv, xlii, 21–26, 62, 115

Self concept; altered, xxxv, 4, 129; challenged, xviii, xix; fidelity to, xxxvi, 69
Self definition, xxvi
SeNgwato language, 90
Seretse Khama, 84
Serowe, 77, 79, 90
SeTswana language, 83
Sexual harassment, xxviii, xxx, 23, 32
Shona, xii, 14, 15
Social history, xi, xiii–xi, xxiv, 135; Tio, xxiii, 113n2, 120, 122–123, 126, 127
Social milieu, xxxiii–xxxiv, 28, 136
Sociology, xi
Soldier, 20, 23, 67, 97, 102
Sorcery, 46, 48, 57–74. *See also* Witchcraft
Sources; diversity of, xlii–xliii, 135–36; feedback, 16; independent confirmation by, 92; inside, xi; quantity of, xi, xv, xlii–xliii, 8; novelty of, 140; variability of, 138. *See also* Heuristics; Message; Oral evidence; Traces; Written evidence
South Africa, 14, 15, 77, 84, 90, 91
Spouses in the field, xxxii, xlii, 9–10, 34, 49–54, 113–21
Spy, xxv, 15, 48, 63n10, 107
Status, xxix, 5, 14, 36–37, 91; dual, xxviii, 105–106; and initiation, 46, 47, 51, 53, 55, 56. *See also* Insider; Marital status; Outsider; Student
Stranger, 7, 8, 65, 66; researcher as, xxviii, 24, 65, 81, 96, 99, 110; Wise, 97, 99, 100, 101
Stress, xix–xxi, xl, 9, 106, 109–111
Student; assistants, 25–26; category of, xxvi, 50, 55; researcher given student status, xxviii, xxix, 62, 10; researcher's student status disputed, 55, 56, 73
Subjectivity, xiv, xviii, xxxviii, 28, 137–38
Sudan, xxiii, 94–103

Tanganyika: Lake, 19, 22, 42, 43, 47
Tanganyikan African National Union (TANU), 41, 44
Tanzania, xxii, 18–20, 27–28, 41–56, 132
Taqali, 95–103
Tax collector, xxxi, 91, 138

Teacher; of Islam, 32, 34; itinerant, 33, 97; local schoolteacher, xxv, 12, 28, 66, 98, 115; researcher as, xxxiii, xli, 4, 29, 40, 104–107; other expatriates as, 31, 107, 130. *See also* Professor
Teachers Training College, Kasulu, 27
Text and context, 90–92, 112
Text as document, 21, 92
Textiles, xxxiii, 1, 7, 8
Theory, 112, 129
Tio, xxiii, 113–26, 130, 132, 138
Tolerance, 73
Torday, Emil, 134, 139
Tourists, xxvii n33, 115, 116, 118; researcher as, 109–110, 111
Town meeting, xlii, 25, 27–28, 62–63, 119
Traces of the past, 94, 103, 136–37
Trade unions, xiv, 13–16
Transnational orientation, 105, 107, 108, 109, 112
Translator, xii,xviii
Translation, 65, 136; cultural 137, 140
Transvaal, 77, 79, 81, 90
Tribe, 14, 21
Truth, xxiii, xxvi, xlii, 28, 75–93, 103
Trust, xxxvi, xli, 4, 14, 24, 25; and women's initiation, xxii, 45, 46, 50, 53, 56
Tshekedi, 81, 82, 83, 84, 88, 91
Tutsi, 20n2, 26, 28, 133, 135
Tswapong Hills and people, 77, 78, 79, 81–85, 88, 89–90, 92
Tswana, xii
Typhoid, xx, xxxiii, 35, 40

Ujamaa mentality, 27–28
Ujiji, 41–56
Universities. *See also* Professor; Student; Teacher; individual universities
United States; Africans at universities in the, 21, 27, 54, 99; estranged from; xxxvii, xl, 104–112; officials, 21–22, 35, life in the, 40, 54

Urban reader, 117
Urban environment, xxxiii, 6

Van Onselen, Charles, xii
Vidal, Claudine, 123–26

Wife. *See also* Marital status; Spouse; Terms of address, xxviii, 8
Williams, Ruth, 84
Wissmann, Hermann von, 58n4
Wisconsin–Madison: University of, xiii, 21, 27, 36, 98
Witchcraft, xxii, xliii, 48, 49. *See also* Sorcery
Work centered fieldwork, xxxv–xxxvi
Working class, 12, 13, 14, 16
World Bank, 12, 30
Women; interviewing, xxxvii, 20, 27, 62, 115, 120; invisible, xlii n67; research about, xiv, xxii, xxxix, 7n14, 29–40, 41–56, 62; researchers, xxvii, xxviii–xxx, xliii, 63, 68, 70, 132
Writing: rejected, 103
Written evidence; and corroboration of oral data, 14, 101, 114, 125; and dating, 105; and feedback, 16; interpreted by fieldwork, xv, 122–23, 125; information used in interview, 16, 84, 119; oral tradition in written form, 134–35; and poetry, 29, 30, 33; and recollection, 126; scarcity of, 103

Yale University, xiii
Yellow fever, xxxiii, 52
Yoruba, xii, 1, 2, 7, 8, 108

Zaire, xxii, 43, 57–74, 130
Zambia, 43
Zanzibari, 46n13
Zero time, 129, 133, 138
Zimbabwe, xxii, 11–17; University of, 13, 15, 17; National archives, 13, 16; Congress of Trade Unions, 14
Zulu, 14, 15